D0648025

HER ACT *and* DEED

Number Three:

SAM RAYBURN SERIES ON RURAL LIFE

SPONSORED BY TEXAS A&M UNIVERSITY–COMMERCE

JAMES A. GRIMSHAW, JR., GENERAL EDITOR

ANGELA BOSWELL

HER ACT *and* DEED

Women's Lives in a
Rural Southern County,
1837–1873

TEXAS A&M UNIVERSITY PRESS

COLLEGE STATION

Copyright © 2001 by Angela Boswell
Manufactured in the United States of America
All rights reserved
First edition

The paper used in this book meets the minimum require-
ments of the American National Standard for Permanence of
Paper for Printed Library Materials, z39.48-1984. Binding
materials have been chosen for durability.

LIBRARY OF CONGRESS
CATALOGING-IN-PUBLICATION DATA

Boswell, Angela, 1965–
Her act and deed : women's lives in a rural southern county,
1837–1873 / Angela Boswell.—1st ed.
p.   cm. — (Sam Rayburn series on rural life ; no. 3)
Includes bibliographical references and index.
ISBN 1-58544-128-7
1. Rural women—Texas—Colorado County—History—
19th century. 2. Colorado County (Tex.)—Rural conditions.
I. Title. II. Series.
HQ1438. T4 B67 2001
305.42′09764′253091734—dc21
2001000707

Contents

TABLES

SERIES EDITOR'S FOREWORD

Her Act and Deed: Women's Lives in a Rural Southern County, 1837–1873 is the third book in the Sam Rayburn Series on Rural Life, a series established on the Texas A&M University–Commerce campus under the auspices of the Texas A&M University Press book-publishing program. Designed to be diverse in scope of topics, the series focuses on the eastern half of Texas and the surrounding region. Angela Boswell has written a compelling account about the nature and place of women in Colorado County in the nineteenth century, a time frame that touches on the frontier, antebellum, and reconstruction eras in the South.

Boswell captures the cultural mix of Spanish heritage, German immigrants, and southern ideals in her snapshots of the political, economic, religious, familial, legal, slave, and Civil War involvement of women in this small rural community. Her research in the county records and local newspapers and in diaries and private letters affords valuable insights into the role of women, African American and white, during this transitional, formative period of the region.

Still affected by the southern values, traditions, and myths of the Old South, Colorado County settlers homesteaded on a frontier where customs and manners had to be redefined. In the middle of the century, women who moved with their families endured the well-chronicled hardships of frontier life, shared in the unrelenting toil, and still remained under patriarchal domination. And as southerners in general continued to seek their identity, so women sought their own identity. Their searches are, in some ways, the same search. Boswell provides specific cases to illustrate women's quests for legal rights and their struggles against physically and mentally abusive husbands. Her findings underscore the dominant metaphor identified by Louise Cowan in John Crowe Ransom's poetry: "the victimization of women" and the southern myth of womanhood.

The German immigrants in Colorado County faced similar frontier hardships. And their cultural differences were soon melded into a bouillabaisse of German-southern-Texan culture. Over time second generations of Texas Germans had subordinated, if not lost, their ancestral traditions. After the Civil War, public education, the critical intellect, and modern Christianity weakened patriarchal ideas and prepared the way for the idea of equality for race and gender, according to historian Keith F. McKean. Boswell finds the seeds for that idea and for increased opportunities for women during the antebellum period, and she traces the added responsibility that women assumed while their husbands were fighting in the Civil War.

From Boswell's minute research into details of property rights, slavery, and marital status of women, readers now have additional background on the issue that became particularly prominent in the last half of the twentieth century: women's rights. Objective but focused in her presentation, Boswell relays the "facts" and provides additional glimpses of life that is reflected frequently in the historical consciousness of southern writers in the last century. From the information presented in *Her Act and Deed* will surely emerge similar studies, as well as the potential for understanding better past writers of the South. Creative writers will also find new material for their stories, poems, and plays. Angela Boswell's work provides yet another snapshot for the Sam Rayburn Series on Rural Life album.

—JAMES A. GRIMSHAW, JR.

ACKNOWLEDGMENTS

My debts of gratitude are numerous, as many people assisted me directly and indirectly in the completion of this work. First and foremost I want to acknowledge the crucial role of and assistance from John Boles in the research and writing of the dissertation from which this book grew. As adviser of my graduate work, he encouraged my interest in the topic of Texas women, was constantly and tirelessly available for discussions in which I formulated my ideas, gave invaluable advice in the research process, and used his vast editorial skills in many readings of drafts of the dissertation. Above all, he encouraged me and had faith in my abilities throughout my graduate career, especially at times when I lacked faith in myself.

I also want to thank the other members of my dissertation committee: Harold Hyman, Jane Dailey, and Elizabeth Long. A fellowship from Rice University contributed invaluable financial assistance, and a scholarship from P.E.O. enabled me to finish the dissertation.

After a year of intense research in Colorado County, I owe thanks to many citizens of Columbus, Texas, for accommodating me in the process. The staffs of the District Clerk's Office and the County Clerk's Office particularly deserve praise, as they allowed me with my computer to camp out in the records' vaults every day for nearly a year. Both offices' staffs were extremely cooperative and courteous in allowing me access to the county's records and helpful in finding even those hidden ones. The extreme care taken to preserve the records in Colorado County made it a historian's paradise. I especially want to thank Bobbie Elliott of the District Clerk's Office, not only for her assistance in using the records there but also for her friendship. I gladly acknowledge Bill Stein's enormous contribution to my research in Columbus. His great care in collecting historical documents and histories of Colorado County at the Nesbitt Memorial Library, as well as his editing of the *Nesbitt Memorial Library Journal,* offered a wide range of historical materials in a convenient location. Additionally he offered continual insight into the history of the county and its residents and advice on further research.

For research done beyond Colorado County, I wish to thank the staffs of the

ACKNOWLEDGMENTS

Center for American History at the University of Texas in Austin and the National Archives in Washington, D.C. I also want to thank Barry Crouch for helping me make the most efficient use of my time in Washington, D.C., by directing me to the records on Colorado County held by the National Archives.

Many persons have read and commented on portions of this work at conferences and meetings and in the halls of the Rice history department, including Elizabeth Turner, Laura Edwards, Barry Crouch, Sylvia R. Frey, Randal Hall, and the members of Houston Area Southern Historians. Advice and mentoring such as they gave me cannot be overrated, and in recognition of mentoring I would also like to thank Jan Dawson, my adviser from my undergraduate years at Southwestern University and my friend and supporter ever since. I must also note the importance of the Southern Association for Women Historians, which not only gave me a venue to present portions of my work but also validated the research into southern women's history and provided role models for women in the field of history.

On personal notes of gratitude, I first wish to thank my parents, Buford and Wyma Boswell, for their encouragement and support as I pursued my dream of a college education and graduate degree. They were instrumental in instilling in me a love of history from the youngest age, as many a family vacation was spent traveling to visit the location of whichever historical event enamored me at the time. As I engaged in the often painful process of writing in sometimes isolated areas, many friends at sometimes great distances prodded me along with encouragement and intellectual stimulation, particularly Tracy Harting, Amy Wink, Vanessa Davis, Jan Dawson, Cathy Gurney, Janet Ryan, and Eileen Scholpp.

Finally, I wish to acknowledge the debt of gratitude that I owe to Barbara Boswell, who patiently encouraged me through the years it took to revise the manuscript. In addition she read draft after draft, proofread footnotes numerous times, and in many other ways aided in the preparation of the book. Above all, she helped me maintain faith in the project and in myself.

HER ACT *and* DEED

INTRODUCTION

She has always been a virtuous and dutiful wife and has performed
all her marital duties as a good wife would do, but she avers that [her
husband] has not performed his duties as he was in duty bound to do.
— ADELADE LEWIS TO COLORADO COUNTY
DISTRICT COURT, 1873

In her divorce petition to the district court Adelade Lewis did not have to
describe what the duties of a husband or a wife were. Although they were
not specifically written into any law, she, the judges, the juries, and the rest of
the nineteenth-century South shared the same understanding of the roles
men and women in a family were obligated to perform. And, of course, in the
nineteenth-century South these duties and obligations differed for men and
women.[1]

The roles of husbands and wives were defined not just by the ideals of the
marriage relationship, but also by the ideals of members' places within the
household. As the nineteenth-century South was predominantly rural and relied still upon agriculture, the household remained the main unit of production even after the Civil War. Although everyone was expected to contribute
to the well-being of the household, the duties and obligations of each member varied according to age, race, and gender.[2]

As the male head of household, the husband held authority over his wife
and all dependents in the household: children, servants, and slaves. He also
supposedly represented the entire household's interests in the broader public.
As a result, laws allowed only white men to vote, serve on juries, and serve in
the army to protect the interests of the household. In addition to representing his dependents' interests in politics or war, southerners expected the male
head of household to make the financial decisions as well.[3]

The head of the household, however, had different relationships with his
various dependents. As a loving and caring husband, he embodied and symbolized his care and affection by being "willing to protect and support his

wife," as one antebellum divorce petition specifically claimed. Specifically, the white male saw to it that his family's primary needs were provided, either by overseeing the production of those needs on the farm or plantation or by earning the money to purchase those needs. As a male, he was expected to perform the heaviest labor or oversee its performance if he had slaves.[4]

The southern wife was supposedly protected from heavy labor and was not expected to represent the household's concerns in the public sphere. She, however, had many duties. As a member of the economic unit, she contributed to the household's welfare by producing as many goods as possible. Wives were responsible for making clothing, tending the gardens, canning and preserving food, preparing meals, and cleaning. In addition, or probably most important, wives increased their families' wealth, reputation, and sustenance by bearing and raising children.[5]

While all wives were expected to contribute to the economic production of the family, slaveholding women and nonslaveholding women experienced their duties differently. The model sturdy farm wife served as a helpmate to her husband by performing all the wifely chores herself. In addition, although rarely remarked upon by southern society, a farm woman sometimes found it necessary to join her husband in the fields. The southern "lady" was not expected to perform field chores at any time, and her responsibilities for the laborious work inside the home often merely entailed overseeing the coerced labor of her slaves.[6]

Besides their economic contributions, ideally both husbands and wives were loving, caring, affectionate, and considerate of each others' feelings. The ideal of the companionate marriage held forth in the South as well as in the industrializing North. Marriage was the relationship between two loving partners drawn together by mutual attraction. As men in the North increasingly left the home for a separate workplace during the day, women gained authority over a separate sphere in the home. Far from equal in political rights, women held positions in society that were at least theoretically equal and complementary to those of men.[7]

Because in the South the two partners in a marriage worked together in one productive household, wives did not develop a separate sphere of authority in the home. Even though specific duties were relegated to the women, the husbands, as they worked at their duties within the household, had the opportunity to direct and advise. Husbands remained the authorities over home, work, and public life. Southern women did not develop a separate sphere over which they had authority, but the duties in the home consumed their time and energy. As southern women had no duties outside the home according to the social ideals, the home encompassed their lives.[8]

Although southerners did not develop the same ideology of separate spheres for the sexes, they shared many beliefs about women's nature that resulted from this ideal. Southern women imbibed the basic tenets through books, prescriptive literature, and even the local newspapers. True women were pious, pure, domestic, and submissive whether in the North or the South. Their pious and pure "natures" gave further justifications for the necessity of protecting women from the corruptive influences of public life. While the southern "lady" remained the embodiment of these ideals, nonslaveholding women also embraced these basic assumptions.[9]

The other dependents of the household had different relationships with its head than did the wife. Although these dependents had reciprocal duties, they were unequal. Children, of course, were expected to obey their fathers and to perform extremely valuable labor. In return, fathers supported their children, ensured their education, and worked for something tangible to give them either when the children married or when the father died. Children's labor was divided by gender. Girls assisted in the traditional female roles while boys labored in the fields or in the business and political world with their fathers. Thus they contributed to the household and prepared themselves for the roles they would accept as adults.[10]

Above all, at least ideally, the relationships between the heads of the households and their children and wives were based on love and affection. As a result, children and wives saw their places in the household and their obedience to their father/husband as natural and self-fulfilling. The relationships with slaves, however, were a different matter.

Southern slaveholders asserted a paternalistic ideal regarding the system of slavery: they appropriated the labor of slaves and in return sheltered and protected them. The most benign expression of this ideology occurred when a slaveholder referred to his "family, black and white." However, the actual force necessary to coerce labor from slaves belied these assumptions, at least on the part of slaves. Some persons held in bondage might have seen the relationship between master and slave as organic and natural, but enormous evidence exists that masters did not consider the best interests of their slaves nor did slaves accept the theoretical underpinnings of slavery.[11]

Nevertheless, slavery and the defense of slavery, even more than the rural nature of the South, reinforced the need for southerners to uphold the authoritative roles of white men in the household. Maintaining southern society required that the authority of husband, father, and master not be challenged. Southern society found it as crucial to maintain restrictions on women's exercise of authority in male realms as it was to maintain masters' power over slaves.[12]

As a result, the district court to which Adelade Lewis presented her case shared the nineteenth-century assumptions about men and women, husbands and wives, and masters and slaves, as did the southern politicians, legislators, and judges who made the laws. Legislation and interpretation presumed that these aspects of women's and men's lives were appropriate to each's nature and the proper actions to ensure an ordered society. Assumptions about men and women showed most obviously in laws regarding voting, holding office, marriage, property, crime, and death, but all laws assumed this basic makeup of society. The passage and enforcement of laws reflected the social context of the time and reinforced and enforced it as well. Thus men and women faced both social and legal pressure to conform to their respective ideals. The ideal woman in southern society was married, thus claiming the protection and representation of a man and having no right to vote, serve on juries, or hold office.[13]

Married women who ideally relied upon their husbands to provide for their families suffered the further legal disabilities that prohibited their agency in financial transactions. Even in southern states where married women could own property, their husbands exercised "the sole management of all such property." Legislators and jurists wanted to ensure that married women could not challenge the authority of their husbands. Since a married woman legally had no control over any property, she could not sue, be sued, or make contracts. She could not conduct business in her own name or execute a security bond to serve as an administrator or executor of an estate or even as guardian of her own children. Many southern states even restricted or refused a married woman's right to write a will.[14]

Historians who studied the laws and the ideals behind the laws recognized that neither laws nor ideals accurately described women's actual lives. The vast majority of women who lived less than elite lives had to contribute labor considered to be men's work at least occasionally, especially during harvest time. During extraordinary circumstances, such as the Civil War, even elite southern women abandoned ideals—first to contribute to the war cause and then to survive. In a few cases the laws that embodied and reinforced the ideals of womanhood contradicted those same ideals by requiring or allowing women to exercise rights or perform duties in that realm ideally reserved for men.[15]

In order to explore the varying and sometimes diverging pulls upon southern women—ideal, law, and reality—this study examines in depth the women of one southern county: Colorado County, Texas. Several historians studying southern women have proved the value of investigating these issues at the local level using public records. However, this study of women of the westernmost portion of the South expands the knowledge of southern women's different experiences, despite the similar ideals to which they held. Although beginning as a frontier region only some twenty years before the Civil War, Texas had enough time to develop distinctly antebellum southern traits and culture before the outbreak of hostilities which would forever transform the South. Therefore, the important periods that all southern states experienced can be studied in Texas in a rather compact time period: frontier, antebellum, Civil War, and Reconstruction.[16]

Finding an appropriate Texas county with adequate records was a difficult task. Urban Texas counties have been much more successful at keeping their records. However, a rural county (despite the smaller numbers of people and records it might provide) is more representative of the majority of nineteenth-century southern women who lived their lives in rural areas. Most rural counties' court records in Texas, however, have fallen victim to tornadoes, hurricanes, or fires. Based on the survey of extant county records, only three rural cotton-producing counties in Texas have relatively complete records for any length of time before the Civil War.[17]

Colorado County's courthouse records proved to be virtually complete and invaluable, even if other valuable historical documents in the area have been lost or destroyed, including church minutes, city records, women's diaries, and many women's letters. However, district and county court records from 1837 to the present are well preserved and give details of hundreds of court proceedings involving women, both married and single. Marriage records, probate documents, and deeds and bond records from the Colorado County courthouse are virtually complete. Other sources, such as Confederate Widows' Pension records, marks and brands records, a few extant Justice of the Peace record books, scattered issues of local newspapers, and a few letters, diaries, and reminiscences, help fill out the picture of women's lives in this nineteenth-century southern county. The exhaustive reading of every extant public document in Colorado County from 1837 to 1873 provided the contours of this group's lives in ways that private letters and diaries could not. The stories of women who might otherwise have left no record because they were not literate, leisured, elite, or introspective enough to write a journal are included in these public documents.

The women of Colorado County are not expected to exemplify or typify all southern women. The South was never one homogeneous cultural and economic monolith but rather ranged from the urban and industrial eastern seaboard towns to the extremely rural western farming and plantation communities of Colorado County, Texas, including nearly everything in between. Located approximately seventy miles west of present-day Houston, Texas, Colorado County was one of the first counties in Texas, created under the Republic of Texas in 1836. Originally part of the first colony of three hundred

Anglo settlers under Stephen F. Austin, a portion of it was surveyed to be the capital of that settlement but was passed over in favor of San Felipe de Austin (now in Austin County). Settlers organized Columbus, one of the few towns and the county seat, in 1823. It remained the only town of significant size in the county yet did not have a large enough population to be listed in the census until after the Civil War.[18]

Nineteenth-century Colorado County was unique in some ways. The Spanish legal heritage in Texas made the adaptation of a basically southern legal tradition distinctive from that of some other states yet similar to southern states such as Louisiana and Arkansas. Because it was the last of the southern states to be settled before the Civil War, Texas passed laws that possessed a frontier quality, including more liberality in areas that older southern states did not and could not adopt because of tradition. Neither Texas nor the county had the time necessary to diversify the economy as land became scarcer—at the time of the Civil War land was still available for cultivation in the county even if it was not of the best quality. Colorado County was also unique in its large number of German immigrants who perhaps diluted the essential southern ideals brought to Texas by the majority southern population.

In spite of its uniqueness, Colorado County embraced southern ideals and held some important commonalities with the rest of the South. These included an economic dependence upon cotton, a commitment to slavery as an economic and social institution, and the willingness to contemplate or actually enter a war to protect a way of life built upon the previous two commonalities.[19]

Colorado County sat on the very western edge of the southern, cotton-producing, slaveholding society. The county consisted of three soil sections: "a rolling blackland suitable for cotton, corn, small grains, and fruit"; "a post oak timber country"; and a "flat country" suitable for potatoes and rice. However, its agricultural and economic strength was cotton. Colorado County produced more cotton than any other Texas county in 1850 and the fourth largest cotton crop in the state in 1859. While it fell behind other, more productive counties in 1860, cotton and corn continued to be the most predominant and important crops for its residents. Reliance upon the cash crop of cotton and other agricultural products impeded the development of industries: three small sawmills and a blacksmith shop were the only productive industries in 1860. After the Civil War a few more industries developed, including a canned-meat packaging company. However, like the rest of the rural south, Colorado County remained mostly rural and struggled to make the shift from slave to free labor in producing its mainstay of cotton.[20]

As the residents of Colorado County relied on cotton as their primary cash crop, they depended upon slave labor to make it profitable. In 1850, 723 slaves comprised just 32 percent of the county's population, but 3,558 slaves comprised nearly 45 percent by 1860. The increase in the number of slaves by 392 percent in ten years outpaced the percentage increase in Texas as a whole. In addition to the growth in number of slaveholders in Colorado County during this period, the number of slaves each owner held increased. In 1850 only ten slave owners qualified as planters by holding more than twenty slaves; by 1860, fifty-five were planters, and four of those held over one hundred slaves each. Because the economy of the county depended heavily upon cotton and slaves, it is not surprising that the editors of the county's primary newspaper, the *Colorado Citizen,* defended slavery and castigated those who would question the institution. The district court even indicted one of its citizens, Richard Putney, "for bringing the institution of slavery (African) into dispute in the mind of a free inhabitant of this state."[21]

In addition to sharing southern values due to their dependence upon cotton and slavery, the vast majority of the Anglo and African American populations had their origins in other southern states and thus brought their attitudes with them to Texas. However, while there were extremely few Native Americans or Mexicans, Colorado County also had a large population of settlers and inhabitants from German-speaking provinces of Europe. (Germany was not yet a unified country, and so technically the immigrants were not German; however, for the sake of simplicity they will be referred to as Germans throughout this work.) Germans or their recent descendants made up nearly half the county's white population in 1850, 40 percent in 1860, and 46 percent in 1870.[22] The most famous Germans in Texas came as part of the Society for the Protection of German Immigrants in Texas in response to the upheavals of 1848, settling in central Texas near New Braunfels. However, Germans had begun settling in the eastern part of Texas as early as 1821. These first Germanic settlers formed a community along the border of Austin and Colorado County and were joined by other immigrants throughout the nineteenth century, even after the more popular and culturally distinct central Texas settlement had begun. Most Germans in Colorado County settled in separate areas such as Bernardo and Frelsburg. However, many lived in the predominantly Anglo county seat of Columbus or in other Anglo areas. Even while maintaining much of their cultural distinctiveness in these communities, Germans in Colorado County associated more frequently with Anglo southerners than did those Germans who settled in central or west Texas. They quickly adopted southern agriculture and commercial practices that forced them into the matrix of southern society. While many Germans eschewed slavery, a few of the wealthier Germans not only grew cotton but owned slaves.[23]

In the crucial presidential election of 1860 the county newspaper's editors urged caution and espoused unionism. After Abraham Lincoln, the symbol of an increasing northern threat to slavery, was elected, the *Citizen* endorsed secession wholeheartedly, and the rest of Colorado County seconded the opinion. Although a large portion of the German population opposed secession and expressed their opinion at the polls, the secession referendum carried the county by a large majority. Predominantly German districts of the county mostly returned votes against secession, but even there many prosecession votes were returned.[24] The large German presence did not significantly modify the essential southern character of Colorado County.

This book, then, is as much about how southern ideals regarding women took root in and pervaded Colorado County's society and laws as southerners settled this eastern portion of Texas as it is about how these southern laws and ideals affected the choices and realities of women of all races, ethnicities, and classes. Chapter 1 describes women's lives and roles in settling Colorado County after Texas gained its independence from Mexico and how the frontier shaped their daily lives and realities. Chapter 1 also traces the Texas evolution of the most important laws affecting southern women: married women's property rights. Although drawing initially and heavily from the Spanish legal heritage, Texans adapted this tradition in such a way that by the end of the frontier period the operation of the laws practically replicated that of the southern legal codes.

Chapter 2 continues a discussion of the frontier period of Colorado County and particularly the actions and reactions of women who found themselves without husbands. Their experiences show how the frontier was less than hospitable to women and to single women especially. Most women found it absolutely necessary to marry and remarry because of the realities of frontier life even more than because of the dictates of southern ideals.

When Colorado County became more settled, it developed antebellum traits more characteristic of the South as a whole. Chapter 3 describes how the ideals regarding antebellum southern women exerted more influence over women's lives in this period of the county's history. These ideals were reflected in the choices women made as well as in the constraints placed upon them by the southern laws and legal tradition.

African American women's experiences of the changes in Colorado County contrasted enormously with those of white women. As slaves, black women had choices, family lives, and legal access that diverged so significantly from the lives of white women as to warrant a separate discussion in chapter 4.

Chapter 5 explores how the Civil War affected women in Colorado County. Spared the physical destruction caused by the military conflicts in other southern states, the people of Colorado County still experienced enormous upheavals in their economy and in their social ideals. Women took up the roles of their men absent because of the war, challenging the social ideals of what women's nature enabled them to do, as well as forcing legal rigidity regarding women to become more flexible.

Chapter 6 explores the postwar years in Colorado County and the meanings of the changes brought about due to war, women's increased presence in business and law during the war, and especially emancipation. African American women challenged and changed their relationships as dependents to the white male heads of households. In wake of this challenge, white women's dependence and submissive position in the household became ever more important in the attempts to uphold the ideals of southern society.

Political, social, and economic conditions; the social ideals regarding women's nature and place; and laws regarding women all played different parts in shaping southern women's lives in the nineteenth century. Historians have studied how each of these aspects changed and developed in the nineteenth-century South or how they affected individual women. This in-depth study of one small rural southern county seeks to reveal how one group of women reacted to these formative factors in their lives. By concentrating on a small county, this study is able to take into account the many facets of women's lives and to show how changes occurred not only in their individual lives but in the larger ideology, conditions, and legal aspects that provided women the framework in which they chose their actions. Women were not just passive recipients of the defining characteristics of their lives, whether it be ideology, politics, or law; they made active decisions within the confines of the factors governing their society.

CHAPTER I

WOMEN, WORK, FAMILY,
and LAW *on the* FRONTIER

I came to Texas in 1842. . . . We settled on the Colorado River,
near Reels bend. The country all around was a perfect wilderness,
and the people had no houses to live in. . . . We pulled through
until we could clear land and raise something to eat.
— CORDELIA SIMMONS

The adage "A woman's place is in the home" is hard to follow when families
have no homes. Ideas of women's place, women's work, and women's duties
were all stretched by the challenges of carving new homes and new livings out
of wilderness on the frontier, as indicated in a letter written by Cordelia Simmons.[1] Yet the men and women who settled Colorado County, like others
who traveled west, clung to traditional gender ideals despite the day-to-day
exceptions they were forced to make in order to survive on the frontier. Social ideals shaped women's perceptions of themselves and their abilities. These
ideals also shaped the formation of statutory and judicial law in frontier Texas.
However, frontier living challenged both women's expectations of their roles
and the laws that were drafted to conform to the ideals of women who stayed
out of the fields and public life. Frontier women who shared men's duties at
home also sometimes performed men's roles in public. Both society and the
courts made exceptions for these women when conditions seemed to warrant
it, but otherwise most women tried to maintain standard gender roles despite
their seeming inadequacy on an untamed frontier.

Colorado County experienced an unusually long frontier period. Before
Texas won its independence from Mexico in 1836, only a few places in Texas
could have been considered anything but frontier because of the sparse population, rudimentary government, and undeveloped community structures.
Nevertheless, the area that is now Colorado County had been growing in population and becoming increasingly developed. During the 1836 war for independence Colorado County and its fledgling town, Columbus, found themselves directly in the path of Sam Houston's retreating forces. In the resulting

"runaway scrape," as the retreat was called, the settlers scrambled to the east fleeing Santa Anna's army. As they left, Houston's forces often burned private homes and other buildings to prevent them from falling into the hands of the Mexican troops. After the surrender and retreat of the Mexican army at San Jacinto, the inhabitants began slowly filtering back into Colorado County to find most of their homes, buildings, fences, crops, and stores of foods destroyed and their livestock missing. Those who returned faced a virtual frontier again as they started from scratch rebuilding their homes and reestablishing their community. Despite owning land grants in the area, many could not bear to return; as a result, some of the most attractive land in the county remained inactive, unsettled, and unavailable. Colorado County residents slowly rebuilt their lives, but the momentum toward growth had been stifled.[2]

In the painful aftermath of the Texas Revolution population, prosperity, and other evidence of civilization in Colorado County grew slowly. The county was officially organized in the new Republic of Texas in 1837. The county seat of Columbus was described by a traveler at that time as "a small town, consisting of two public houses, two small stores, and half dozen shanties. . . ." Ten years later another traveler found a few additional houses, but only one additional store. The number of taverns remained at two, and he recorded that there was no evidence that the place was growing. In 1850 the entire county held only fifteen hundred white persons.[3]

Those who chose to move to Colorado County in the 1830s, 1840s, and 1850s therefore found a virtual frontier. The majority of those immigrating to Texas came from the southern states. Colorado County was no exception: by 1850 immigrants from southern states outnumbered those from northern states 478 to 42. These southerners brought with them their culture, gender ideals, and, of course, slavery. The Germans who migrated to Texas before 1848 settled primarily along the border of Colorado and Austin Counties. Like the southern immigrants, German immigrants faced frontier life that challenged their cultural ideals. In addition Germans had to obey the law of the land, shaped primarily by southerners.[4]

As with most frontier areas, more males than females migrated to Colorado County. Most Mexican and Republic of Texas censuses enumerated only heads of household, so the total number of women and men in the county before 1850 is difficult to determine. Wives, sisters, and daughters in the 1825 Mexican census were not named, but they were counted; at that time, of the ascertainable white population of 174 persons, 62 were women (36 percent) and only 25 of the 59 male heads of household had wives (42 percent). As late as 1850, near the end of the frontier era in Colorado County, men still outnumbered women, with 675 females comprising only 44 percent of the 1,534 residents. Among adults, the disparity between males and females was even greater: 275 women made up only 40 percent of the adult white population.[5]

There were many reasons for the disproportionate amount of men in Colorado County. Moving to the West represented to many men the idea of independence and freedom. Thus younger, unmarried men were more likely to move to frontier Colorado County than were older, married men. However, married men did move west as well, although their wives did not always go with them. Many wives stayed farther east waiting for their husbands to make homes or buy land or just get settled before moving their entire households.[6]

Other wives were purposely and permanently left behind. The difficulty of obtaining a divorce in the eastern seaboard states had, since colonial times, made the West an attractive place for men wishing to escape unhappy marriages. Texas was particularly inviting to men who no longer wanted to fulfill their marriage vows. Travel to Texas was difficult, thus making it harder for men who deserted to be found. Texas also had more liberal divorce statutes than did the southern seaboard states. Especially before 1845 the fact that Texas was not part of the United States meant that courts were less strict about ensuring that spouses left behind in a foreign country (the United States) were notified of impending divorce proceedings. Even the president of the Republic of Texas, Sam Houston, had left his wife in Tennessee when he moved to Texas, and only years later when he wished to remarry did he get a divorce.[7]

Three out of nine men who filed for and received divorces in Colorado County during the frontier period had left their wives behind in other southern states. For instance, John Hope's wife Rusha remained in Florida after he moved west to Texas. Either he had purposely abandoned her or she had been initially recalcitrant about the move. After he filed for divorce, she made the decision to move to Texas but was too late to save the marriage. William Dunlap simply left behind his wife (or perhaps wives) and married another.[8]

While some wives were not given the choice to migrate with their husbands and other wives were waiting for better opportunities before joining theirs, undoubtedly some wives just absolutely did not want to go. There were many reasons not to want to travel to frontier Texas. Even the wealthiest families faced untold hardships. Reminiscences of frontier Colorado County residents describe the area through 1850 as "pioneer" days when "settlers lived in log cabins, on dirt floors and ground their corn at home on steel hand-mills," but not because they "were indigent and thriftless. On the contrary many of them were well to do, owning many negroes, large tracts of rich land, cattle, horses and sheep."[9]

Many wives, though, chose to accompany their male family members to Texas. By 1850, 239 married women resided in Colorado County. The move itself was no doubt extremely difficult. Many families traveled to Colorado County overland from the Southeast, and a few traveled from the North. The wealthiest and luckiest women rode in carriages with other women and children while wagons carried their belongings. Other women rode in wagons sitting on top of everything they owned. Most women, however, walked the fifteen miles each day on their two- to three-month trip from, say, Tennessee. Other families traveled to Galveston by boat and then traveled the one hundred or more miles overland to Columbus.[10]

These trips, of course, were exhausting and even dangerous. Even when women were spared the difficult work that men performed, such as driving wagons and watching the stock, the duties of washing, cooking, cleaning, and child care on the trail were strenuous and belied the myth that women were fragile or delicate. Colorado County resident James Holt remembered how his mother walked from Georgia to Alabama and then from Houston to Columbus carrying a five- or six-month-old baby the entire way. Although the sickly baby was nursed through the move, it died a few years later when the family settled on a stagnant creek and everyone came down with the "chills and fever."[11]

Once the families survived the trip, the work for women was far from over. Women's labor was absolutely necessary to create a successful farm or plantation, especially for young families. Unlike in the rapidly industrializing North where urban women's duties were more to consume than to produce, women in the South had always played a valuable role in the economic production of their households. Wives in frontier Colorado County carried on the traditional responsibilities of caring for gardens, preserving meat and vegetables, making soap and candles, preparing meals, keeping the houses comfortable and clean, and bearing and raising children. However, they performed these duties in new ways under adverse conditions.[12]

Few families were fortunate enough to move into houses once they arrived in Colorado County. Because planting crops took priority over building shelters, immigrants sometimes continued to live in tents. Even when the first shelters were built, they were crude and hastily put together. Families lived in primitive, difficult-to-clean homes that often were built of cane or pin-oak board and had dirt floors. Rarely were families able to bring kitchenware to make life easier for women cooking for large families. Instead, with a minimum of utensils women learned to cook over open fires. In addition, everything had to be made or produced because there was no place to buy necessities. James Holt remembered that "there was no market for chickens, eggs, butter, honey, etc.," and so they raised or made that food themselves. Corn had to be ground with a hand mill and meals made without a cookstove or matches. Because beef was scarce and expensive—even in the state destined to become famous for its cattle drives—and bread scarcer, frontier families harvested the plentiful deer of the area, and women learned the new techniques of drying it for both meat and bread.[13]

As difficult as it was for women to carry on their usual responsibilities in frontier conditions, wives were often called upon to do much more. In most immigrant families a wife was the only other adult besides the husband, and she most likely helped perform traditionally male duties that were too numerous for one man alone. A typical woman probably directed her labor as much as possible toward the bare necessities of life and making a success out of the farm—pulling through until the family "could clear land and raise something to eat." First and foremost, land had to be cleared and crops planted. In order to survive those first years wives had to assist with duties atypical for women. In order to have a shelter at all, the frontier wife probably had to help in its building. Concentrating on survival and not domestic niceties is probably what led Seaborn Trumbul Stapleton to remember that he was seven or eight years old before he got his first pair of pants. His family lived in the county for several years before taking the time to construct a hand-operated cotton gin and loom to weave cloth.[14]

Families that owned and brought with them slaves probably spared the women from the most back-breaking labor in the fields and building shelter. Yet even the wives of slave owners faced the same difficult chores of performing traditional women's duties under adverse conditions and for a larger number of people in the household, slave and free. Because getting in crops was a priority for slaveholders as well as nonslaveholders, slave labor was probably directed to the field work and away from the homes.[15]

Women's labor was difficult but invaluable on the frontier and as part of the family project. In 1837 David Wade estimated that his fifteen-year-old daughter's services were worth two thousand dollars when he filed a civil suit against a group of men who had "stolen" her away. If Wade had recovered that amount in cash in 1850, it would have put him into the top quarter of the population in terms of wealth in Colorado County. Although he undoubtedly exaggerated the harm caused by his daughter's loss for the purpose of punitive damages, this still shows that even a young girl's labor was highly valued.[16]

Men who brought their wives or could find wives on the frontier undoubtedly appreciated their economic and physical assistance and contributions to the household. However much Texans might have recognized and valued women's contributions to individual families and building the frontier generally, they continued to hold onto the ideal of the southern household, including the importance of upholding male authority within that household. Lawmakers continued to see women primarily as wives dependent upon and sub-missive to the authority of their husbands. Because Texas inherited the idea of community property from its Spanish heritage and because laws in frontier states were generally more favorable to women than in the established eastern seaboard states, many contemporaries and historians alike have claimed that married women in Texas had substantially different, even better, rights than women in other southern states. If this was ever true, by the end of the frontier era in Colorado County married women had almost the same rights as else-where in the South.[17]

Former southerners made up the majority of the rebellious inhabitants when the Republic of Texas declared its independence from Mexico in 1836. Mexican civil law had been in force until 1836, however, and certain rights, in-cluding married women's property rights, had come to be taken for granted by all Texans. Yet most citizens of Texas were more comfortable with the political opinion and customs, common law tradition, and governmental organization of the United States. In the midst of revolutionary turmoil and uncertain fu-tures, however, the framers of the constitution of 1836 considered it expedi-ent to declare that all Mexican laws should remain in force until such time as "the common law of England, with such modifications as our circumstances [warrant]" could be introduced by statute.[18]

In most cases the Texas Congress began acting immediately to introduce common law, and Spanish civil law prevailed for only a few years after the constitution was adopted. However, in the area of married women's property rights, the Texas Congress and later the legislature vacillated, torn between three different impulses: Spanish civil law as it had been practiced in Texas under Mexican rule, common law as practiced in the United States, and the ideas of equity law that offered special remedies when common law gave none.

From independence in 1836 until 1839 the Texas Congress allowed Spanish civil law as it had been practiced in Texas under Mexican rule to define married women's property. These laws considered that a husband and wife formed a partnership by their marriage, in which each accrued an equal share in the "ac-quisitions, fruits, profits, and gains of whatever nature" during the marriage. Although the wife equally owned this community property, as the business manager of the partnership, the husband administered it with only slight ex-ceptions. He could sell any or all of their community property without his wife's consent, and he was the only necessary party in suits concerning the property. However, a husband could not alienate property fraudulently or dis-pose of more than his half share by last will and testament. Spanish civil law also allowed both spouses to hold separate property in their own names. For a wife, this separate estate included all real assets she owned at the time of marriage and legacies, inheritances, or donations made to her during the marriage. Again, although the wife owned the property, only in special instances could she control it.[19]

The finer points of Spanish law regarding married women's property, however, were probably lost upon the inhabitants of Texas as a whole and Colorado County specifically. One legal historian has suggested that lawyers in Texas, some of whom had legal training in or law books from Louisiana, assumed that the civil laws of Louisiana and Mexico were "essentially the same, and in most matters of concern to them, they were correct." Most frontier Texas lawyers had little training or law books of any kind. In the earliest years after independence the laws and the legal system remained confusing and unsystematized.[20]

The Colorado County District Court's first session exemplified the irregularity of court proceedings in the earliest years of the Texas Republic. It was held outside, and its sole action was to fine those who had been summoned for jury duty and failed to appear. With the rapid changes in laws and courts, a lack of learned lawyers, and the primitive knowledge of Texas law even by judges, "arguments and decisions (even of the Supreme Court) were based more often on common sense than on citations." In 1842 the Supreme Court of the Republic of Texas recognized that irregular proceedings were bound to come out of Texas' chaotic early years and allowed for them.[21]

Therefore, it is not surprising that the early Colorado County courts exhibited little consistency in their approach to married women's rights. This lack of consistency allowed some married women to act as individuals on their own behalf. For example, on several occasions Martha Bronson sued, and was sued, in her own name for her separate property in both the county and district courts. She continued these suits with little reference to her husband in the official papers and without his express approval, despite the prenuptial marriage contract they had signed, which gave him half interest in her estate and sole management of it. The judges both allowed these suits to be defended and prosecuted in her name and ultimately recognized her defense of her separate property against a debt incurred by her new husband before their marriage. Spanish civil law recognized that Bronson had a premarital legal identity and allowed her to continue that identity after marriage. However, without claiming abandonment or mismanagement, even Spanish civil law would not have allowed her to prosecute and defend these suits without her husband's express authorization. Judges and juries probably took into account the fact that Martha's husband, Zeno, was a less than ideal husband and head of household. Thus, in the chaotic frontier legal system Martha Bronson was allowed to protect her individual rights even against the authority of her husband.[22]

However, even in the frontier courts not all married women were allowed such liberty. While Martha Bronson was defending her separate property as if she had a legal identity, another married woman's identity was subsumed under that of her husband. In December, 1838, Nathan Barr instituted a suit in district court on behalf of his wife's separate property. Nathan Barr had married Rachel Newman within the preceding ten months, and the suit was to enforce a contract she had made with Jacob Lynch while still a widow. Although the property and the gains of the suit were clearly Rachel's separate property, the suit was prosecuted solely by her husband.[23]

Less than a year later the Barrs were involved in another suit that led the courts to allow for yet another precedent of a married woman's involvement in court. Nathan Barr was embroiled in other lawsuits with Jacob Lynch besides the one regarding his wife's separate property. When Jacob Lynch won a judgment from the district court, the Colorado County sheriff levied two hundred bushels of corn to satisfy the judgment. However, the corn belonged not to Nathan Barr or even Rachel Barr, but to her son Andrew Newman. While she was still a widow the probate court had granted to Rachel the coguardianship of her son Andrew. Along with her coguardian Andrew Rabb, Rachel sued the sheriff on behalf of the minor son to recover the corn. The sheriff promptly asked the judge to dismiss the suit because one of the parties to the suit was "a feme covert and incompetent to appear as above without joining her husband in the writ." The sheriff argued that Rachel Barr was "covered" by the protection of her husband (feme covert), and it was her husband who should be in court regarding her legal matters. Under the precedents of Spanish civil law the court could have easily authorized the prosecution of the suit by the wife only. No law had yet been passed instituting the English common-law concept of coverture, by which a married woman's entire legal identity was subsumed under that of her husband, and thus a feme covert. The judge, however, sustained the defendant's objection and required that Rachel's husband join the suit in order for it to continue. According to the courts, Rachel had a husband capable of representing her interests and therefore had no right to challenge his authority in this public business.[24]

While judges and juries in Colorado County struggled to determine the rights of married women, the Congress of the Republic of Texas attempted to institute the common law of the United States as its constitution had instructed. In 1839 the Texas Congress finally addressed the issue of married women's property rights. The statute that the Texas Congress enacted, however, established the law of dower with little forethought as to what that establishment would mean. English common law did not allow a married woman to own property separately or commonly with her husband: upon marriage all of her real property became her husband's. Common law did, however, grant married women dower rights allowing the widow a lifetime interest only in one-third of her deceased husband's estate. In United States locales that recognized this law, married women received an interest in all real property acquired by their husbands during their lifetimes. Consequently, even during his lifetime a husband's conveyance of that property was incomplete without the wife's relinquishment of her dower rights to it. The January, 1839, act did not specifically address the relinquishment of dower rights. However, because it indicated that a widow was entitled only to dower in her deceased husband's estate, it directly contradicted the idea of joint ownership of property and technically stripped all married women of any separate property they had acquired under Spanish law.[25]

Judges and clerks in Colorado County paid no heed whatsoever to the statute granting women dower rights. Not a single widow applied for dower rights in probate court, not a single deed in 1839 relinquished a married woman's dower rights in her husband's property, and not a single district or probate court case maintained a married woman's lifetime interest in one-third of the property of the marriage. In May of that year the estate of Robert Gray Cummings was partitioned among his heirs, a widow and four children. Cummings left no will, and so the partition was decided by the Colorado County court. The judge distinguished between the property brought into the republic and that acquired in Texas. Each child and the widow received one-fifth of the property brought into the republic—a decision not entirely inconsistent with English common law. But of the property acquired in the republic, the widow Isabella was given one-half in fee simple and the children received one-eighth each—a decision consistent with Spanish civil law and community property ownership. While the judge recognized that the property brought to Texas from the United States might be subject to English common law, he ruled that the property in Texas should be divided according to Spanish legal precedents. The judge made no provisions at all for dower.[26]

The institution of the dower law and the swift break from the Spanish legal system of married women's property proved unpopular in Texas. Just a year later the Texas Congress repealed the statute and codified married women's property rights according to rules of equity. Equity law was a separate set of rules in England and the United States that had arisen to consider on a case by case basis what was "right" and not just what was statutorily legal. Most courts in the United States followed both laws of statute and equity, and Texas did the same. The constitution and subsequent acts never recognized separate courts of equity but endeavored instead to incorporate common law and the ideals of equity into the same court.[27]

Equity law as practiced in the United States offered married women an al-

ternative to the rigidity of the common law by recognizing antenuptial contracts, premarital contracts that gave the wife control of certain property, trusts,
separate estates, and mandatory contractual agreements between the husband
and wife. The use of these contracts and trusts increased enormously in the
United States during the first half of the nineteenth century, and by midcen-
tury significant numbers of women used these equitable rights, subject to interpretation of the judge.[28]

However, disputes over the contents of separate estates, the need for overly
specific wording of trusts and deeds, untrustworthy trustees, and the expense
of court proceedings worried those who wished to use equity to protect married women's interests. So in 1839 (as Texas endeavored to meld common law
and married women's property rights by introducing dower rights) Mississippi passed the first married women's property rights act and thus began a
trend in the South and the United States by codifying the laws of married wom-
en's property found in equity. Married women's property acts in the United
States, such as the one passed in Mississippi, systematized and offered to all
married women the rights and privileges wealthy women had enjoyed under
equity in the courts of common law. Neither Mississippi's act nor the act of
any other southern state gave the wife control over her own property.[29]

Following Mississippi's example of codifying equity into statutory law, the
Texas Congress passed an omnibus act in an attempt to clarify which of the
three legal traditions Texas law would follow. In 1840 the Texas Congress specifically repealed all Mexican laws and adopted the English common law. However, the act made exceptions in cases of land grants, colonization, and min-
erals and continued the homestead exemption, whereby a certain amount of
land inhabited by a person as his or her home was protected from confiscation
by creditors for debts. The act further explicitly outlined new laws regulating
married couples' property that incorporated ideas of all three legal traditions.
Community property provisions of Spanish law were adopted, giving married
women the outright ownership of one-half of all real property acquired by the
couple during marriage. The equity law tradition and its codified example in
the Mississippi Married Women's Property Act contributed to a recognition
of married women's right to own property separately from their husbands.
That property included all lands and slaves that a woman owned at the time
of marriage and all that she might gain by gift, devise, or descent during marriage, as well as the paraphernalia that she owned before marriage. Finally, English common law and Spanish law might allow her to own property, but both
stripped a married woman of her right to control any of that property and
gave her husband "the sole management of such lands and slaves."[30]

Although husbands had management and control of their wives' separate

property, in 1841 Texas Congress clarified that a married woman must be consulted before her separate real property could be sold. The tradition of English
common law required a married woman to relinquish her dower rights to property to validate a deed. A married woman in Texas did not have dower rights,
but after 1841 the transfer of any of her separate "estate or interest in any land,
slave or slaves, or other effects" required a relinquishment: the wife was to be
"examined privily and apart from her husband, [and] shall declare that she did
freely and willingly seal and deliver the said writing (to be then shown and explained to her,) and wishes not to retract it, and shall acknowledge the said
writing so again shown to her, to be her act" before a judge or chief justice of
the court.[31]

Colorado County had virtually ignored the statutes on dower rights, but
the new married women's property rights acts made more impact on married
women in the county. Before 1840 few deeds included a wife's name, signature, or consent to the sale. Husbands continued, as they were allowed to do
under Spanish law, to sell both the community estates and their wives' separate estates without their wives' consent. After 1840, however, married women
seemingly became more involved in the public financial affairs of the couple.
The number of deeds requiring a married woman's signature rose dramatically
and continued to rise throughout the frontier era.[32]

Compliance with the 1841 statute requiring a wife's relinquishment of her
rights in Colorado County was slow and halting at first. Of the fifteen deeds
conveying property in Colorado County in 1841, only one wife was examined
separately from her husband. In the following years most of the deeds contained the verification of a woman's separate examination although in a less
than systematized procedure. Sometimes her exam was conducted months or
years after the sale; sometimes the examination seemed not to follow the intent of the law. For example, Nancy Morris acknowledged the deed to be her
"act and deed" in a separate paragraph, but not necessarily in a separate room,
from her husband.[33]

The 1841 statute applied only to a wife's separate real property. Although
Texas law seemingly liberalized a married woman's ability to own property by
enacting the Spanish community property laws, it actually gave her less control than English common law. She could own separate property and owned
one-half of the joint property, but she managed none of it and had the power
to refuse to relinquish her rights in the sale of only her separate property. She
had no similar power over any community property as married women under
English common-law heritage had due to their dower rights. Dower rights in
the United States and during the brief year that they were recognized in Texas
specifically stated that a widow's one-third life estate included the dwelling

house and surrounding land and outhouses. Under Texas law this property was usually part of the community estate and only rarely a married woman's separate estate. Therefore, women in Virginia could block the sale or mortgaging of their homes, but married women in Texas could not.

In 1846 the legislature of Texas (no longer an independent nation, but a state in the Union) sought to rectify this situation. The legislators did not require that a husband consult his wife before selling or mortgaging all community property, but it did require a married woman's consent before the sale of the family homestead became complete.[34]

Texas laws regarding married women's property therefore drew from a mix of legal traditions. By 1846, however, they closely resembled those in other southern states where equity was recognized and especially where married women's property acts had been passed. Texas law differed from law of other southern states by entitling a wife to one-half ownership of community property. However, while she was married, the extent of a woman's ability to manage and control property and the amount of property over which she had any power was almost identical to that of married women in the rest of the South. The heritage of Spanish law added a distinctiveness to married women's property ownership, but it did not represent a greater advancement for married women's rights than those in states elsewhere in the South.[35]

Texas legislators, like others in the South who passed married women's property acts, did not enact these statutes because they believed that women suddenly deserved or were even capable of handling the responsibilities of property ownership. The Texas Married Women's Property Act was a way to shelter the family fortunes by allowing some property to be held in the wife's name, free from the claims of creditors. Fathers could rest more easily knowing that the property they transferred to their daughters would not be easily wasted or gambled away by their sons-in-law in the uncertain financial situation of the Texas economy. Paralleling state legislatures throughout antebellum America, Texan lawmakers strove to guard families' financial resources without elevating women's power within the home.[36]

Although a gradual change in attitudes toward married women's rights and abilities may have preceded these acts, the primary cause of the revisions in the law was the unstable nineteenth-century economy and particularly the panic and depression of 1837. Texans understood the economic pressures all too well. Many Texans were southerners who had moved west in an attempt to remake fortunes lost in the panic or to try to avoid their debts by moving to a different country. Legislators' concern over debtor-creditor relations and their proclivity for debt relief is evidenced by the Homestead Exemption Act passed the year before the Texas Married Women's Property Act. The homestead act protected a certain amount of a person's land from creditors even in complete bankruptcy. Like the married women's property act, the homestead protection act performed at least two purposes: it maintained the inviolability of a family unit and kept that family from becoming a burden on society.[37]

The separate examination of the wife whenever her separate property or the homestead was sold is an indication that lawmakers believed not in women's increased abilities but in their need to be protected. The emphasis on "privily" and apart, or separate and apart, in married women's relinquishment of their rights was important for the legitimization of the sales. As in the United States, legislators and judges in Texas adopted with great hesitation the idea that married women might be able to make their own judgments about or question their husbands' handling of financial matters. The outside influence and protection of the court and, in particular, the judge was necessary to insure that the wife's small degree of control was preserved. The separate exam began with an explanation of the deed to the wife, whether or not she could read. This examination was an opportunity for the wife to "retract" her signature. Before a standard examination form was adopted, Colorado County judges' descriptions of their private exams of wives often included the words "voluntarily," "without fear," and "without constraint."[38]

The judges assumed that a married woman was unaccustomed to financial decisions and therefore must receive a private, not public, opportunity apart from her husband to have the matters explained to her before she could make a decision. The Supreme Court of Texas recognized this fact when it allowed a wife to withdraw from a contract up to the last moment. Associate Chief Justice Abner Lipscomb reminded the court: "Such is the influence the husband acquires over the wife, that however worthless and profligate he may be, he would be able generally to procure her assent to transfer her property with all forms required by the statute; and the proceeds would be spent by him in riot and debauch, if so inclined."[39]

As a result of the 1846 statute requiring a wife's relinquishment of her rights to the homestead, married women more often left their homes to appear before a judge or justice. Less than 10 percent of the deeds involving wives in Colorado County before 1841 included a separate acknowledgment or examination of the wife; between 1841 and the end of the frontier era in 1852, 90 percent did. In a conservative estimate, an average of 11 percent of married women every year were required to go to the courthouse and sanction their husbands' actions regarding their own property during the frontier period.[40]

The importance of married women's trips to the courthouse is difficult to measure. A separate exam was possibly a mere formality. Every woman who was examined privately and whose deed appeared in the county clerk's record had agreed to the sale of property, of course, or the deed would not have been recorded. After the 1841 statutes a few deeds did find their way into the record without the wives having been officially examined: 32 of the 302 deeds transferred the interests of wives in separate or homestead property without separate acknowledgment by the wives. Nevertheless, the vast majority of the deeds that made it to the courthouse did include the wives' consent. It is hard to imagine that many married women would or could oppose their husbands' wishes in selling their property even with the intervention of a county official. Wives accustomed to submitting to the authority of their husbands in household management would not easily challenge that authority in a public place. If any women did object to their husbands' financial dealings, most did not make their objections known publicly. Despite the 10 percent of the deeds without wives' acknowledgment, no one sued to contest their validity.[41]

In fact, no frontier wives challenged their husbands in court over the transfer of separate or community property. Nor did any sue a third party to recover property that she believed her husband had improperly or wrongly conveyed. Except in cases of divorce (to be discussed later), the slight share of control granted to married women in these series of acts was never exercised in a Colorado County courtroom by a wife against a husband.

One frontier-era Colorado County court case, however, suggested that a husband and wife not involved in divorce proceedings might possibly have differed in their opinions on financial matters. This was not a case brought against a husband but a defense by the wife after her husband's death to avoid paying a debt. In 1844 a recently widowed Susan Ann Stevenson answered Alexander Brown's petition to recover a debt on a promissory note that she and her husband had jointly signed. Stevenson claimed that "at the time of signing said promissory note [she] was a married woman incompetent to contract[,] that she derived no benefit therefrom directly or indirectly[.] [D]efendant further states that she was persuaded much against her will and desire to sign the aforementioned note for the sum specified therein."[42]

The judge accepted a "judgment by default" against Susan Stevenson as administrator of Robert Stevenson's estate and allowed the question of whether Susan Stevenson's property should be held liable to be submitted to the jury. The jury found in favor of Susan Ann Stevenson, and her property was not subject to the debt. Even in this case it is probable that had her husband not died during the trial, Susan Stevenson would not have pleaded this defense. She might have disagreed with her husband's financial decisions, or she might have seen this as a good defense after his death. Regardless, during her husband's life she did not use the legal resources available to her to challenge his authority over the financial matters of the household.[43]

During the frontier era husbands in most cases exercised exclusive control publicly over legal and financial matters. Even though married women owned property and needed to protect or defend their legal title, they were required to do so with the consent and in joint agency with their husbands. At least seventeen cases involving married women's property came before the frontier-period district court after the Married Women's Property Act of 1841, and in fifteen of those cases the husbands exercised nearly exclusive control over the proceedings.[44] In one case a husband even acknowledged "service" of the suit for himself and on behalf of his wife: "I Dempsey Pace hereby acknowledge service of the written petition and waive writ and copy of petition for myself and my wife Elizabeth Pace." Not only did he and other husbands control the proceedings, but their wives may never have even received notice that their property rights were being questioned. A judge dismissed the sole case in which a married woman attempted to pursue a case in her own name for being brought in a "wrong name." In another case a wife whose husband was "absent" sued by a "next friend" to halt the foreclosure of their homestead.[45]

Although the district court granted little latitude in the prosecution of suits by married women after the introduction of the Married Women's Property Act, it did recognize that in some circumstances a married woman might exercise financial rights and responsibilities. Statutes granted married women the right to contract for family "necessaries" for which the community property would be held liable. Husbands only needed to conduct transactions that disposed of community property or potentially transferred such property.[46]

The Colorado County District Court, however, allowed married women to contract in their husbands' absences, whether that absence be temporary or permanent. Joannah married William Dunlap in 1837. As a widow with many mouths to feed, circumstances forced Joannah to remarry as quickly as possible. Within three months she discovered that Dunlap was actually married to someone else and he abandoned her. With the ability to remarry removed from her because Texas still had no legal provisions for divorce, Joannah set out to provide for herself and her children however she could. In the process she bought some property and to pay for it signed two promissory notes for $750 each in 1839. Without their husbands' permission married women's "contracts, agreements, covenants, promises, and representations were regarded as void," according to English common law and Spanish legal tradition. Seemingly, Samuel B. Mixon, the person to whom the still-legally-married Joannah Dunlap promised $1,500, had no hope of recovering his money if Joannah refused to pay.[47]

Nevertheless, on November 5, 1840, Mixon instituted proceedings to recover the debt Joannah owed him. The wording of Mixon's petition to the court indicates the importance of Joannah's marital status, both at the signing of the note and at the filing of the suit. He pointedly, but erroneously, stated that she had been a single woman, "sole and unmarried," at the time she signed the note. Since then Joannah had "contracted marriage and united herself in the bonds of wedlock with Jacob Tipps also of the said county of Colorado, who is her present husband." Joannah in the interval had indeed married Jacob Tipps. They were married less than one month after she had successfully sued her former husband William Dunlap for the first recorded divorce in Colorado County.[48]

Mixon's petition needed to describe Joannah's matrimonial state at the time of the suit to identify the legally liable parties. Mixon could not sue a married woman unless he also named her husband as a defendant, for upon marriage husbands assumed the debts of their wives. Although Joannah had contracted this debt before her marriage, her new husband not only had to participate in her legal defense but was also liable for the payment of the debt if necessary. Joannah's marital status at the time of the suit, therefore, made a difference to Mixon's case.[49]

At first in defending their case the Tippses did not challenge the assertion of Mixon's petition that Joannah had been "sole and unmarried." Their defense rested on other points, but they lost the case in December, 1840. When the judge ruled for Mixon, the Tippses filed an injunction against the execution of the judgment. Up to the point of filing the injunction, Joannah's husband Jacob had managed the entire case and defense himself. Despite Joannah's independence prior to her marriage, the Tippses apparently took seriously the laws regarding the husband's right to manage his wife's property—and his duty to settle her debts. Whenever the documents or minutes referred to the defendant(s), they did so in the singular and as "he."[50]

However, both Joannah and Jacob signed the injunction, which claimed that there were two liens on the lots for which Joannah owed the money; an addendum was signed by Joannah alone. From this point forward the minutes always referred to the defendants in the plural, there is evidence of Joannah's continuing presence, and the Tippses engaged a lawyer to represent them. A year later a jury canceled the injunction and judgment was issued against the Tippses.[51]

Both Jacob and Joannah Tipps owned land, personal property, and slaves and could have paid the judgment ordered against them. However, they did not voluntarily do so. Samuel Mixon, probably despairing of ever collecting on the debt, sold the promissory notes to Alfred Kelso on December 10, 1840, less than a week after the injunction was filed. Kelso filed for recovery of the debt in November, 1841. Unlike in the previous defense, the Tippses immediately hired a lawyer to represent them. Still, the lawyer did not at first challenge the debt on Joannah's original inability to contract due to coverture. The Tippses' attorney argued in December, 1841, for a continuance "for the want of an Advertisement." The case received this and at least one other continuance until Kelso filed for recovery of the debt on the second promissory note as well. Finally, on March 8, 1843, after almost two years of continuances, a jury heard the case. The Tippses' attorney by this time had a well-prepared defense on multiple grounds, yet no one questioned Joannah's right to make the contract. After deliberations the jury could not agree, and the case was continued again.[52]

After a well-prepared defense, two years of continuances, three total years' experience with the issues involved in the case, and one hung jury the Tippses and their attorney finally decided to try the defense of coverture. On March 9, 1843, one day after the jury could not agree, it was presented that "in this case the defendants come and answer, and say that at the time the supposed promissory was given the said Joannah was then a married woman and that her husband was Wm Dunlap—wherefore they say that she was unable to contract or bind herself and pray that said suit be dismissed." The judge did not dismiss the case but instead continued it again for another year.[53]

When finally the "case was submitted to jury on plea of coverture" in March, 1844, the court's new instructions to the jury were, in effect, to determine if Joannah Dunlap had been acting as a *feme sole* (an English common-law term for a woman legally recognized by the law as able to conduct her own business, usually because she was single), although no Texas statute would allow such a role for a married woman until 1911.[54]

Since William Dunlap's abandonment, Joannah had purchased town lots in Columbus without permission or interference from her husband. "Joana" Dunlap was listed as the sole administrator for John Dunlavy of Austin County in 1840 even though law required that her husband be joined as coadministrator. Under her previous husband's name, McCrabb, the 1840 tax roles listed her as the head of household. And, of course, in 1839 she signed two promissory notes for a total of $1,500. For three years at least Joannah Dunlap acted as feme sole without statutory or judicial authority to do so. Those who did business with Joannah obviously did not worry that she was disabled by law to enter contracts. Samuel Mixon did not even realize that she was married. It appears that Joannah faced no legal or social problems because she was a married woman; she, apparently, did not need a divorce until she wanted to remarry.[55]

When Joannah Tipps pleaded "coverture" in 1844, the same community with whom she had been profitably trading for at least three years had to decide her right to do so. The jury found "1st That Joannah Dunlap was the wife of William Dunlap at the time of contracting 2nd They did live separate and apart at the time the contract was made 3rd She was in the habit of trading generally, 4th We believe the contract was made in the regular course of trade." [56]

Joannah had been married, but she had also been trading as if she were a single woman. The defense in pleading coverture had possibly been looking for a last-ditch attempt to avoid paying the promissory note, but failed. Fortunately for the Tippses, the judge did not make an immediate ruling in favor of either party, and the case was continued for another year. Eventually, on September 1, 1845, the Tippses and Kelso negotiated a settlement and ended the case. [57]

Joannah's extenuating circumstances played a role in the outcome of this case. By recognizing the right of Joannah to conduct business without the protection and permission of her husband, these southerners were not striking a blow against the social ideals in which wives deferred to their husbands' authority. Instead they made an allowance for one woman whose husband did not live up to his end of his obligations. [58]

One other district court case recognized that life on the frontier presented situations in which married women had to act on their own behalf. Men had greater opportunities to pick up and disappear in the West, as did Joannah's husband. But on the frontier men also often had to leave temporarily to conduct business, whether it be driving stock, going to town to get supplies, or fighting in wars against Indians or Mexicans. While her husband Abel was in California, Dolores Beeson contracted with Charles Kesler for store goods. When Kesler won a judgment against the Beesons in Justice of the Peace Court, the Beesons appealed, saying that "the said Dolores being a married woman could not make a contract except for necessaries." The district court did not recognize their defense and dismissed their appeal. When husbands did not or could not fulfill their obligations to wives, married women could assert their authority. Since Abel had left Dolores for such an extended period of time, whatever the reason, Dolores had the right to make financial decisions and arrangements. [59]

However, when husbands were capable of fulfilling their obligations to their wives, married women—even the most capable of married women—had no right to usurp the proper male role. Joannah Tipps had apparently grown accustomed to her role as a feme sole even after her marriage to Jacob. Her husband Jacob was obviously a more active partner in the marriage than her previous husband William Dunlap had been, and Jacob had engineered the defense of Joannah's property in the Mixon and Kelso cases. Joannah, however, had played an active role in that defense and apparently continued her sole merchant and trading practices while married to Jacob. A year after the jury had decided that Joannah was liable for the debt on the promissory notes because she had been in the practice of trading generally, Joannah went back to court on another matter. She sued Martin D. Ramsey in Justice of the Peace Court to recover a debt. She had traded for a promissory note that Ramsey had signed for ten cows and calves. In September, 1845, she won the case and received a judgment against Ramsey for $51.80. The justice of the peace never questioned her right to sue in her own name. However, when Ramsey appealed to the district court in 1847, the suit was "dismissed because it is brought in a wrong name." Joannah lost her judgment from the lower court against Ramsey and was liable for all the district court costs for failing to have her husband join her in the suit. Although it was acceptable for Joannah to conduct her own financial and legal business when married to a husband who refused to fulfill those duties, once married to one who would, the court would no longer allow her to do so.[60]

In the frontier era the district court expanded the laws regarding married women to align them better with the social and economic realities of frontier life. These realities included women who were abandoned by their husbands and women whose husbands left temporarily to do business abroad or fight in wars, and such women often had no other male family members nearby. The judges of the district court, however, were not willing to expand married women's rights at the expense of husbands who were present and capable of fulfilling their duties as heads of households. While the courts might recognize married women's ability to enter business and law, they were not willing to recognize their right to do so unless their husbands abdicated that right to them. Married women in frontier Colorado County, then, did not necessarily receive expanded rights, but concessions were granted them for the actions they made under frontier conditions.

CHAPTER 2

TO FIND *a* NEW HUSBAND

The End of Marriages on the Frontier

> Your poor Aunt Laura is now a widow and her little children
> fatherless. . . . She is, I believe, almost a maniac. John tells me
> that she has his shot-bag swung on her shoulder,
> his hunting knife at her side and his gun in her hand.
> — LIZZIE THATCHER, AUGUST 20, 1852

Despite laws restricting and regulating married women's rights, Colorado County women did not clamor either to change those laws or to throw off the restrictions of those laws by being single. In fact, being married became much more important to women in the frontier South than it had been in the eastern states. The loss of a husband, while always traumatic, could be devastating to women on the frontier, as evidenced by Thatcher's letter above describing Laura Ann McNeill after her husband's death.[1]

Nineteenth-century southern women faced social pressures to marry a first time. Women still single by age thirty were considered old maids and had to attach themselves to male households by some form other than marriage. Once married, women had fulfilled their destinies whether their husbands outlived them or lived only a month. Unlike propertied urban widows, however, even propertied women on the frontier were pressured to remarry by the labor and financial demands of farms. As valuable as women were within a family, the frontier left little place for them to contribute outside the family. As a result, most—perhaps all—adult white women who immigrated to Colorado County were married when they did so, and if those women lost their husbands, they almost always found new ones. There was virtually no place for women alone on the frontier.[2]

Apart from the family farms, widows and other women without husbands had few ways to support themselves. With few schools (mostly taught by men), little mercantilism, and few churches, there were no cultural or economic spaces for women outside the family. The few schools that opened before 1852 had a primarily male faculty. Although women often took in boarders, that could not have been profitable, since the town had only two taverns and a couple of stores. Just eight adult women (of 274, or 3 percent) listed occupations on the 1850 census, and all were single women. Darcas Rize made her living as a seamstress and by boarding the merchant John Mackey and his family. Eliza Hotze was listed as a laborer, along with two male German laborers living and working with another German family. The other six women listed "farming" as their occupation.[3]

The Texas frontier called to many immigrants primarily because it was predominantly rural and unsettled, offering opportunities for inexpensive and unclaimed lands. But farming for single women was almost as difficult as finding another occupation in a frontier community. Without an adult male field worker in the family, women found it practically impossible to make a living from farming. There was the social proscription against women working in the fields, which of course was ignored when necessary. But apart from that, a woman in a frontier farming household had more work than she could handle with the duties set aside for women.[4]

While grown sons could take over their fathers' chores and enable women to remain single, most frontier families did not have grown children. Grown or nearly grown children of immigrants to Texas probably often opted not to go along when the family moved. Even by 1850 most families had not been in the county or state long enough for their children to have grown to adulthood. The opportunities of the frontier drew young men even farther west and away from home quickly when they reached adulthood. In the 1850 census only 36 families out of 295 (12 percent) had male children over the age of eighteen living at home; only 26 percent had boys over twelve. At the same time, only fourteen women (including the six who listed farming as their occupation) were listed as heads of household (out of 283 households, or 5 percent), and of those, nine (64 percent) had sons sixteen or over; four (29 percent) had sons over the age of eighteen. So the majority of women who were able to remain single during the frontier era after their marriages ended were able to do so because they had older sons at home to assist in farming duties.[5]

Nevertheless six women who listed occupations in 1850 were widowed heads of household, carrying on the farms they had built with their husbands, and only three of these had grown children. One option for a widow without grown children was to find a trusted adult male to run the farm for her. Two farming women in the 1850 census had adult men who were not their husbands living in their households. (Two other widows who lived in town had adult males as part of their households: Darcas Rize, the seamstress; and Mary Ann Sapp, whose relative John Berry lived with her and her two-year-old daughter.)[6]

Women throughout the predominately rural South faced this same dilemma, of course. However, in frontier Colorado County the problem of finding a trusted male to assist with the farm was intensified by the lack of kinship networks. When southern widows found themselves with young children, they often turned to the extensive web of kin within their region to assist them. However, during the frontier stage of Colorado County, extended kin were as rare as grown children. Young families who moved to Texas in the early stages of settlement left behind their parents and other relatives. Although brothers, sisters, cousins, and sometimes even parents would later join them, reforming kinship networks, the first families to settle usually were alone.[7]

The isolation of the frontier also contributed to the difficulties of women running farms and businesses alone. Having moved west to establish farms, families most often settled on large tracts of land—the typical land grant to homesteaders in Colorado County was 640 acres. Thus, any neighbors lived quite a distance away, and those neighbors were busy with their own large tracts of land. In addition, in the earliest stages women's opportunities to form networks and get to know trustworthy contacts were limited. Elite women were not supposed to travel without male escort, and it is likely that few women left their farms without men to accompany them. Elbert Tait operated a ferry across the Colorado River that practically ran through the fledgling town of Columbus. Of 2,850 ferry crossings in his account book from 1847 to 1852, only twenty-six women (less than 1 percent) crossed without male escorts. Several of those without accompanying males crossed with other women. The inadvisability of travel without a male escort made conducting the business of carrying on a farm even more difficult. Apart from those who had business that needed conducting in court, women had to arrange for male travel companions for even basic trips such as going to town for farming supplies.[8]

The lack of male kin or grown sons to assist them, the difficulties of finding trusted adult males, and the gossip that ensued when a young woman and young man lived and farmed together while not married forced most widows on the frontier to find new husbands. For those women unfortunate enough to lose husbands in frontier Colorado County, their chances of finding new husbands were good. Men outnumbered women, and most men recognized the valuable labor that women performed. In addition, a widow with a ready-made farm was extremely attractive. Of the widows whose husbands' estates were probated between 1837 and 1852 and can be traced at least one year, thirty-four out of thirty-seven remarried. Seventy-three percent married within two years after the court granted letters of administration on their deceased husbands; 89 percent remarried within four years.[9]

A husband was considered more likely to keep the best interest of the household in mind than a hired hand or overseer. Of the few women who remained heads of household farmers in 1850, Elizabeth Bateman was the only one with neither a grown son nor an adult male household member. Bateman's first husband had died late the previous year, and by the end of 1850 she had re-married. The fact that she had no grown sons may have hastened her into a marriage that ended with a hostile divorce and her new husband imprisoned for assaulting her.[10]

Like Elizabeth Bateman, rushing into marriage sometimes proved devastating. The lack of kin and parents not only presented the need for women to re-marry quickly but also deprived Colorado County women of the screening process that relatives often performed for their children in helping them determine a suitable mate. Because few people had relations in the county, a male without relatives (and therefore references and family lineage) was not unusual. As a result many widows made mistakes, as did Bateman. For instance, Joannah's husband John Dunlavy died one month after moving the family to Texas, leaving her with nine children, the youngest less than a year old. Joannah quickly married Joe McCrabb, who lived barely long enough to get Joannah pregnant with yet another child. Within a year of McCrabb's death she was married again, this time to William Dunlap. Dunlap unfortunately had made a habit of marrying women and had at least one other wife who was still alive. After enduring abuse at the hands of her third husband, Joannah was abandoned.[11]

Despite the difficulties women faced when widowed, that fate was unavoidable for many. Disease, injury, and unsophisticated medical care contributed to the early demise of many men and women. While the loss of any loved one was tragic, the loss of a spouse also fractured the carefully constructed ideal of a family structure in which each spouse performed duties and obligations based upon gender. A man who lost his wife no longer had the domestic counterpart to raise his children and perform the essential economic contributions of household production. A woman who lost her husband no longer had protection—neither physical protection from predators nor the accustomed shelter from the distressing public world and its troubles. Laura Ann McNeill coped with the death of her husband by grieving for him: she remained "inconsolable." But she also immediately took on what she perceived to be the duties of her deceased husband for her now "fatherless" children by arming herself with knife and gun. Of course, this masculine action seemed quite maniacal to her well-educated, well-married, well-protected sister who described her.[12]

Laura McNeill might not have been prepared to take on all the many roles left vacant by the death of her husband. In her relatively wealthy family, education was expected to make girls of her children's age the "ornament[s]" of the "family circle," and a woman expected to be a wife and a mother, and to "alternately sew and read" to "find relief from melancholy." As a minor she had learned only those skills that would enable her to perform her domestic duties while her father performed those duties of provider and protector. Once she married at sixteen, her new husband managed the legal, financial, and political responsibilities of the family, while Laura discharged the domestic duties of a wife and mother, including bearing four children in their eight years of marriage. John Shelby McNeill died when Laura was only twenty-four with four children between the ages of seven and three. Fortunately for Laura Ann McNeill, she did have family in the area. After the funeral her sister wrote that Laura "cannot go home to stay. She will remain with Pa and Ma for sometime and then decide for the future." [13]

No doubt many factors affected Laura Ann McNeill's decisions in the months to follow, including her and her society's ideals of a woman's place and duties in that society. Although Laura's upbringing taught her that her place was in the home as dependent and not as protector and provider, she had suffered through the hardships of the frontier with her husband. Whether or not she believed it to be her place, when necessary she would take the gun in hand to fulfill the more masculine roles required. One of the difficult decisions she had to make was to take on the legal responsibilities of John McNeill's estate and to become her deceased husband's administrator.

Serving as an executor or administrator and untangling the business and legal interests of any deceased's estate could be daunting. It required that a widow finish both the business and legal transactions of her husband at the same time that nineteenth-century social ideals denied that women, even widows, had any place in business and law. Texas laws and Colorado County courts denied or discouraged married women's participation in business or the courtroom unless abandoned by their husbands. Courts and laws further discouraged women from entering the courtroom at all: women of all ages regardless of marital status were not compelled to appear in court to give testimony except in criminal cases. Compelling the appearance of women in court to give testimony was as distasteful as calling a man who was "old and infirm." In general, the probate court seemed no more accessible to women than the district court had been: between 1837 and 1853 only one woman administered the estate of a person other than her deceased husband. Melissa Ann Silvey's husband James had been administering her father, William Watt's, estate when James died, leaving Melissa Ann to finish some business on Watt's estate. However, as soon as she could present an account of her father's estate, she resigned the administration and allowed one of her sister's husbands to take over the role of administrator. [14]

With the notable exception of widows, most women avoided the probate court, the main responsibility of which was overseeing the unfinished business of deceased persons. While the court structure and practices, statutes, and social dictates conspired to constrict the number of women involved in the probate court and its business, these same factors encouraged women of one category—widows—to become active participants in these public legal proceedings.

John McNeill left an unfinished estate—debts, claims, or court cases pending—and needed an administrator (or if he had left a will, an executor) to conclude his business. Laura McNeill's decision for the future was to assume the legal and financial responsibilities her husband had left behind. Despite other factors that might have served to intimidate her from entering the courtroom, four months after John McNeill's death Laura McNeill applied for letters of administration on his estate and posted a six-thousand-dollar bond. McNeill was one of the last widows to become the administrator of her husband's estate in the frontier era of Colorado County. Although she sat at the very edge of the transition to the antebellum era, her decision to administer her husband's estate was typical of the frontier period. Over half (53 percent) of the forty-three widows whose husbands' estates required administration in this era acted as sole administrators of the estate. Another four (9 percent) served as sole executors, and eleven (26 percent) served as coadministrators. Only five widows out of forty-three (12 percent) did not actively participate in the court settlement of the legal affairs of their deceased husbands.[15]

Of the thirty-eight widows active in the estates of their husbands, four were appointed executors of their husbands' wills and estates. A total of twelve men left wills in this period, but only four who wrote wills had surviving wives. Three testators appointed their wives sole executors in their wills, and their wives all chose to accept the position. One other testator appointed his wife coexecutor, naming two men to administer with her. She chose to accept the position, but neither of her coexecutors did, allowing her to act as sole executor. Frontier husbands trusted their wives with their estates, and the widows often agreed that they could handle the duties.[16]

For those widows whose husbands did not leave their last wishes in a will, twenty-three, including Laura McNeill, decided to take sole responsibility for the business of the estates. In most cases this responsibility required a degree of financial and legal expertise, as well as a great deal of work and confidence. First, an administrator (or executor) had to post a bond at least equal to double the estimated value of the estate. Then she had to oversee the initial appraising of the estate, submit periodic inventories, petition the court at the correct times for sale of property, sell the property at public sales, publish notice to all potential creditors, settle accounts with all claimants, answer summons to court sessions, prosecute and defend suits the deceased had been party to before death, and instigate suits based on unrecoverable debts.[17]

A few widows filed their initial reports in probate court and never returned. Perhaps in these cases the estates did not need administration and the widows merely needed court authorization to perform some duty. For instance, Sophia L. Jesse applied for letters of administration on her deceased husband Charles Jesse, posted bond, and asked for permission to cancel a contract Charles had made before his death, all in one day. She never returned to court to administer the estate further and was never challenged by other heirs.[18]

Other widows faced difficult challenges. The widow of Robert Stevenson was determined to control the administration of her husband's estate despite encountering one difficulty after another. Susan Ann Stevenson's husband had written a bad deed that needed to be corrected, the estate was bankrupt, and creditors continued to sue the estate. Instead of resigning her post, she hired an attorney, former county judge Kidder Walker.[19]

Ellender Earp similarly administered the complex and troublesome estate of her deceased husband, William. Family turmoil poisoned the proceedings from the beginning. The probate court granted Earp guardianship of her and William's two children. Ichabod Earp, one of William's children from a previous marriage, challenged Ellender for guardianship of the other child in the family, also William's from a previous marriage, and won that guardianship. Ichabod Earp also petitioned the court for partition of the estate and raised questions about Ellender Earp's accounting of separate and community property. He maintained that much of what Ellender Earp claimed as community property had been acquired by William Earp during his first marriage and therefore should be considered separate. The controversy caused the men who had pledged securities for bond to request permission to withdraw. Ellender Earp then had to find further security, which took her more than one term of the court. After giving a new bond in June, 1844, Ellender challenged the inventory that court-appointed commissioners had made of the property. The court favored her suit: "Therefore upon the premises of law and equity, the administratrix Ellender Earp be and she is forever discharged from all liability to said estate of more than four hundred bushels of said corn." The original inventory had listed eight hundred bushels. Unlike Susan Ann Stevenson, Ellender Earp did not seek the legal assistance of a lawyer or joint administrator. For over three years and at least eleven court appearances Ellender served as sole administrator. Even when she remarried two years after her first husband had died, the court records show that Ellender still appeared to pursue and administer the case.[20]

Fourteen of the twenty-three widows who solely administered estates also pursued or defended cases in district court, averaging about three cases per estate. Susan P. Carter, for instance, eventually found herself involved in nine district court cases as administrator of her husband Amsted's estate. One case had been filed before his death, she filed seven more to recover debts, and in one she defended the estate. Other women, like Ellender Earp, suffered challenges from other heirs, creditors, and frequent problems with security bonds in probate court. Isabella Adair even found herself challenged in both courts by another woman claiming to be her late husband's "true" legal wife.[21]

Despite the difficulties, the majority of widows administered estates. Some did so to save money and others to make it. Executors and administrators generally were not expected to work from duty or charitable feeling alone, and it could be a profitable enterprise. Texas' 1840 act provided that executors, administrators, and guardians received 10 percent of all the business they transacted "for their care, trouble, and attention." This money was significant to widows of even small estates who were suddenly left to support themselves and their children. But the profits could not have been as large as the headaches for Ellender Earp or for Susan Ann Stevenson, who hired an attorney to settle the estate. Another motivating factor for administering an estate was that by efficiently settling it, more property was left to inherit. A less conscientious administrator might not collect as large a portion of the debts or track down all the debtors. In the estate of Robert Stevenson, though, efficient handling to insure a larger inheritance was not the motivating factor for his widow Susan Ann: the estate was bankrupt. From the percentage of profit allowed by law, she had to pay an attorney to sort out the tangled legal and financial mess.[22]

Nancy Colwell, Isabella Adair, and Jamima Wright also administered the bankrupt estates of their husbands. When the amount owed to creditors was more than the estate was worth, the homestead law provided certain protections for these widows. The Homestead Act passed in January, 1839, protected from creditors an amount of property of both those living and dead. It reserved for the insolvent, or the insolvent's surviving spouse, fifty acres or a town lot including the homestead, household and kitchen furniture, tools of the profession, five cows, one yoke of oxen or horse, twenty hogs, and one year's provisions.[23]

An administrator arranged a sale of all other property, both personal and real, and paid the creditors a prorated portion of the debt. The widow administrators in Colorado County were often instructed to sell all property "except that portion exempt by law." Susan Ann Stevenson's husband unfortunately did not leave her with any land, but the court set aside five cows and calves, "one horse called Jack," twenty head of hogs, farming material and implements, household and Victorian furniture, and one year's provisions, worth a total of $238.75.[24]

One obvious reason for widows to remain in control of the administration, despite the complications, was that those who avoided the burdens of administration had to worry about who would administer in their place. Widows might have been more willing to relinquish control of the estates when there were reliable or competent men willing to take on the duties. Of the five frontier widows who chose not to execute, administer, or coadminister the estates, four of their husbands' estates did not have letters filed until after the widows had remarried. In all four cases the new husbands became the administrators. The other widow, Nancy Zumwalt, had a brother-in-law capable of and willing to administer the estate. Even in this case, two years after the final account was given and the administration closed, Zumwalt went back into court for permission to sell property to pay some debts, essentially acting as an administrator over unfinished business. In December, 1851, Rebecca Kuster officially declined the administration of her husband's estate in favor of her son. Just three weeks later she applied for the letters of administration herself "based upon the refusal of my son to administer the same." As discussed earlier, during the frontier era most families did not have grown children; and only few had other male relatives close enough to take on significant financial and legal duties. Just as women on the frontier acted in male roles by building homes and farms because they were the only adults besides their husbands, women went into the public arena of the courtroom because there too they were the only adults left in the family.[25]

One option for widows who doubted their own abilities to handle all the legal and financial difficulties but were unwilling to relinquish all their authority over the estate was to administer it jointly. Eleven widows chose this option, about half the time serving with administrators who did not claim to have any relation to the deceased. Four widows applied for letters of administration on their deceased husbands after they remarried, but instead of allowing only their husbands to serve, they served as coadministrators. The other two widows served with relatives. Even when they had trusty alternatives, some frontier women were not willing to give up control over estates. Isabella Cummings (alias Adair, alias Izard) coadministered the estate of her first husband. When her second husband died, she administered his estate alone. By 1841, only two years after her first husband had died, she felt confident at handling both administrations alone and petitioned for the removal of the joint administrator of her first husband's estate.[26]

Age, ethnicity, and wealth did not seem to have overwhelming influence on women's decisions to administer in the frontier era. Unfortunately, little is

HER ACT *and* DEED

TABLE I.
FRONTIER WIDOWS ADMINISTERING ESTATES
OR EXECUTING PROVISIONS OF WILLS, BY WEALTH

Quarter of Wealth*	3	2	1	Top 10%	Unknown	Total
Administrator	2	6	9	5	1	23
Coadministrator		4	7		0	11
Executor		2	1		1	4
Declined administration	1			1	3	5
Total	3	12	17	6	5	43

*No estates probated fell into the bottom quarter of wealth.

Source: Probate Records, CCCC; Schedule 1 (Free Inhabitants), Eighth Census of the United States (1860), Texas, Colorado County.

known about the six widows who declined to administer, but of the thirty-eight who did administer their husbands' estates, all ages, degrees of wealth, and both German and Anglo women were represented. The youngest widow to administer was fifteen, while the oldest was fifty-five. Of those whose ages can be determined, about half were thirty or younger. Their ages did not seem to affect their decisions of whether to administer solely or jointly. As many women in the lowest half of the age range solely administered as in the top. No matter what their ages, married women on the Texas frontier seemed equally willing to handle the business left behind by their husbands.[27]

It is more difficult to determine the effect that wealth had on the decisions of widows to administer. The overall population of Colorado County can be divided into roughly four quarters according to wealth. (See table 1.) Of the thirty-eight widows whose husbands left estates for which wealth can be determined, no estate fell in the bottom quarter of wealth. Where wealth can be determined, widows were much more likely to take active roles in the estates in the top two quarters of wealth. One out of twenty-three widows refused to serve in the administration of the estates in the top quarter. Significantly, this widow was not only in the top quarter of the population in terms of wealth, but she was actually in the top 10 percent. In the next wealthiest quarter all the widows took active roles, either administering, coadministering, or acting as executor. In the third wealthiest quarter, however, only two of the three widows acted as administrators. Clearly most widows did not shy away from administering estates, but large amounts of wealth might have intimidated them more and the smallest amounts of wealth may not have seemed worthwhile. However, the value of the estate was not necessarily the determining factor in the decision to administer, since widows at the highest and the lowest rungs of wealth more often than not chose to administer.[28]

Ethnicity affected the character of administrations, but not necessarily the decision to administer. Germans (immigrants or descendants of immigrants from German-speaking countries), in general, were less likely to have estates probated in county court than their southern and Anglo counterparts. Although Germans made up approximately half the population, roughly only a fifth of all estates probated in Colorado County were those of German decedents. When administrations were required, though, German widows were just as likely to be in court as not. Nineteen percent of the widows administering, coadministering, or executing wills were German. German widows served a public role in their husbands' estates in the same proportion as German estates appeared in court.[29]

The character of German widows' administrations differed somewhat. German women did not seem any more likely to decline administering their husbands' estates; of the four declining widows whose ethnicity can be determined, only one was German. Many more Anglo widows served as sole administrators than coadministrators: 23 percent of all Anglo widows were coadministrators. However, German women were much more likely to choose coadministration: four of the eight German widows who probated their husbands' estates were coadministrators. During the frontier era Germans were less likely to use the court system overall. In addition, German women who did not often venture into the public world had much less opportunity and motivation to learn English than did German men. Widows who did want to serve as administrator, even if they spoke English, probably would want someone to assist them who spoke the language well and was better acquainted with the Texas courts and familiar with Texas law. German women faced similar frontier situations as Anglo women and were as willing as Anglo women to take on financial, legal, and other public responsibilities when their husbands absented themselves or died.[30]

The most striking aspect of frontier widows' administrations and choice to administer is that so many of them chose to do so. More frontier widows administered estates in Colorado County than during the antebellum, Civil War, or Reconstruction periods (see appendix A). Eighty-eight percent of the widows chose an active legal role in their deceased husbands' estates (as administrator, coadministrator, or executor), while only 60 percent of the widows in the other three time periods chose such a role. Most significantly, the percentage of frontier widows who took active legal roles is double the percentage during the antebellum era. In antebellum Colorado County only six out of twenty-one widows solely administered the estates of their deceased husbands, and only three more coadministered (43 percent). Over half, twelve, chose not to administer at all. The number of wills drastically increased in that era as well, from four written by men with widows in the frontier era (all executed by their widows) to thirteen in the antebellum period—with only six executed or jointly executed by the widows (46 percent).[31]

Not only did frontier widows often not have other male relatives available to take on these roles, but the character of their marriages made women more responsive to taking on the task. Life on the frontier may have made women more self-reliant. Laura McNeill, for instance, had male relatives nearby who could have taken on the responsibilities her husband left behind. But, just as she took up her husband's gun and hunting knife at his death, she and widows like her were willing to take up other male roles. Frontier marriages may have been partnerships in which wives at least knew more about the financial transactions of the husbands, even if they did not necessarily take a greater role in those decisions. Even in the antebellum period as widows increasingly declined the business of administration, widows of marriages entered into in the earlier frontier period were more willing to engage actively in settling the estates. Of the nine marriages whose dates can be ascertained, over half of the widows who were married before 1850 administered, coadministered, or executed their husbands' estates. Of those married after 1850 only one out of seven administered the estate. In other words, women widowed in the antebellum period but married for at least two years in the frontier era were more likely to take on a public role in their husbands' business after their husbands' deaths.[32]

If frontier widows were so willing to take on male roles even in court after the death of their husbands, they might have been willing and able to do so before those deaths. The judges of the district court did not recognize this willingness or ability, however, and allowed a married woman to conduct business only in the absence of her husband and to enter the courtroom only with the consent of her husband. Widows in probate court, acting nearly unanimously on their own behalf, no doubt influenced the judge of that body to have different expectations of women, even when the widows remarried. Widows of husbands whose estates required court action in Colorado County before 1853 tended to remarry more quickly than during any other period. Sixty-five percent of the widows in the frontier period remarried before administration of their husbands' estates was completed, whereas in all the other periods only 13 percent of widows did so. Administrations lasted longer during the frontier era than they did in other eras—an average of 4.1 years compared to 2.5 in the antebellum and 2.3 years during the Civil War.[33]

Long administrations and quick remarriages presented many situations in which married women continued (or began) the administration of their previous husbands' estates. Texans may have believed that a wife should submit to her husband's authority in business matters if he competently fulfilled that role. At the same time, in the passage of the Married Women's Property Act, they also recognized married women's contributions to building a couple's wealth and that she deserved a portion of that wealth—if not for herself, then for her children.[34]

A widow might have earned her right to possess and control property in her actions during marriage and after, but by law and custom her new husband assumed all the legal and financial duties. Still, the statute clearly allowed a widow to be administrator of an estate. The new husband was required to join in executing a security bond, but "such bond shall bind *her* estate in the same manner as if she were a feme sole." In language reminiscent of the Married Women's Property Act, it also required that "whenever an executrix or administratrix may be a married woman, she and her husband shall act jointly in all matters pertaining to her said representative capacity." Allowing her to administer but requiring her husband's approval on all actions did not seem to the legislators to be a contradiction. Exactly what the joint action of the husband was to be was left up to the probate court.[35]

Frontier petitioners presented and judges allowed a variety of interpretations of that matter. Of the four widows who began administration after remarriage and coadministered with their new husbands, three exhibited their own agency at some point in the proceedings. Mary Thomas petitioned for the removal of the previous administrator and was appointed in his place. Her new husband was later added as coadministrator. Elizabeth Pieper took to heart her duties as administrator; her petitions referred to herself as the administrator who conducted the business: "Your petitioner represents that she as administratrix aforesaid proceeded to pay and has paid all debts due by deceased in his lifetime and also all debts accruing at and after his death." At the bottom of the petition was an addendum: "And Peter Pieper husband of the said Elizabeth Pieper and Saml. J. Redgate joint administrators of the estate aforesaid join in the above petition."[36]

Catherine Schimmer Miller did not attempt an administration of the estate of her first husband until after she had remarried, less than a year after Bernard Schimmer's death. In 1851 the judge entered the decree that "in the matter of the petition of William Miller and Catherine Miller praying that the said Catherine be appointed admx of the estate of Bernard Schimmer, decd. . . . it is ordered, adjudged, and decreed by the court that letters of administration shall issue to the said Catherine Miller on her and the said William Miller giving bond."[37]

The decree clearly indicates that Catherine Miller was considered the administrator of the estate, and her husband was not named as coadministrator or even "joined" in the suit. On the approved bond, Catherine Miller was listed alone as the principal, Casper Heimann and A. Mirator as sureties, and "William Miller as the husband of the said Catherine."[38]

Similarly, some widows who married after beginning administration of estates continued to be actively involved in the process. Of seventeen widows who remarried before the end of their administration, at least eleven exhibited some type of individual agency in the courtroom. Isabella Izard married twice during her administration of her first husband, Robert Cumming's, estate. Controversy surrounded her as she administered her second husband, Joseph Adair's, estate and that administration was contested by his *other* wife. Isabella, however, despite a third marriage, struggled through the administration and the resulting court cases as the sole petitioner, so recognized by the court despite her legally feme covert status. Court minutes never noted whether Nancy Slaughter's new husband ever appeared in court with his wife. She continued her petitions and business in the court after remarriage, and the only change was her name.[39]

Although the probate court allowed remarried widows more liberty to conduct business and petition the court in their own behalf, it was not so lenient with other women. When Ann Elizabeth Stockton attempted to challenge the men who were executing her father's will, her most difficult obstacle was finding status in the law under which to petition. First, she was still a minor, so she sued by a "next friend," Richard Stockton. However, when only she appeared in court to sue, Richard Stockton was summoned. He appeared in court and asked the judge to dismiss the suit because he "never authorized said suit to be instituted or prosecuted in his name." When Ann Stockton married a short time after filing the petition, she was no longer considered a minor by law, but she was then a feme covert. Her suit was then dismissed for "informality" because it was not brought also in her husband's name.[40]

Judges in both county and district courts might discourage and disallow independent activity by married women, but widows (even married widows) found more room to maneuver within the law. Their abilities to conduct business and legal proceedings in their own interest and on their own behalf were not questioned or challenged by the courts. The probate judges exhibited less concern in protecting them from themselves and recognized the widows' rights and interests in their former husbands' estates.

Frontier widows in Colorado County were not the only women who functioned in public. As discussed in the previous chapter, the district court recognized that some married women had to conduct business and legal transactions in order to survive because of the permanent or temporary absence of their husbands. Women on the frontier who were without husbands faced special difficulties and circumstances that statutes and the courts eventually sought to alleviate.

For example, complications arose from an abandonment. In August, 1837, less than a year after Joannah McCrabb's second husband died, William Dunlap "induced" her to marry yet again. The couple lived together for three months, during which time "the treatment of the said William was cruel, violent, and unkind to her." William attempted several times to compel her "to deliver to him the said William her money and other articles of value." Joannah's challenge of her new husband's authority was undoubtedly rare and bold. However, perhaps Joannah assumed the same basic attitudes of the court: as a widow, she was entitled to the property left behind by her previous husbands. When she would not give William her money and other valuables accumulated with her previous husbands, William abandoned her. Before he left, however, he confessed to Joannah that he had been married three previous times, "and that his wife was still living." Left again to her own devices in late 1837, Joannah confronted a problem her already difficult life had not before presented. Even though her husband had abandoned her, they were still legally married. Joannah was without a husband and unable to marry another.[41]

Because of the lack of economic opportunities for wives, abandoned women on the frontier were especially vulnerable because they could not remarry. When Louisa Muller filed for divorce in 1843, she complained that her husband had "failed to provide the food necessary to sustain life," that he finally abandoned her, and that she was "now dependent upon her own labour and charity of her friends for a support." Her labor alone could not support her. Six of the thirteen women who filed for divorce in the frontier era complained that their husbands had abandoned them without support.[42]

As with many other widows, Joannah's need to remarry had pressured her into a bad marriage. In 1838, however, Joannah found herself alone with her family before Texas courts had recognized any uniform divorce law. Although the Texas Congress in Austin would hear individual petitions for divorce, the illiterate, financially impoverished, and burdened-with-family Joannah had no resources to discover these faraway possibilities for obtaining a divorce. With remarriage virtually eliminated as a possibility, Joannah struggled for three years to supplement the farm income of her large family by becoming a "public merchant or trader."[43]

Although Texas did not pass a divorce statute until 1841, Joannah did eventually file in district court for and obtain a divorce from William in 1840. Joannah struggled under her disability for three years before pressing the courts to stretch its judicial boundaries for her benefit. Although the documents do not indicate if anyone acted as her lawyer, she had clearly made the acquaintance of a man who was somewhat acquainted with law: Jacob Tipps, a justice of the peace in Colorado County, whom she married a few days after being granted her divorce. Additionally, her son William Dunlavy had reached an age that allowed him to serve on the jury that annulled his mother's marriage with William Dunlap because of bigamy.[44]

Texas Congress made divorce more accessible in 1841 with the enactment of a statute allowing district courts to hear and grant divorces on the grounds of adultery, abandonment, and cruelty. This new divorce law helped a few women in Colorado County sever ties with their husbands and allowed them to remarry. Six of the thirteen women who filed for divorce cited abandonment as one of their complaints against their husbands. However, three years on the frontier was still a long time for a woman to wait for a divorce before having the opportunity to remarry. All six women filed for divorce before the requisite three years had elapsed since the abandonment, and therefore they could not be divorced on those grounds. Joannah Dunlap received an annulment on the grounds of bigamy, while Louisa Muller and Caroline Kahnd won divorces on the grounds of cruelty. Julia Shoemaker and Virgillia Woolsey could not find other grounds for divorce and had their cases dismissed.[45]

Only one woman who cited abandonment in the frontier era, Elvira Perkins, actually won her case on that grounds. She had originally filed for divorce less than a year after her husband left and charged him with cruelty. Elvira let the case be continued until three years had elapsed since his abandonment and then filed an amended petition to receive her divorce. She probably did so on the advice of her lawyer or the judge because without a solid case the odds were against her winning on the grounds of cruelty. Despite the fact that the Texas divorce statute was modeled after laws in other states that expanded the cruelty clause to benefit women, it was men who reaped the benefits from these grounds for divorce in frontier Colorado County. The cruelty clause had no inherent gender bias; district court judges could grant either the husband or the wife a divorce for "excesses, cruel treatment, or outrages towards the other, if such ill treatment is of such a nature as to render their living together insupportable." Nevertheless, during the frontier period judges and juries at the local level in Colorado County interpreted the cruelty clause to men's benefit.[46]

Jesse Robinson's divorce from his wife Sally in 1843 involved a man taking advantage of the liberal interpretation of cruelty to win a divorce. Jesse did not claim that Sally threatened him or physically abused him in any way. Rather, Sally committed cruel acts against her husband by refusing to live up to the nineteenth-century ideals of southern women. In addition to accusing her of being a "scold and termagant," he alleged that "she conducted herself towards other men with the most unjustifiable familiarity" and abandoned her husband and one of her children. Jesse did not have to prove that Sally committed adultery; the jury granted the divorce "on the grounds of excesses and cruel treatment on the part of the Defendant." [47]

Sally was certainly no saint. Her later life became the grist for legends. Better known as Sally Skull, she became "notorious for her husbands, her horse trading, freighting, and roughness." She was a sure shot and a "champion cusser," and she loved poker and dancing. While violence, drunkenness, and gambling were accepted, if not adored, attributes of southern men, the southern lady was supposed to be fragile, charming, submissive, and without temper. Indulging in such indiscretions brought a woman censure in her community, while a man's drinking, cussing, gambling, and fighting were overlooked as severe expressions of his masculinity. Her cross-claim for divorce denied the allegations, but it expressed much more concern with the division of property and custody of the children than with protecting her reputation from the scandal of divorce. [48]

Other women less flamboyant and notorious than Sally Skull also found themselves accused of cruelty for exhibiting behavior deemed improper for a woman. John Hope at first attempted to win a divorce based on abandonment and charged that his wife Rusha "left the house of your petitioner about three years since." Rusha, in actuality, had never left Florida where they had previously lived together. While other men successfully abandoned their wives in other states and then quietly sued for divorce in Colorado County, Rusha Hope foiled John's attempt: she hired a lawyer and came to Texas to fight the divorce. John then submitted a new petition. According to John, Rusha "invariably wreaked her *incorrigible* temper and disposition upon [him] whenever in her reach . . . in a manner unbecoming her sex, a wife or a mother and disgraceful to humanity. She . . . would break forth into fits of furious jealousy and conduct herself more a fiend, than a human being, or a wife." [49]

In addition to referring to the obvious torment a mean temper could cause a spouse, John also relied on gender ideals to show that his wife stepped out of the roles considered suitable for "a wife or a mother." Like Jesse Robinson, John did not cite physical violence or threats, but the jury considered him a "wretched victim" and found Rusha Hope "guilty of ill-treatment, excess and outrages," thus allowing the judge to declare the bonds of matrimony dissolved. John evidently was delighted; he married again just three days later. [50]

James Dickson's primary complaint against his wife Hetty was "that she was in the habit when in company of using the most obscene and vulgar language such as the rule of society forbid." He procured the depositions of two witnesses who swore that they "heard Hetty use vulgar and very unbecoming language to her husband and in fact talk more than any woman I ever did hear talk to her husband." James Dickson received his divorce. James, much like John Hope, had particular reason to rejoice at the jury's finding: he remarried twenty days later.[51]

Whereas men pursued and won divorces on grounds as slight as their wives' profanity or scolding language, women in frontier Colorado County had to prove a greater degree of cruelty in their marriages to receive divorces. Ten women, compared to only four men, cited cruelty in their petitions as the primary justification for their suits for divorce. However, the wives enjoyed a much lower success rate than the husbands in obtaining divorces. Two cases were voluntarily withdrawn after a year or two of protracted legal opposition. The judge dismissed three cases before they reached a jury. Another wife lost her case when her husband countersued, charging her with adultery. The four successful cases in this frontier period, less than half those brought on the grounds of cruelty, demonstrate what constituted "excess and outrage" against a wife by a husband.[52]

Two of the four cases described physical abuse. According to Margaret Pinchback, her husband James, "without cause or any provocation whatever, unlawfully beat and bruised" her and drove her from their home "with the marks of the rod upon her body inflicted by his cruelty and abuse." Mary Dresler complained that her husband made an "attack upon her person with a drawn knife in his hand threatening to take her life and inflicted severe blows and bruises on her body with his fist and with a large club," and that he attacked and beat their daughter. Significantly, both causes included rewritten petitions. After their first appearances in court, these wives submitted amended petitions placing more emphasis upon the physical and threatening nature of their relationships. Both cases received continuances, allowing the plaintiffs to amend their petitions. Margaret Pinchback's first petition had alleged only generic "divers acts of unkindness and ill treatment," instead of the detailed amended account that described her flight from home with "the marks of the rod upon her body." While Mary Dresler's first petition did include a description of her husband striking her with a chair, her second petition added the attack with the knife.[53]

Another case documented no physical cruelty but alleged that the plaintiff had reason to fear for her life or safety. Caroline Kahnd's husband "abused and ill treated her by threats of violence and [she] was only protected by the interposition of others from beatings and injur[y]."[54]

Only one petition filed by a wife cited no instances of physical abuse, threats of physical abuse, or viable legal grounds other than cruelty. Louisa Muller lived with her husband for only three months, "during which time [Frederick] Muller treated her in a harsh, cruel & unkind manner." Like the men who alleged that their wives had failed to live up to expectations of womanhood, Louisa charged that her husband had failed his expected role of providing for his family. "He failed to provide the food necessary to sustain life," leaving her "in a destitute situation," and finally abandoned Louisa altogether. Abandonment for under three years alone did not constitute grounds for divorce, but a cruel manner combined with failing to support his family apparently earned Louisa enough sympathy from the jury for a verdict in her favor.[55]

Although this case brought by a wife on the sole basis of nonphysical cruelty was granted, three other petitioners who did not demonstrate physical cruelty or threats of such cruelty did not obtain divorces. Virgillia Woolsey, whose husband had abandoned her for less than three years, claimed that her husband was "guilty of great excesses, cruel treatment, and outrages," but she did not claim that he was dangerous to her health. Her suit never reached the jury; the judge dismissed her case and ordered her to pay the court costs. Another unhappily married woman, Susan Bostick, brought suit against her husband Sion in 1851. She charged that he "refused to recognize or speak to her" for over a month and that "he drove her from his house and home, and has repeatedly declared since that he will never speak to nor live with her again." Sion evidently wanted the divorce as much as Susan did, since he later filed actions twice to obtain it. However, a great deal of property was involved and guilt would greatly influence its distribution, so Sion fought Susan's divorce action. At the next term of the court the judge dismissed Susan's case entirely.[56]

During the frontier period women in Colorado County might have won as many divorces based on cruelty as did men, but women also lost more cases on that ground. Ill treatment by a wife and ill treatment by a husband were based on gender assumptions of how men and women should behave. Husbands did not need to prove much more than that their wives used profane language, had a jealous temper, or otherwise deviated from societal expectations of women, even in contested cases. By comparison, a husband could curse his wife, drive her from the house, and vent an impossible temper upon her and still successfully block his wife's suit for divorce. Wives seemingly could not win contested cases unless the abuse was life-threatening.[57]

The double standard in cruelty cases worked against women in Colorado County only during the frontier era. Three of the four men who won divorces on the grounds of cruelty did so before 1848, when the Texas Supreme Court handed down a decision stating that only threats to the life or health of the victim should be considered cruelty. The fourth frontier male divorced on the grounds of excesses and outrages after 1848 by vaguely and unconvincingly claiming that he feared physical violence. His wife "did curse, swear at, and threaten to beat and maltreat your petitioner and other wrongs and outrages." Only two other men received divorces under the cruelty clause before the end of Reconstruction; both charged that their wives abused not them, but the children from the husbands' previous marriages.[58]

The accusation of cruelty offered more opportunity for men to divorce women than for women to divorce men. Yet the bias in the grounds of cruelty was not the only reason for the higher success rate among male petitioners. Twenty-two petitions in total were filed during the frontier era, and fourteen divorces were granted (63 percent). Women filed more of these petitions than men (thirteen by women, nine by men) and received fewer divorces (six to women, eight to men). To an extent, the high population ratio of men to women in the county increased the number of men's petitions and also the chances of their success, as many married men in Colorado County had left their wives behind. The grounds of abandonment especially worked in men's favor since they could leave their wives behind and three years later file for divorce. Four of the men who won divorces specifically stated that their marriages had actually ended elsewhere, usually in other southern states. These men had moved west leaving families behind, and they sought and won legal divorces even after abandoning their wives. The grounds of adultery also favored men's success since the husband had to prove only a single act of adultery. A wife, on the other hand, could divorce her husband for adultery only if he abandoned her and lived with another woman. As a result, no frontier wives cited adultery by their husbands in their petitions, whereas over half the men complained that their wives had committed adultery or "received the addresses of divers other men."[59]

Another possible reason for men's greater success than women in the divorce court was that some women used the divorce proceeding not because they truly wanted to be single with the limited options that position offered, but because they wanted to force their husbands to support them or behave in a financially responsible way. Polly Reels claimed that her husband "neglected to furnish her with the necessaries of life although appropriating to his own her individual estate." Margaret Zimmerschitte filed for divorce, claiming that her husband Frederick "has been and still is waisting [*sic*] away in intoxication and dissipation all the property that he can possibly so dispose of and that to no advantage to himself or family." Over half of her petition was dedicated to detailing the property that they owned and which he had wasted. Both women also charged their husbands with cruelty and presented convincing evidence of physical abuse of the type that won divorces for other women. Zimmerschitte's husband threatened to shoot her and assaulted her with an ax, "inflicting a severe wound [on her hand] and permanently disabling her." He also threatened her with the ax, "whereby she was put in fear that he would kill her." [60]

But Margaret put aside all her fears, dropped the suit, and lived with her husband again when he agreed to transfer all of their property to more reliable relatives. The importance of property in these proceedings was still evident nine years later, when after her husband's death Margaret wrote to her daughter: "I know well if murderers had shot me, my family would shed few tears. Why—I know it and many know it unfortunately. . . . If I had let my husband do as he wanted, I would have had no quarrels and would have had none with you either. Then you would not have had a foot of land nor would I either." [61]

Because Margaret had lived through years of bad times as a German immigrant in Texas and feared "in their old days com[ing] to want and sufferance," she chose to use the threat of a divorce action to challenge her husband's control of their property. Although the details are less clear, Polly Reels also came to an agreement with her husband, at least part of which was financial, and he paid the costs of the suit after she dropped it. [62]

Although their concerns were clearly financial, neither Zimmerschitte nor Reels could pursue a divorce solely on the grounds of financial mismanagement or even lack of support. Failing to support one's wife was not grounds for divorce, but it was a nineteenth-century expectation of a husband's duties. Wives should be pure and submissive, and in return husbands should protect and support them. Yet there were some legal remedies for women whose husbands did not support them. A wife could contract or enter debt for family necessaries for herself and children if she could convince someone to advance her credit or supplies, and her husband remained legally responsible. By 1848 the Texas legislature passed a law enabling wives who had separate property to complain to the county court "should the husband refuse or fail to support his wife from the proceeds of the lands or slaves she may have, or fail to educate her children as the fortune of the wife would justify." For Polly Reels, this statute came too late—she complained to the district court in a divorce petition in 1843. Margaret Zimmerschitte, however, never would have benefited from such a law. Her complaints were about how her husband handled their joint property, not her separate property. [63]

Divorces occurred across lines of class and wealth. Women with wealth, such as Zimmerschitte and Reels, were concerned with keeping property or wealth and having access to it. Poorer women, such as Mary Dresler, who took the poverty oath in order to pursue her case without posting bond, wished to have a legal option of remarrying and have assistance in making a living. The parties to divorce proceedings were distributed nearly equally among categories of wealth. Four divorces were filed by people in each of the lowest three quarters of the population in terms of wealth. Parties in the top quarter filed six suits, with two of those being in the top 10 percent. Divorce might have been an opportunity for poorer women to better themselves financially by re-marrying, but it was also an opportunity for couples with wealth to settle property questions. Of the female petitioners in divorce, a much higher per-centage came from the upper two classes than did divorces overall. The six successful divorce suits brought by women, though, were distributed equally across lines of wealth.

Germans made up half of the Colorado County population in the frontier era, but less than half of the divorce petitions were filed by Germans. Forty-one percent, or nine of the twenty-two divorces, were filed by Germans. Con-sidering that Germans overall used the district court less than Anglos in this period, this figure suggests that there was not much of a cultural difference with respect to divorce. However, eight of the thirteen divorces filed by women were German, and half of their cases were successful. German women were more likely than German men or Anglo women to seek divorce or take their husbands to court to gain concessions. German women were as likely to face abandonment as Anglo women were in Colorado County: five of the eight cases claimed abandonment or failure to provide.

Polly Reels and Margaret Zimmerschitte—both Germans—believed that once their husbands agreed to their financial demands, they were better situ-ated financially and personally to remain married women. Of the six women who filed for and received divorces in frontier Colorado County, four of their husbands had already abandoned them, and a fifth complained that her hus-band did not provide for her. Married women, whether Anglo or German, sought and received divorces not because their marriages failed to live up to some ideal of companionate union, but because their husbands left them on the frontier and they needed the option to remarry. At least four of these women remarried in the county shortly after receiving their divorces.

In divorce cases, women of both ethnicities and all classes were most con-cerned with financial matters. Whether forced into public transactions be-cause of abandonment by their husbands or frustrated at their attempts to influence their husbands' financial decisions privately, married women in di-vorce proceedings exhibited a knowledge of and desire to change the financial and legal exigencies of their marriages.

As in most of the nineteenth-century South, in Colorado County marriage defined a woman's identity and shaped her destiny. A poor marriage could bring unhappiness, suffering, and even destitution. A good marriage might bring happiness and prosperity but even then might end suddenly with the death of one of the spouses. Women in frontier Colorado County relied on marriage for more than a fulfillment of social expectations. In a society in which there was virtually no place for single women and in which eligible men outnumbered marriageable women, marriage was a financial transaction and a partnership.

Immigrants to frontier Colorado County asserted this ideal and attempted to establish its reality in society and in law. However, the conditions of an uncivilized frontier sometimes precluded protection for wives from men's duties. Frontier realities often required women to move beyond the traditional role expectations. Wives accustomed to performing some normally male roles and participating in private financial and legal decisions were more likely to take those abilities into the public realm when necessary. Women, with a few exceptions, did not exert independence from or attempt to gain authority over their husbands. However, they expected and received, both from society and the courts, a certain amount of influence over their own public lives in and out of marriage. Exigency often forced frontier women to abandon temporarily the nineteenth-century social ideals relegating them to a subservient role in all public and many private matters. Laws and rules founded on traditional ideals often resisted the women who pushed the boundaries of their assumed duties and obligations, but both the local courts and the legislature recognized and accommodated many of these frontier realities.

SETTLING UP

The Ascendance of Antebellum Society

"Is man superior, intellectually, to woman?" We would propose . . .
that woman is superior, morally, to man. If the question was which
is the greatest we would answer, if greatness consists in goodness,
woman is by far the superior.
— EDITORS, *COLORADO CITIZEN*, MARCH 27, 1858

It is difficult to establish a definitive conclusion to the frontier era, but sometime between 1850 and 1860 a dramatic population increase finally occurred
in Colorado County. The population of the county, as of Texas as a whole,
nearly tripled. Based on contemporary observations, 1852 to 1853 were the years
of the most astounding growth for the county. Reminiscences in the *Weimar
Mercury* from 1915 and 1916 describe the period through 1850 as "pioneer"
days. Lizzie Thatcher described Eagle Lake, a community in the eastern portion of the county, in August, 1852, as "being almost depopulated." [1]

Around 1852 or 1853 "the country was beginning to settle up," and a growth
spurt occurred in Colorado County, as resident Seaborn Stapleton remembered much later. According to tax records, land values were increasing rapidly during this period, up nearly 40 percent in 1851 and almost 25 percent the
next two years. The number of cleared acres was gradually increasing as well.
Cheap frontier land was giving way to more valuable cleared land. But the tax
records show other significant attributes of population growth and settlement
too. The number of town lots increased in 1852 by 70 percent, and their overall value increased by 125 percent. Property not as affected by its location, such
as slaves and cattle, only increased slightly in value (13 percent and 23 percent
respectively). [2]

The *La Grange Texas Monument,* published in adjacent Fayette County, reported rapid growth in Colorado County in 1852, whereas neither the *Texas
Monument* nor the *Texas Telegraph* ran such stories in 1851. The February *Texas
Monument* related that "within the last year the number of buildings has been
doubled [in Columbus], and built of substantial materials. The surrounding

country is also improving, and with the tide of immigration locating every-where, this rich county is receiving a fair proportion of wealthy and enter-prising settlers." In March the *Texas Monument* reprinted a travel account that claimed that "not less than $100,000 worth of property had been brought into [Colorado County], within the last three months! and that within the same time lands had almost doubled in value." In 1852 Columbus and Colorado County showed "evidence of great prosperity" worthy of mention.[3]

The increase in population and prosperity meant much to Colorado County women. The greater number of citizens provided greater safety. While isolated women on widely separated farms might have made easy targets for both In-dians and desperadoes, the greater density of population and increased num-ber of households discouraged plundering. Other potential dangers also de-creased with the increase in human population. Charles William Tait wrote in 1854 that "the bears are so scarce now that I do not have much use for hounds." The year before he had been unable to shoot a single bear.[4]

More residents also meant broadened markets. As additional families settled their land and began to raise food besides the essentials, women could diver-sify their families' meals by trading among neighbors for eggs, vegetables, but-ter, and other garden surplus. Bread could even be bought. The demand for merchandise of other kinds also grew in the early 1850s. The population and prosperity of the county could finally support merchants' costly transportation of an expanded variety of goods. In 1852 merchandise in stores increased by nearly 70 percent. Women could buy cloth instead of weaving it themselves, cooking utensils to decrease the difficulty of preparing meals, and luxuries such as bows and pins. Even timesaving novelties such as matches became available.[5]

The crude housing and buildings of the frontier gradually gave way to more substantial and comfortable homes. Once the land was cleared and crops were planted regularly, both men and women could devote more time to improv-ing housing. Additionally, greater availability of labor, capital, and materials in the county provided the wherewithal to build new homes and public build-ings. In 1852 Colorado County outgrew its "wood frame courthouse" com-pleted only three years earlier. The county commissioners met to commission a new two-story concrete and rock courthouse with a jail—a vast improve-ment over the small wood frame structure.[6]

The most significant improvement for frontier women that came with in-creased population was relief from their isolation. Time allowed daughters and sons to grow to maturity and become adult company for their parents. Larger, more comfortable homes also meant more room for visitors and guests to stay, thus increasing the ability of women to visit and be visited. Although many frontier settlers came as individuals or as individual families, later settlers often came together with people they knew. One large group of settlers, mostly from Tennessee, formed the new community of Osage in the eastern portion of the county in the early 1850s. Those individual families who planted roots in the county during the frontier era encouraged family members from their previous homes to join them. After Charles Tait had written to his family for six years about his success in Colorado County, Charles Tait's brother James finally in 1854 decided to bring his family to live in the county. Charles arranged for James to buy the land adjacent to his so that they might share resources. He suggested that "if James gets out time enough to let his [slave] women pick cotton for me, I can put my [slave] men to building for him."[7]

Charles Tait considered the financial benefits of having family nearby, but his wife Louisa probably looked forward to the social benefits of having other white women, especially family, nearby. In 1854 Louisa was a twenty-five-year-old mother of two. She had given birth to her two children in Texas far away from her family in Alabama and was destined to have more children. Although the Taits owned slaves, no other white women lived in the Tait household. From the description of the adjoining landholders, few other white women lived close by. Louisa's isolation was broken in the early 1850s as other female family members came to Colorado County and as other families with adult white women finally settled on the surrounding lands. Women like Louisa depended less upon their husbands as their sole support and adult company as other family members began arriving. Antebellum women who lost their husbands to death or desertion had family and friends on whom to depend and thus had options available to them besides quick remarriage.[8]

The lives of white women eased somewhat, at least for those who could afford to buy timesaving conveniences and manufactured goods. As the initial labors of clearing land and building farms out of the wilderness gave way to routine crops, women performed fewer male chores on the farms. Their lives remained far from leisured, but the decreased amount of work to achieve the bare necessities coupled with the increased number of women in the county led to more organized efforts by women to build communities. By 1860 the gap between the number of males and the number of females had decreased: 1,925 females now made up 45 percent of the 4,325 white inhabitants.[9]

Religious services had long been held in Colorado County, but in the mid to early 1850s many churches began erecting buildings and securing ministers. Both Frelsburg and Columbus formed at least two congregations each between 1848 and 1856. The Methodists, who had devoted members in Colorado County as early as 1822, finally built their church in 1850. In 1853 Reverend G. Scherer moved to Columbus, Texas, as the first English Lutheran minister in Texas.[10]

Religious services and institutions served an important role for white women in taming the frontier. Churches gave women an opportunity to meet with and form a community with other people. In a primarily plantation and farming community, Colorado County neighbors necessarily lived far from one another. Social functions centered around work had always brought people together. The greater density of population in antebellum years allowed for barn raisings, hog butcherings, and even canning and quilting to become larger social events for women. Frontier men, however, had much more opportunity to interact with one another as they conducted business and law in the small towns. The rise of antebellum churches gave women a reason as well to congregate socially on a regular basis with other people in the area. Fannie Darden moved to Columbus in 1853 and became actively involved in Saint John's Episcopal Church in Columbus. The first women's session shortly after her arrival "consisted in the meeting of three ladies, Mrs. Mackey, Mrs. Foshey and myself for a sewing society. We met in faith and love, had nothing to work with but a few hands full of scraps. But the Lord blessed our efforts."[11]

Women became involved in other social institutions about this time too. The Sons of Temperance formed in 1849 voted itself out of existence in August, 1854, transferring its "assets and liabilities" to the Lone Star Circle of the Order of Social Circles No. 2 of Texas in Columbus. While the Sons of Temperance allowed only male members, the new temperance society had female members as well. Of the twenty charter members, half were women.[12]

After 1852 the more settled social and economic conditions of Colorado County eased life for white women there, allowing them to make more choices. Instead of being driven by financial necessity, the need for male protection, and limited opportunities, women made their decisions in this new era based on social and cultural ideals. The culture that shaped their decisions was primarily that of the antebellum South. In the frontier era the German-born and southern-born populations had been almost equal. Although southerners had greater impact during the frontier because the laws were framed by southerners at the state level, both had exerted influence over the development of society and culture in the county. The new surge of immigration beginning in 1852 brought many more Germans and southerners to Colorado County than immigrants from any other region of the world. Most Germans settled in distinct locations, such as Frelsburg and San Bernardo. Germans attempted to replicate as many of their traditions and ways as possible, establishing German schools and churches to serve as the centers of those communities.[13]

Try as they would, Germans could not duplicate their homeland cultures completely. As historian Terry G. Jordan pointed out, the numerically dominant "southerners provided the matrix into which all other Texas settlers were

TABLE 2.

GERMAN AND SOUTHERN POPULATION INCREASE

	Germans			Southerners		
	Total	Abroad	Texas	Total	Other states	Texas
1850	710	567	143	732	478	254
1860	1745	1094	651	2385	1582	803
Increase	145%	93%	355%	225%	231%	216%

Source: Schedule 1 (Free Inhabitants), Seventh and Eighth Censuses of the United States (1850 and 1860), Texas, Colorado County.

placed." Between 1850 and 1860 the German population in Colorado County increased by 145 percent. The population increase due to births significantly outpaced the increase due to immigration from German-speaking countries. There were nearly twice as many Germans who had been born abroad living in the county in 1860 as there had been in 1850. But four and a half times as many Germans had been born in Texas. A second generation of Germans who knew nothing of the old homelands came of age in Colorado County, contributing to a distinctly German-Texan culture.[14]

At the same time, the number of southerners in the county increased almost twice as fast as the number of Germans. This southern growth was distributed more evenly between birth and immigration. Overall, southerners increased in Colorado County by 225 percent between 1850 and 1860. The number of these southerners born in other southern states increased by 231 percent, while the number of southerners born in Texas increased 216 percent. Table 2 provides the figures for the population increase between 1850 and 1860. Significantly more adult or older children were immigrating to Colorado County from other southern states than from Germanic countries, or from any other region in the world. These southerners brought with them the ideals, culture, and social expectations that dominated the county. German immigrants may have continued to foster a distinct cultural identity, but that identity borrowed from and was influenced by their southern neighbors.

Southerners and their culture increasingly guided the development of law, commerce, and social standards in Colorado County after the population boom in the early 1850s. From 1852 until the beginning of the Civil War, Colorado County most resembled the antebellum South of which it was a part, and women in the county reacted to their similar situations in ways familiar to women throughout the antebellum South.

As the frontier came to an end in Colorado County, women's opportunities expanded financially as well as socially. By 1860, 6 percent of adult women listed occupations in the census, twice the 3 percent who listed occupations in 1850. As in the frontier period, many were head-of-household farmers, but the county's growth enabled some women to find other opportunities to earn a living. One seamstress and nine servants all provided for themselves through their work. In 1851 the Columbus Masonic Lodge founded the Columbus Female Seminary, "the first educational institution in Columbus." Other schools opened in the county around 1852 and after. The larger schools employed primarily male faculty, but smaller ones consisting of only a few pupils, often meeting in women's homes, provided at least four women on the 1860 census with the profession of schoolteacher or music teacher.[15]

The census, though, gives only a small glimpse of the women who entered moneymaking occupations. Neither E. C. Crawford nor C. A. Connelly, who ran the most advertised female-headed schools in the county, had an occupation listed in the 1860 or 1870 censuses. Advertisements for other schools indicated the employment of other women who claimed no occupation on the 1860 census. Fannie Darden was a locally renowned poet. Emaretta C. Kimball combined her writing talents with the tales of one Colorado County pioneer to produce the first known literary effort in the county. Earning income was possible in ways only hinted at in public documents. The county court reimbursed Mrs. E. Gilbert for washing clothes and attending to prisoners' wounds in 1856, while in 1858 testimony in a court case showed that Miss Cate Mooney was hired for one dollar per day to wash for a family. Although Mary Ward listed no occupation, she most likely took in boarders. Her husband was a blacksmith, not a hotel keeper, but their household in 1860 contained seven adult men with various occupations and last names and from assorted birthplaces. One seventeen-year-old female student also lived in the house.[16]

More women had greater opportunities to remain financially independent in the antebellum era. However, they did not look upon their independence as an opportunity to take on male roles or question their husbands' authority. Unlike Laura McNeill in the frontier, who took up a gun and other male duties when her husband died, when antebellum women absolutely had to provide for themselves they used their domestic skills at home rather than venturing into public or performing male duties. The occupations that supported them were easily pursued from their homes or were thought to be appropriate to women's domestic nature: washing, boarding, serving, or teaching children.

The majority (63 percent) of women who listed occupations, however, were head-of-household farmers. Most women, married or single, in 1860 Colorado County remained part of a farming household. Yet most antebellum farmers had a different life than that of frontier farmers in the county. Families had more and older children to help work the farms. Fifteen percent of the families in 1860 had sons eighteen or older living at home, while 30 percent had sons thirteen or older. The increased population also provided more labor for hire. As the county became increasingly populated, land became both more scarce and more expensive, delaying a farm purchase for many. The new immigrants to the area, or sons of poorer farmers, worked on others' farms and plantations. Combined and larger families contributed labor to many farms. The number of slaves working on farms also increased in the antebellum era: nearly five times as many slaves lived in Colorado County in 1860 (3,559 slaves) as did in 1850 (723 slaves). Wives were much less often the only other adults on the farms and were no longer required to perform whatever functions were necessary. With more labor available, duties could more easily be divided by gender.[17]

Women antebellum farmers, even when single, did much less actual farm work than frontier women farmers had done. In addition, the assistance of additional laborers allowed many to continue farming, which they might not have been able to handle alone. Of the twenty-five women who carried on farming after being widowed or divorced in 1860, all but two had either adult sons (eighteen or older) or slaves. Twenty had sons thirteen or older, and sixteen had sons eighteen or older. In 1850 only one woman out of seven who listed farming as an occupation had owned slaves. In 1860 thirteen out of twenty-four (54 percent) farming female heads of households had the assistance of slave labor. Four of these women held planter status with more than twenty slaves. Another five had five or more.[18]

Women, especially those with large labor forces, usually turned over the management and overseeing of slaves to their sons or hired farm managers. H. B. Burford's "farm manager" Woodson Coffee lived in her household, while Clarissa Ann Eason's farm manager lived in the house next door with his family. The business of farming, hiring overseers, choosing crops, and buying and paying for supplies could be turned over to male relatives. Rebecca Grace's son-in-law lived with her, assisted her on the farm, and probated the will of her deceased husband. Thirty-six-year-old George Turner and his wife lived with his mother and ran the farm.[19]

A few single women did run the business of their farms or other businesses. Like men who entered into financial dealings, women sued or were sued when financial difficulties or differences of opinion arose. Women appeared in court records six times as plaintiffs and four times as defendants. While at least half of these cases involved a title to land or partitioning property among family members, a few cases demonstrate that women were involved in financial transactions in the community. Widow Susan A. Shepherd had loaned money to a merchant before he left for a buying trip in the North. When the note came due she sued for the $135, and the lawsuit that ensued focused on whether her accounts at the store should or should not be a separate matter. Eliza Y. Hopson had rented her plantation, for which she wanted repayment. Ann Upton had hired out her slave. All three women won the cases they brought before the court.[20]

Despite the evidence that some women were active in financial transactions, antebellum single women were parties to lawsuits less often in relation to their population than frontier women had been. Even when they were named as parties to a suit, they were not necessarily involved in the business that brought the suit to court or in the particular business of the court case. While some women, such as Susan Shepherd, obviously took care of business themselves, giving the money and negotiating for its repayment, others, such as Eliza Hopson and Elvira Earl, had agents taking care of business on their behalf. Earl's brother Marvel McFarlane acted as a "voluntary agent" for his sister (and not as a legally appointed attorney). He in turn hired an attorney, Vincent Allen, to collect the money. The case was so far removed from Elvira Earl that when it was filed, she, the plaintiff, was erroneously listed as Elizabeth Earl.[21]

Antebellum Colorado County courtrooms were commonly all-male chambers, but women's knowledge was sometimes necessary. During the antebellum period women's evidence in cases became more crucial as the number of women in the county increased, and they sometimes outlived husbands and other men who would otherwise have presented the testimony themselves. Antebellum women also began presenting testimonies related to cases in which they were not personally involved, whereas frontier women had nearly always presented evidence only in their own personal lawsuits. Yet antebellum women, at the same time that their testimonies became more sought after, avoided public places, such as the courtroom, that were not considered suitable for ladies. As a result, lawyers served more women with interrogatories during the antebellum period in order to record their testimonies.

The party desiring the testimony of an aged and infirm man, an out-of-county resident, or a woman would submit a list of questions, or interrogatories. The opposing party would then have the opportunity to submit cross-interrogatories. The questions would then be sent to a commissioner who would ask the questions, record the answers, and return the deposition to the court. Although available as an option during the frontier, taking the depositions of women increased in the antebellum years, allowing women to add necessary information to court cases without necessarily leaving their domestic settings.

Sometimes the questions of plaintiffs and defendants assumed that women knew much about the business affairs around them: Mary E. Garrett was asked about a horse her husband had bought, Mary F. Ward about the worth and payment given for slaves one of her houseguests had sold, and Wilhelmina Kessler about whether her grandfather alone had paid the purchase price for a contested piece of property.[22]

Often women were asked about their own transactions or financial deals made on their behalf. Emelia Gilbert answered with certainty questions about horses she claimed to own, including what their ages were and where she got the money to buy them. The bill of sale, however, was not in her name because her son A. J. Shannon "had done the trading for me about the ferry and executed the bill of sale . . . to prevent me from being troubled about the horses." Mrs. R. L. Davidson "did intrust the care of her negroes to her stepson" but did not have any knowledge about the doctor's care provided to her property.[23]

These interrogatories and answers show that women, married and single, did understand the world of business around them but often chose to defer to men regarding that business when possible. The judges and lawyers of the district court honored and protected that wish. Most interrogatories focused on questions that women would be assumed to know best: domestic situations. Women were much more likely to be asked the dates of births, marriages, and deaths than the dates of property conveyances. Women's depositions appear most often in divorce cases in which they reported upon private relationships: for example, letters between illicit lovers, that a husband was violent, or that a wife had refused to live with her husband.[24]

When a party asked a woman to comment on a series of financial activities, cross-interrogatories filed by the opposing party often expressed concern that the woman was being somehow manipulated. In cross-interrogatories to Susan Shepherd the defense asked if she knew whether anyone had ever resided on a certain lot and if she knew the lot number and blocks. The follow-up question tried to ascertain who might be coaching her testimony: "If so who told you so?" Many cross-interrogatories ended with the question "Who has been present during the taking of this interrogatory?" The question was a prelude to claiming in court that a particular woman's testimony was unreliable because an interested party had coaxed her. The answer to that question sometimes elicited the desired response. Elizabeth Steward and Pamilia R. Lynch, both witnesses to their stepfather's deed, gave their depositions together and gave the same answers. This saved time for the commissioner asking the questions but allowed no opportunity for them to contradict one another's testimony.[25]

Other answers to the question of who was present during the deposition did not produce the response desired by the interrogator but do illuminate the nature of these depositions. Mary Garrett answered, "There has been no person present while my testimony has been taken, except the commissioner and his family occasionally passing about the house." Isabella Bagwell answered that Mrs. Bonds and Miss Mary Silvey had been present "nearly all the time and some of Mrs. Bondses little girls." Though encompassed firmly in her domestic circle, a woman could contribute her knowledge to the legal business being conducted by men.[26]

The sanctity of women's domesticity in the home became more protected in other ways as well. Ownership of separate property had often forced frontier women out of their homes to the courthouse for the purpose of approving their transfer. Laws regarding married women's property changed little during the antebellum era. A wife still had to be examined by a representative of the court and sign a relinquishment of her rights before the transfer of her separate real property or of a couple's homestead. From the frontier through the antebellum periods married women were examined and signed their relinquishments at essentially the same rate. About 10 percent of married women every year signed such documents transferring their interest in separate or homestead property. The laws requiring the relinquishment of a married woman's right to her real property became more strictly enforced and more systematized in the antebellum period. Only 3 percent of the deeds requiring a wife's examination did not record it having been performed, much lower than during the frontier era. Increased awareness of the necessity of a married woman's examination, more alert county clerks, and an increase in the number of lawyers assisting in drafting conveyances of property all contributed to married women's property rights being more strictly observed.[27]

While her legal ownership of property was recognized more often, subtle changes took place in the control a married woman exercised over her property. During most of the frontier period a married woman had to appear before a judge of the district court or the chief justice of the county court whenever a deed conveyed her property. In 1846 the state legislature changed the law, easing the requirement so that justices of the peace and notaries public could take a wife's acknowledgment. Before 1847 conveying her separate property required a married woman to go into the courthouse and see a judge. In the antebellum era the use of notaries public to comply with this law increased considerably. Notaries public advertised their availability to "take the examination and acknowledgment of married women to all deeds and instruments of writing, conveying their separate property and their interest in the homestead." These men, especially in rural areas, usually had offices in their homes and would also travel to the home of the wife to take the acknowledgment. One of the simple acts of ownership that had required a married woman to specifically state her understanding and agreement with a sale had become less formal and less public.[28]

Married women rarely appeared in district court during the frontier era, but even those rare appearances virtually disappeared in the antebellum era. Husbands made the necessary appearances for their wives when their property came into dispute. The exception in frontier years was wives left by their husbands, either temporarily or permanently, who conducted their own business in the community and pursued cases in court when absolutely necessary. The settling of the county led to a settling of the men of the county as well. Although permanent abandonment still occurred, it was much less prevalent, especially among those with property. There was much more business in Colorado County, so fewer men had reason to travel abroad often. In addition, wars and battles with Indians took fewer men away from home in this more settled period. Men who still traveled and left their wives now more often had business partners or male relatives with whom to trust their financial affairs.

In the antebellum district courtroom lawyers, judges, and husbands articulated a new rationale for removing their wives even farther from the public workings of law and farther from control of their separate property. As the husband had "the sole management" of his wife's property, lawyers argued that he acted as the "legal manager" of his wife's property and as such was "legally authorized" to act as her "general agent" even when binding her separate estate. In other words, if a husband were managing his wife's property, any money he borrowed or any contract he made on behalf of her property bound her property for payment, even though she may never have been consulted or agreed to the acts.[29]

This argument was most frequently used in cases against William J. Darden, a prominent attorney in Columbus, and his wife Fannie Darden, an artist and poet. William Darden's law practice did not support the family; his wife's separate property did. While Fannie Darden owned eighteen slaves in 1853 and twenty-two by 1860, William Darden was described by plaintiffs in lawsuits as wholly insolvent. When William Darden was unable to pay debts, his creditors sued hoping to win judgments against Fannie Darden's separate property. In seven suits filed between October 10, 1856, and March 14, 1861, William fended off attempts by lawyers to levy and sell his wife's slaves at sheriff's auctions. The five petitions of various merchants alleged that although William Darden had made the purchases or signed the promissory notes, the articles "were *necessaries* suitable to her position and proper for the support of her family and separate property." An 1848 statute clearly stated that debts for necessaries or expenses benefiting her separate property contracted "by the wife" bound her separate estate. According to the merchants' attorneys, William had acted as his wife's agent because he was the general manager of her, her family, and her separate property. Therefore, the expenses were contracted by her, the wife, and her property should be bound for the debt.[30]

William Darden used his skills as a lawyer to protect most of his wife's property from the merchants. He came to an out-of-court agreement with the merchants in three cases, and the merchants dropped their suits. When the agreement in one case failed, the merchants, Blum and Mayblum, filed suit again. While other suits had been filed against William and Fannie Darden, Blum and Mayblum had sued just against William Darden, and only in a belated amendment to their petition did they argue that Fannie Darden's property should be held liable. William submitted an answer that maintained that her separate property was "in no way liable for the payment of individual debts of the said W. J. Darden." In this case the judge ruled that Fannie Darden was not liable for the debt and that William's property be levied for its satisfaction. William's property that was sold to cover the debt was six bales of cotton. These bales of cotton, of course, were the results of the labor of Fannie's slaves, but the bales were considered community, not separate, property. The fifth merchant's case did not come to trial until after the Civil War. Because Fannie Darden's most valuable "property" had finally gained freedom, the merchant's lawyers dropped the case against her and pursued William Darden as having some potential to pay the judgment eventually.[31]

William Darden's success at protecting his wife's property against merchants failed against the prosecution of two overseers. John Williams served as overseer for part of 1856 and part of 1857, while Woodson Coffee finished out 1857 as the overseer. In 1858 both sued William and Fannie Darden to recover their wages. William Darden had hired both overseers to work on a plantation that Fannie Darden did not own. John Williams, however, demanded that because his duties had been to oversee Fannie's slaves, her separate property should be sold to pay his bill: "his services as overseer were rendered for the benefit of her negroes and were beneficial to her separate property." Both overseers argued that "William J. Darden as husband was legally authorized to contract for the management and preservation of his wife's property." In May, 1858, the district judge agreed and awarded $64.33 to John Williams and $149.20 to Woodson Coffee, the writ of execution to be served on both Fannie and William Darden, allowing the sheriff to levy her separate property.[32]

Other wives also lost some separate property in similar cases. Charles Harrison won an 1856 judgment against George and Mary Hatch, and particularly against Mary's separate property, for "work and labor" and "articles furnished . . . for the use and benefit of the said separate property the said Mary."

On the motion for new trial, the Hatches argued that there was no evidence proving that there was any benefit to Mary Hatch, her children, or her separate property. Nor did the plaintiff show that Mary Hatch had requested the work or articles furnished. The motion was denied.[33]

The detailed arguments of the attorneys in the case against Agnes Hawkins are worth noting. Logue and Whitfield charged that the debt should be paid for out of Agnes's separate property because "M. T. Hawkins, acting by the authority and as the general agent of his said wife and in the judicious exercise of his trust, as the legal manager of his wife's separate estate, did at various times purchase . . . merchandise necessary for family supplies, and for the use and benefit of his wife, her children, and separate property."[34]

Agnes's attorney on her behalf filed a lengthy answer, maintaining that among other things, she had no separate property. And "for further answer she denies that M. T. Hawkins is her general or special agent or that she has any general or special agent."[35]

Logue and Whitfield filed an amended petition describing more specifically how a husband could become a wife's general or special agent: "And said plaintiffs further say that by the custom of said Agnes, she conceded to her said husband for five years past the power and authority to purchase for her and her family, not including her said husband, such articles as named in said Exhibit and without objection on her part, he from year to year for five years past did purchase for her and her family articles of necessaries, such as named in said Exhibit."[36]

According to Logue and Whitfield's argument, if a husband bought merchandise, claiming it to be "necessaries and family supplies furnished to my wife Agnes Hawkins and her family," no notification or authorization of the wife was necessary to bind her property. By not objecting to the transactions, whether she knew the nature of them or not, she conceded that her husband was her "special agent" to bind her property.[37]

Based on other rulings of the court, Agnes Hawkins might well have lost the case. However, when neither Agnes nor M. T. Hawkins showed up for the trial, Logue and Whitfield chose to take a default judgment against M. T. Hawkins rather than prove the liability of Agnes. They dismissed their case against her.[38]

Husbands, by law, had always had the legal right to sue alone on behalf of the assets of the wife, or to take any other necessary legal action. Only in transferring real property were married women required to sign their relinquishment. However, when a married woman was forced to sue a third party to recover her separate assets because of the failure of or unauthorized act of her husband, she necessarily had to become a participant, while his taking part was optional. If a married woman's separate property were improperly levied for execution by the sheriff, she could sign an affidavit and give bond "to try the right of property." Even in this case the antebellum district court allowed a husband to act as agent for his wife. When the sheriff levied Jamima McNeill's slave to satisfy a judgment rendered against her husband only, Archibald McNeill made the oath and signed the affidavit as her agent. The merchant W. H. Secrest must have been maddened by the action since Secrest's original case had argued that Archibald as Jamima's agent had contracted for the debt. As in the Hawkins case, rather than try to prove their case against Jamima when the McNeills defaulted, W. H. Secrest's attorneys took judgment against Archibald only.[39]

The trial for the right of property, when the property was the separate estate of a married woman, could be conducted by the wife alone. However, as in the case of the McNeills, it was much more likely that the suit would be conducted by the husband on behalf of the wife. Even in the case *Mahala Smith v. C. R. Perry and J. Kauffmann,* Mahala signed the bond and affidavit, but her husband Asa was the one who went into court and "made oath that he cannot safely go into trial of the above suit for the want of evidence."[40]

Married women rarely conducted the business of a lawsuit, much less appeared in court. Throughout the antebellum years and seven lawsuits, Fannie Darden never appeared in court, nor did any paper, bond, or petition suggest that she was in any way involved in the case, other than being a named party. William Darden, like most antebellum husbands, conducted all the legal business in the district court on behalf of his wife. Antebellum courts were much more careful than frontier courts had been to ensure that a wife at least knew about the cases pending against her: husbands and wives in all cases after 1852 received separate summons. Yet of the fifty-one cases in the antebellum era that named a married woman as a defendant or a plaintiff (not including divorce cases), only six cases indicated that the wife participated in any way in the suit. Four women signed bonds or affidavits in trials for right of property. One wife gave testimony in her own behalf but did so by deposition and did not appear in court. Only one complicated case, in which the husband was accused of fraudulently conveying property to his wife to avoid his creditors, induced a married woman actually to appear in court one day. Married women eschewed the public aspects of business and law, allowing their husbands to sue, defend, and even sign necessary legal documents as their agents.[41]

Even Agnes Hawkins (who luckily did not lose her property in the case brought by Logue and Whitfield above) might not have been an active participant in the suit. Her answers were signed by her attorneys, which was not unusual for men or women. Although she at least seemed to be involved, her case might have been orchestrated by her husband and attorney. Only once was there any complaint over the absence of a married woman or her consent. A plaintiff objected to the affidavit of T. S. and Mary Anderson "because it [was] only sworn to by one of the defendants." The judge never ruled on the objection.[42]

The argument that husbands could bind their wives' separate property by acting as their wives' agents greatly diminished the small power that married women had over any property. Antebellum married women found less and less to draw them into the public sphere. The general acceptance of husbands as their agents excused them from attending to any legal business. Even transferring their interest in their own property became less public, as public officials could examine married women privately in their own homes. Men as husbands and as legal officers acted upon laws in the antebellum era in such a way as to reinforce women's ability to remain focused on the domestic duties more suitable for women. Men and women alike assumed that men's greater intellectual abilities provided women with better protection than would women looking out for their own concerns.[43]

The number of women without husbands to look after their concerns, however, increased during the antebellum era. More occupational opportunities during the antebellum period allowed many widows to remain single. Of the twenty-eight widows whose husbands' estates were probated between 1853 and 1861 and who can be traced at least a year, only 46 percent remarried, a vast drop from the 89 percent who remarried during the frontier era. Only 32 percent married within two years after the probate court granted letters of administration on their deceased husbands' estates; nearly 60 percent never remarried or remarried only after five or more years.[44]

Widows did not remain single in order to assert their independence and take on male duties. Even as more widows from all ranks of wealth declined to remarry, they also declined to participate in the aspect of law that had been most open to them: the probate court. Only six out of twenty-one antebellum widows solely administered the estates of their deceased husbands, and only three more coadministered (43 percent). Over half (twelve) chose not to administer at all.[45]

The number of wills probated also dramatically increased during the antebellum years. While only four frontier men with widows left wills, thirteen were probated during the antebellum era. The four frontier widows all probated their deceased husbands' estates, while of the thirteen in the antebellum era only six executed or jointly executed the wills of their deceased husbands (46 percent). The increase in the use of wills gave husbands opportunity to express their beliefs about whether their wives were capable of administering their estates. In the antebellum era eleven of the thirteen male testators named their executors, and five of those named parties other than their wives. One of the six wives named executor or coexecutor chose not to accept her role. Men and women alike believed that a widow's place was not in the public business of settling an estate or that she was not capable of conducting that business, and when given an option, they chose even unrelated men over widows.[46]

Men showed less distrust, however, of their wives' abilities than the wives themselves showed in declining administrations: 45 percent of husbands named parties other than wives, while 57 percent of widows chose not to be administrators of estates or executors of wills. Widows, therefore, chose to defer to other men the business of finishing their husbands' estates more often in the antebellum era than they had in the frontier period. And they did not just passively allow others to take over; they actively declined their right to serve that duty. After the frontier period passed, law became more formalized and lawyers more meticulous in addressing all legal details. Most widows (nine of twelve who declined) signed statements specifically declining to administer the estates of their husbands, appeared in court to waive their rights, or never challenged petitioners' claims that they had specifically waived their rights. Because the law still gave widows the first right to administer, people who agreed to administer probably insisted upon this safeguard. After a declination was signed, challenging the administrator was more difficult and had to be mounted on the basis of negligence or fraud.[47]

Statements declining to administer give some hints of why a widow would not want that duty. Antebellum widows frequently mentioned the difficulty of the estates or their ignorance of business because of their gender. In 1856 even Mary Smith, who eventually became sole executor, pleaded with the judge to allow her brother-in-law to coadminister with her and "that being a female and in feeble health she would be greatly benefited by [his] services." After initially applying for letters, Martha Logue realized that she was "entirely unacquainted with business."[48]

The antebellum era with its denser population did provide widows with more relatives in the county to whom they could turn over the administration of their husbands' estates. However, this alone does not account for all the declinations. Seven out of the nine who specifically declined administration did so in favor of specific males. Yet less than half of those declined in favor of male relatives. Of all the antebellum estates not administered by the surviving wives, only half were administered by male relatives instead.[49]

Antebellum widows believed that even unrelated men would take better care of estates than they would. Married women had deferred those presumed "male" duties of business and the district court to their husbands. Antebellum single and widowed women acted in business and law through agents as well, even in the probate court.

As during the frontier period, the age of the widow did not seem to affect her willingness to administer or her decision to decline. Of those widows whose ages can be determined, the average age of those who took active roles in their husbands' estates was thirty-six, while the average age of those who declined was thirty-seven. The youngest to accept administration or execution of her husband's will was twenty-two years old; the oldest was fifty-four. The youngest to decline was twenty-three, the oldest sixty-five. Likewise, ethnicity played little role in accepting or declining. Four German widows accepted, while six declined. Eleven Anglo women accepted, while fourteen declined. Whether German or Anglo, more widows declined than accepted.[50]

Disorganized record keeping probably discouraged widows from taking on the responsibility of administration as much as any other factor. The affidavits declining administration often cited the complexity of estates. Martha Logue petitioned to become coadministrator of her husband's estate but a month later officially declined to have any part of it, citing its "complicated condition." Logue's estate was indeed complicated. He owned twenty-two separate tracts, most of them containing more than one hundred acres, thirteen sets of town lots, slaves, sheep, goats, mules, cattle, and other livestock. Additionally, he held extensive lists of claims, accounts, and collectible debts, most of which were out of date, bad, or already paid. The administration required extensive work collecting, paying debts, and other business transactions. It also required frequent visits to the courtroom, justice of the peace, district courts to recover debts, and probate court for frequent reporting and requesting permission to settle court cases or sell property. Martha Logue was wealthy enough that the 10 percent commission she would have received straightening out the mess was not worth the trouble. To administer the estate in her stead she chose the experienced Cleveland Windrow, who served as the county clerk and therefore was already familiar at the courthouse.[51]

Some planters had even more complicated estates than did merchants. The most involved estate in the antebellum probate court was that of planter Alfred Smith, administered by his widow Mary M. B. Smith. Mary did not initially wish to administer, but when forced to choose between administering or allowing one of her husband's creditors to do so, she preferred to coadminister. However, the court frowned on her choice of coadministrator, so Mary administered the estate solely for eleven years, through eighteen suits in the district court as both defendant and plaintiff. Although in her unique case circumstances pressed Mary Smith to administer a complicated estate, a few other widows administered difficult estates without such pressure. Susan E. Rivers

TABLE 3.

ANTEBELLUM WIDOWS ADMINISTERING ESTATES
OR EXECUTING PROVISIONS OF WILLS, BY WEALTH

Quarter of Wealth	4	3	2	1	Top 10%	Total
Administrator	1	1	1	2	1	6
Coadministrator			2		1	3
Executor			3	1		4
Coexecutor				2		2
Declined administration		5	5		2	12
Declined or not appointed executor		3	1		3	7
Total	1	9	12	5	7	34

Source: Probate Records, CCCC; Schedule 1 (Free Inhabitants), Eighth Census of the United States (1860), Texas, Colorado County.

administered the estate of her deceased attorney husband, completing, defending, or suing fourteen separate cases. Four of the six women who administered handled multiple district court lawsuits.[52]

Complexity may have affected the decision of some widows in choosing or declining to administer, but a high-valued estate did not necessarily intimidate women (see table 3). Widows in the top half of the wealth bracket were more likely to choose to administer estates than those in the lower half. Widows of two estates who were in the lower half of the population according to wealth administered, while eight declined. In the upper half thirteen widows acted on the estates, while eleven did not. Husbands leaving wills and widows choosing to administer had greater faith in women's ability and willingness to complete the husbands' affairs when the widows had lived within the top two quarters of wealth. However, even among the top half, the wealthiest of men had reservations. Of five men who in wills appointed their wives executors and one whose will appointed no executor, none of the estates was in the top 10 percent of wealth. Four men appointed persons other than their wives, but three were in the top 10 percent of wealth. Given a choice to administer, widows of even the wealthiest top 10 percent of estates chose or declined to do so in even numbers (two in each case).[53]

The most striking predictor of whether a widow would choose to administer the estate of her husband or execute his will, as mentioned in the previous chapter, was whether she had been married in the frontier era. Of those whose marriage dates can be ascertained, over half of the nine widows married before 1850 administered, coadministered, or executed their husbands' estates. Of those married after 1850 only one out of seven administered the estate. Women widowed in the antebellum period but married for at least two years in the frontier era were more likely to take on a public role in their husbands' business after his death.[54] These widows were less accustomed to having their husbands or any other male act as their agents in business or in court. Carving out homes with their husbands on the wilderness in the frontier era both forced them into male roles and gave them more opportunity to be intimately acquainted with their husbands' business.

As the antebellum era allowed more women to focus solely on domestic and female duties during marriage, they chose less often to venture into the public and take on male duties as widows. Antebellum women had opportunities to work for money, were expected to know about business and financial transactions, and were even essential to establishing facts in lawsuits. Yet although antebellum women had increased opportunities to perform male duties, they chose not to. The laws based on gender assumptions protected women from the male world of law, business, and politics. Women raised with the social ideals of male and female duties chose to defer more often to men in those public arenas because they had more opportunity to do so in the antebellum era than during the frontier period.

The settling of the frontier, the increased number of kin and other trustworthy men, and the greater number of grown sons allowed women to defer more often to males in public and financial matters and allowed women to remain single longer. These changing attributes also had an effect on divorce in Colorado County.

Antebellum women sought divorces for different reasons than frontier women had. Frontier women had looked to divorce as the opportunity to force husbands to be more financially responsible or to enable them to remarry when their husbands were not, as when they abandoned their wives. Seventy-one percent of divorced women in the frontier era can be ascertained to have remarried, while only 30 percent in the antebellum did so.[55]

The legal grounds for women obtaining divorce did not change from the frontier period to the antebellum era, although their motives may have. Abandonment might have been the prime motivation for almost half the women who filed during the frontier era (six of thirteen), but it served as legal grounds for only one. A woman in the frontier could not wait three years for legal abandonment before she remarried. In the antebellum era women much more often had other relatives, grown male sons, or increased occupational opportunities to support themselves when abandoned. Five antebellum women were able to wait the requisite period of time before petitioning for divorce on the grounds of abandonment. Even then the abandonment was usually local; most petitioners knew where their husbands were. Women did not necessarily need to remarry, and several tried to work out terms of separations, instead of divorcing. Sophia Illg after her divorce stated, "Illg and myself had agreed to divide our property and separate without any law suit and I left and went to [William Byar's] house to board." Sophia and William Byar both expected that even though separated, Jacob Illg would remain responsible for Sophia's boarding expenses.[56]

Charlotte Cherry waited three years before claiming that her husband had abandoned her. Charlotte, like most of the women who claimed abandonment, knew where her husband was. When he was notified, Thomas answered the petition claiming that he had left Colorado County to make a living, "and that he endeavored to induce and persuade his wife the s[ai]d Charlotte to come and live with him so that he might more fully protect and care for their children, but that she has wholly disregarded his earnest desires in this respect and refused to live with him and discharge her duties as a wife or mother."[57]

In his answer Thomas effectively denied neglecting the expectations of him as a husband and shifted the blame to Charlotte, who refused to submit to her husband's requests to move to Houston. By mutual agreement, the case was withdrawn.[58]

Two other wives who claimed desertion but obtained no divorce had the unfortunate timing to file during 1859, the first year of George W. Smith's tenure as district judge. Smith stated clearly in his charges to the court that he opposed divorce. He allowed it to occur, of course, when the parties met all the rules of law, but he granted absolutely no leeway. Judge Smith's views were widely held throughout the South, wherein he saw divorce as a challenge to the authority of male heads of household; only when that authority was abused to the extreme that it cast doubt upon the legitimacy of the marital institution should a wife be released from that authority.[59]

Margaret Miller alleged a series of verbal abuses and lies and abandonment by her husband for more than three years. When she went to court, Judge Smith heard her evidence apparently with little sympathy, and she chose to "prosecute no further." Odelia Besch proceeded with her suit against her husband, who had over three years before told her that "she might go to Hell and he was going to California." She produced witnesses that "stated she was a faithful and affection [sic] wife to deft." She even called the county sheriff, who testified that he had four-year-old writs of execution against the property of Charles Besch that he had never been able to serve. Despite this evidence, the judge's instructions to the jury were simple: "You are charged to find a verdict [against] the plff. she having failed to make out her case in proof." The jury complied by finding the allegations in the petition not proven.[60]

In the antebellum era women had mixed results alleging desertion (only 33 percent granted), but their prospects when alleging cruelty improved. Cruelty, the grounds on which most frontier women won their cases, was expanded and utilized by women in the antebellum era. In frontier-era divorces the grounds of cruelty had greatly favored men, requiring a lesser degree of physical cruelty to win a divorce for men than for women. In antebellum divorces the cruelty clause began to resemble what contemporaries and historians assumed it was meant to be: a modification "favoring women."[61]

Eleven women petitioned for divorce on the grounds of cruelty, and six won their divorces. All but two cited physical cruelty, and only one was dismissed by the judge before reaching the jury. The two nonphysical-cruelty suits filed by women, surprisingly, won divorces—even in the courtroom of the difficult Judge George W. Smith. These actions heralded the beginning of a new pattern in divorce for Colorado County: slander against a wife's reputation by the husband could constitute cruelty.[62]

Elizabeth and Jacob Hahn had been married for ten years and had four children at the institution of the suit for divorce. Elizabeth's petition carefully painted her as "a true and faithful wife" who received "in return for her affection, and the faithful discharge of all the duties of a good wife," cruel and unnatural treatment. The petition read: "at the birth of each and all of said children the Deft charged your petitioner with infidelity to his bed, and in the presence of company charged her with adulterous intercourse with divers persons. . . . [A] day or two after the birth of their last child which was on the 25th Dec 1858, the Deft in the presence of company charged her with adultery and that the child just born was not his, and that he would not have anything to do with it."[63]

After the 1840s false allegations of adultery came to be considered extraordinarily cruel treatment in divorce cases throughout the United States. Texas followed this national trend when in the 1850s rulings of the Texas Supreme Court indicated that false accusations of adultery or even thievery made in public constituted cruelty. Destroying a lady's reputation and visiting disgrace upon her was considered nearly as dangerous and every bit as cruel as physical abuse.[64]

By 1859 the Colorado County District Court saw a fraudulent charge against a woman's virtue cruel enough to justify divorce. Presiding judge George Smith took the occasion of Elizabeth Hahn's divorce suit to discuss at great length his views on divorce, giving seven pages of instruction to the jury. He charged the jury that "the marriage relation is the most important that can be formed and that it should not be broken up and dissolved easily." His charge quoted Texas Supreme Court decisions and Lord Stowall's writings that discouraged divorce, admonishing couples to recognize the indissolubility of marriage so as not to "foment the most frivolous quarrels and disgusts into animosities." Elizabeth's petition detailed other abuses, including the exact day that Jacob took a gun and threatened to kill her, but Judge Smith informed the jury that Jacob's charge of adultery "in an insulting and slanderous manner" was the only action on which she could sue. Despite his prejudicial opening, Smith did instruct the jury, "if you find from the evidence that the deft did maliciously and with intent to injure the plff did falsely charge her with adultery publicly and in a manner calculated to injure her character and destroy her happiness then you will find the allegations in the plffs petition setting forth that the deft charged her with adultery is true." The jury found in Elizabeth's favor, and the judge pronounced the bonds of matrimony dissolved.[65]

Nancy Jane Cundiff claimed that her husband had begun "to treat her in a cruel and outrageous manner" by accusing her of criminal intercourse and publicly calling her a "lewd strumpet." She carefully stated that the allegations were false. Her petition read, "she has been delicately and respectably raised . . . [and] she has always been known as a virtuous and pure woman." Although chief justice of the Texas Supreme Court John Hemphill had allowed that false charges of adultery might constitute cruelty, he continued to maintain that "no exact definition of legal cruelty can be given." Even "mere blows . . . among persons of coarse habits may pass for little more than rudeness." By stressing her delicate, respectable raising and position in society, Jane Cundiff claimed that allegations of adultery were as cruel to her as physical cruelty was to any woman of a lower station. The district court judge charged the jury that if the allegations of adultery were publicly made and the jury considered them to be false, then Jane Cundiff was entitled to a divorce. Cundiff received her divorce. Two other women also cited slander by their husbands. One received her divorce because of physical abuse, and the other woman's husband obtained a divorce in another county before her case came to trial.[66]

Although not overwhelmingly successful, the charge of slander in the antebellum era signified the shift in social attitudes toward marriage and divorce. Women were no longer satisfied with husbands who might act financially responsible but otherwise treated them poorly. Elizabeth Bateman, or the lawyer who wrote her petition, found it important to note in the first section that her husband "has not performed the duties of a kind husband . . . rendering himself very disagreeable in his family and especially to your petitioner, that he has for more than two years shown feeling of dislike to your petitioner and a total disregard for her comfort and happiness."[67]

Many other antebellum women seeking divorces made similar complaints about their husbands' "total want of affection and regard," and some accused spouses of "utterly disregarding [their] feelings." Petitions also frequently referred to husbands' failure to uphold wedding vows, specifically "to love honor and protect" their wives.[68]

Men too complained of their wives' disregard for their wedding vows or for their duties as mothers. The most frequent infraction of women's roles as wives, according to petitions, was adultery. Men in the antebellum period, as they had during the frontier era, relied heavily on adultery to receive divorces from their wives. Of the fourteen petitions filed by men between 1853 and 1861, ten charged their wives with adultery. Sion Bostick and Jacob Illg both filed second divorce petitions when juries found their allegations against their wives not to be proven. Jacob's second suit found more favor from the jury, and he was divorced by the court in Colorado County. Sion's second suit received a change of venue, and his divorce was granted in another county. Of the eight husbands who petitioned for relief because of their wives' "criminal intercourse," five eventually received their divorces. The other three husbands could not complain that their cases never went to court: Antone Rickis never had process served on his wife, and Fletcher Bridges and Horace B. Pendleton both withdrew their suits after it was alleged that they were bigamists and that each had another wife still alive.[69]

The eventual success rate for men charging their wives with adultery was quite high, but it was also the most contested type of case. Divorced women did not necessarily die a social death, but society believed that women found guilty of adultery had only a small hope of a respectable life again. Judge Smith thus charged the jury in the *Jacob Illg v. Sophia Illg* trial:

> **You must be aware of the serious consequence that will result to the deft from a verdict finding her guilty of adultery. It may work blight upon her character that will seriously effect her to the close of her life, hence for this reason the law makes it your duty to be satisfied beyond a reasonable doubt that she did commit the alleged act of adultery before you find the charge to be true . . . for though the husband is let free as he wishes yet in the very act that this liberates him she is sunk to the depths of infamy.[70]**

Understandably, most wives fought these charges with all available resources. As mentioned above, Sion Bostick and Jacob Illg had to try more than once to prove that their wives committed adultery. Susan Pendleton and Rachel Bridges defended their honor by impugning their husbands' reputations and accusing them of bigamy. Half the adultery divorces granted in this period were to husbands whose wives after committing adultery had also abandoned them and "gone to parts unknown," therefore putting up no defense.[71]

Both men and women used petitions to highlight alleged facts that would get them divorces, but these did not necessarily describe the true state of their marriages. Petitions exaggerated in order to place the petitioners in the best possible light compared to their spouses, especially when the innocence of one and the guilt of the other was necessary to sue successfully for divorce. From the frontier era through Reconstruction, husbands and wives alike described themselves in a gendered vocabulary that exaggerated their blamelessness. Sion Bostick claimed that his wife Susan "wholly disregarded *all* the duties and obligations of a wife," even though the petition showed that she somehow had conceived at least four children. All petitioners and respondents described themselves as living up to the ideal of their gender and described their spouses as failing in this attempt. Women who filed stated that they had always acted as "kind and faithful" wives. Nancy Hope, for instance, maintained that "since the period of her marriage [she] has ever endeavored according to the best of her knowledge and ability to fulfill all the duties of a faithful wife . . . [exercising] diligence and assiduity in household affairs, in ministering to the wishes and wants of her husband and his three children by a former marriage and in conforming to all the requisitions of the marriage relation."[72]

Antebellum petitions, whether filed by men or women, increasingly used the rhetoric of gendered expectations of husbands and wives to gain divorces. The overall success rate for antebellum women petitioning for divorce did not improve from frontier days. Only seven out of seventeen divorce suits filed by women were granted (41 percent), compared to seven out of thirteen in the frontier era (54 percent). Men's success rate dropped drastically from the frontier period to the antebellum era, from seven out of nine (78 percent) to seven out of fourteen (50 percent). Women's changing expectations of marriage, however, affected both their legal reasons and their motivations for seeking divorces. Few women used divorce in the antebellum years as an opportunity to wield financial power in marriage or to disengage themselves from abandoning husbands in order to remarry.

Women found many opportunities in antebellum Colorado County that they did not have during the frontier period. Women pursued an increased number of profitable occupations. They enjoyed more leisure and a greater concentration of people, which led to a greater participation in organized community activities, such as churches and social organizations. Almost all women still married, but they exercised a greater freedom not to remarry when widowed or divorced.

The opportunities that women chose to pursue, however, were often related to the domestic duties that a pious, pure, submissive woman was expected to perform. Even the occupations that they held could be performed in their homes or were extensions of their domesticity. In business and law they could and did choose to defer more frequently to male family members and respected male citizens. Yet women's greater options allowed them to expect more from the men in their lives. Women divorced men for reasons other than abandonment and failure to provide. Widows chose to rely on their own sons, sons-in-law, or other nearby kin rather than remarry.

Social customs, laws, and practices also changed to allow the business and law concerns requiring women's attention to be transacted without disturbing women's ideals of themselves as domestic and untouched by the public world. Women increasingly made their own choices not to enter public transactions, even in cases in which frontier women had overwhelmingly chosen to participate, such as in probate court. As labor and capital increased and a general settling of the county occurred, duties on and off the farm could be more easily divided by gender. Women's choices showed that they participated in or agreed with the divisions between their duties and men's, both at home and in public.

CHAPTER 4

THE LAW *of the* MASTER
Slave Women

Carey drove a wagon, I worked in the farm at whatever
I was put at, Jim Irvin drove a wagon part of the time and worked
in the crop or whatever Mr. George S. Turner put him at.
Ann staid in the house to wait on the family.
— AMANDA MILTON, FORMER SLAVE
OF GEORGE S. TURNER

Whereas the ideal antebellum white woman was pure, black women were believed to be lusty, wanton, and sexual. White women were considered naturally submissive; black women had to be forced to be subservient. White women were seen as domestic; black women were suited for all kinds of labor. White women were individuals whose legal rights were best protected by husbands, fathers, and other males in their lives; black women were not individuals but rather property with virtually no legal rights. Amanda Milton and her husband Martin testified in a deposition after emancipation that while a slave on George S. Turner's plantation she "worked in the field" or "at whatever [she] was put at." [1] Nineteenth-century social ideals about women and women's nature did not apply to black women.

Southern male legislators and judges formed the laws regulating relations between white men and women based on their gender ideals. These laws constrained white women's actions. However, these same laws allowed white women to venture occasionally into public. There they could indicate by their actions the degree to which they agreed with the ideals behind the laws. The same southern males made the laws regulating the lives of African American women. But these laws, based upon the nineteenth-century southern ideals about African Americans, did not allow black women to exert even occasional agency in public business or law concerns. As a result, it is impossible to say that black women had public lives at all before emancipation in Colorado County. Public records, however, contain a glimpse of black women's lives and, more explicitly, white southerners' ideals about black women. The foremost opinion southerners held about African Americans was that they were and should naturally be slaves.

The most powerful law affecting black women's lives was the one that consigned the vast majority of them in Texas to slavery. Only African Americans who were free and living in Texas at the time of Texas' independence were allowed to stay there as free persons. All other blacks, whether freed by migrating to Texas or by manumission, had either to leave Texas or "choose his or her master, and become a slave." As a result, few free African Americans lived in Texas as a whole and almost none in Colorado County. As slaves, there were few other legal statutes that affected their lives. It was against the law for descendants of Africans (or Indians) back three generations to marry or "fornicate" with whites; they could not witness in court against white persons; and slaves were not allowed trials except for crimes higher than petit larceny, and then of course by an all-white jury.[2]

These few laws touched few African American women's lives in Colorado County. Legal statute governed their lives much less than the rules and the ideals of the master. Slaveholders had little interference from the government in the way they treated their slaves, and masters could make many decisions for their slaves with little participation from the slaves themselves.[3]

Thus even basic rules differed from plantation to plantation and farm to farm. Charles W. Tait explicitly outlined the rules both for those overseeing his slaves and for the slaves themselves. The rules generally urged fairness toward the slaves in making them work: "1. Never punish a Negro when in passion. . . . 2. Never require of a Negro what is unreasonable. But when you have given an order be sure to enforce it with firmness." Tait's rules, however, went far beyond the basics of governing the amount of his slaves' work. He also interjected himself into personal details of their lives, requiring slaves to eat breakfast before going to work, inspecting slave cabins on Sunday morning to ensure that they were clean, and not allowing profane or obscene language.[4]

Tait's rules and ideals conformed to one of the prevailing views of the Old South that regarded slaves as perpetual children who required supervision, care, and firmness. More than likely, other Colorado County slaveholders also ascribed to this view and endeavored to get as much work out of their slaves as possible through this paternalistic approach. Other masters in the county, however, took more drastic approaches to slave management. John Pinchback gained a particularly evil reputation among slaves. One of his former slaves, James Green, speculated that Pinchback liked "to make niggers suffer to make up for his own squirmin' and twistin'. He was the biggest devil on earth." Among other practices, Pinchback seemed unconcerned about whether or not his slaves ate, and he kept a pack of dogs to intimidate slaves and track down runaways.[5]

Whether masters treated their slaves as working children or working property, they still had the same goal in owning slaves: to use the labor of the slaves to increase the slaveowners' personal wealth and comfort. Thus, southern social ideals about black women's nature reinforced their pocketbooks. According to these ideals, black women were not the delicate, pure, and pious creatures that white women were, and therefore black women did not need to be protected from heavy "male" labor. Even white women believed that the primary purpose for female slaves was to perform difficult labor, thus increasing the wealth and status of the white families, including themselves. Mary F. Ward of Colorado County certainly showed no concern for one female slave other than her earning potential: "I think Mima is an idiot. I do not consider her any account. I would not feed and clothe her for all she could do."[6]

Cotton in Colorado County, as in much of the South, presented the most potential for acquiring wealth. Other crops also allowed southerners the opportunity to increase their fortunes, especially with the help of slaves. Evidence from Colorado County shows that slave women routinely contributed to turning the land into financial gain. In the deposition cited earlier Amanda Milton testified that she worked in the field while a slave on George S. Turner's plantation. When Thomas J. Adams sold his slave Winny to John Hope, he guaranteed that although she had "Phtisic," it "would not prejudice or hinder the said Winny from doing good service as a field hand." John Hope described in another case how much work he had expected the slaves Allen and Rose to perform in farming cotton, with no differentiation between what he expected of Rose than from Allen. When those who hired out the slaves refused to deliver them, he felt that he had been "greatly damaged." Other court documents indicated the assumption that the most valuable female slaves could work in the fields. In describing the services of Sarah, A. Boyd Bonds described the fifty-one-year-old slave as "being entirely useless as a field hand" and "of service only as a nurse for children." He therefore argued that he should be required to pay less for her services after hiring her from Dianah Obenhaus.[7]

As in Texas as a whole, the vast majority of Colorado County slave women lived in farming households and worked in the fields. In 1850, of 723 slaves in Colorado County, 374 were females. Of those female slaves, 95 percent lived in households that on the census listed the occupation "farmer" or in households that produced cotton, corn, or tobacco. The number of slave women who were probably involved in field work did not change much in the next decade. In 1860, of 1,733 female slaves, 92 percent lived in farming households.[8]

While white slaveholders had little hesitancy at putting slave women to work in the fields just as they did male slaves, there still existed some division of labor according to gender in the slave population. The few records in Colorado County that address the types of work performed by slaves correspond with studies of slave labor elsewhere. In addition to Sarah, who worked as a nurse for A. Boyd Bonds, Ellen Lacy mentioned in a court petition that a female servant had been her cook. When adults went to the fields to work from sunup to sundown on large plantations, often younger girls or older women were put in charge of the slave children for the day. Dick Dervin remembered that "each child went to the care of Granny Hannah. She fed them in a long wooden tray, corn bread, milk and peas, mixed."[9]

In one postemancipation case white defendants called former slaves to testify via a deposition and specifically asked the duties of particular slaves on the plantation. The female slaves of James Wright had waited on the family, cooked, taken care of the house, and performed the weaving, sewing, making and mending of clothing, milking, and spinning for both the white family and the slaves. The males mentioned, however, acted as carpenters and "builders," as did other male slaves in other cases. In another case both male and female slaves worked in the fields, but women also worked "at the house," while men worked in the blacksmith shop and drove the wagons. Men seemed to be much more valuable when it came to raising sheep. When John G. Logue's estate was probated after his death, the administrator retained the slave "Tom" to attend to the sheep, while hiring out the other slaves. The only person to own slaves and list "grazier" as his occupation in 1860 held only four slaves, but they were disproportionately male: three adult males to one adult female.[10]

Females were preferred for domestic work. Those who ran hotels or boarded paying customers (such as teachers) relied heavily on female slaves. Of the seven teachers and hotel keepers who owned slaves listed on the 1850 and 1860 censuses, eleven adult slaves were female, while only one was male. When Joseph Holt rented the Columbus Hotel from Arthur Sherrill and his wife, he also specifically rented the slave "Lucy."[11]

Owners of many slaves undoubtedly could divide work according to gender more easily, with certain slaves dedicated to the "house" except under special circumstances (such as picking season). It appears that some of the smallest slaveholders also each owned a female slave or two for the particular purpose of working as a house servant or cook. According to the 1850 and 1860 censuses, those who owned five or fewer slaves were almost four times more likely to own only adult females than they were to own only adult males. In 1850 each of sixteen small slaveholders (five or fewer slaves) owned an adult female slave and no male slaves over ten years old, while only four each held an adult male with no female slaves over ten. The proportion in 1860 was 116 to 40.

These statistics alone do not prove that female slaves were performing primarily household duties. Coupled with the fact that a large portion of those with only adult females listed occupations other than farming, statistics suggest that sometimes a female slave found herself alone in a household where she served primarily as the white family's domestic servant.[12]

At least a few of the female slaves served as household servants for German families. While Germans generally opposed slavery, several Germans in Colorado County followed the lead of their Anglo neighbors and invested in cotton and slaves. In 1850 Christian Kelch owned ten slaves and raised cotton as well as sheep. In 1860 Charles Ehlinger, Henry Obenhaus, C. Kesler, and Wm Frels raised cotton with the help of more than five slaves each. Most Germans who owned slaves, however, only owned one female slave or one female slave and her children. William B. Dewees, who had a young German wife in 1850, owned one adult female with three children. Charles Kesler, a miller, owned one female slave with a male child aged fifteen. In 1860 nine Germans who owned at least one slave each seemingly did not invest in servants to improve their cotton yield. Gerard Heinsohn, Christian Kelch, C. Jordt, Ernst Weishuhn, and Elizabeth Hahn did not even plant cotton or other staple crops. Yet each of these German households, along with four others, owned only one female slave and her offspring in 1860.[13]

Historian Lauren Ann Kattner speculates that German American women in Texas and Louisiana had different attitudes toward their female slaves in America than their southern Anglo counterparts. According to her findings, German women sought to replicate their elitist notions from their home country and were unable to find white women in America willing to be properly subservient as domestic servants. Therefore, they purchased female slaves but treated them less paternalistically and less as property than their southern neighbors did. There is no extant evidence in the words of Colorado County German women to show whether their attitudes coincided with Kattner's findings. However, this could possibly explain why, despite the general distaste Germans had for the institution of slavery, at least several German families with adult white females purchased slaves.[14]

While some slave women were assigned male jobs, especially in the fields, male slaves almost never performed the female duties of cooking, cleaning, sewing, and weaving. Because slave owners did not hesitate to use slave women both for "domestic" duties and for heavy labor, slave women had a very different frontier experience than white women.[15]

Ideals convinced many white women to follow their husbands to the frontier of Colorado County, Texas, even if some did so with reluctance. Other white women, however, chose not to go, or at least not immediately. As a result, single men or married men who would later bring their wives were more likely to move west, and during the frontier era of Colorado County there were many more white men than white women. White women made up only 44 percent of the population. While ideals and expectations shaped white women's decisions, laws and masters gave slave women no choice. As early as 1823, even though slavery was technically illegal in the Mexican province of Texas, of 126 residents in the Colorado District there were five "domesticks," two of whom were female. When Texas declared its independence from Mexico in 1836, slavery became legal, and the number of slaves increased.[16]

At least in the early years most of the slaves in Colorado County seemed to have come with their masters from other states where they had lived together. James Holt remembered how his family of twelve traveled to Texas along with "about the same number" of slaves, at least some of them female. Other white residents also reminisced about traveling with their slaves or wrote letters home to white relatives telling them about slaves whom their relatives obviously knew. Many men planned to clear land and make homes before sending for their wives, and some men took only some of their slaves at first, intending to send for the rest once they were settled. Of course, some bought slaves for the express purpose of taking them west or bought slaves once they arrived.[17]

Because slave women lacked the same kind of choices that white women made when moving west, slave women were, of course, much better represented in the frontier slave population. Even so, it is surprising to find that slave women substantially outnumbered slave men. In 1850 slave women made up 52 percent of the slave population, a stark contrast to white women, who made up only 44 percent of the white population.[18]

It is reasonable to assume that when slave owners made the decision which slaves to take to the frontier of Texas, male slaves would seem the most useful in the labor-intensive work of clearing new land, planting the first crops, and building houses and other structures. According to several historians, male slaves were preferred on frontier farms.[19]

However, ideals about slave women dictated that they could also be put to these duties. More important, slave women could also cook, sew, wash, and clean. In the absence of white women, these types of labor became extremely important to the white slaveholding men of Colorado County. Slaveholding families in 1850 contained a smaller percentage of adult white females than the population as a whole. White adult females made up 37 percent of the slaveholding families, while they made up 41 percent of nonslaveholding families. Those men wealthy enough to own slaves probably preferred taking at least one female to perform domestic duties. Men who bought slaves were more likely to invest in female slaves because they were cheaper and because there were fewer white women available to perform "female" tasks. Men such as Robert Robson, who moved to Colorado County in the 1840s and had no family living with him in 1850, probably found it easier to buy a female slave than to find a wife or another white female to do his washing and cooking. He owned two slaves, one of whom was an adult female.[20]

During the frontier era the presence of more white men than women and more black women than men encouraged miscegenation, especially in areas with a heavy black concentration. James W. Holt remembered that the area around Oakland in 1850 had a ratio of approximately two whites to three blacks. Although miscegenational relationships were illegal, they apparently occurred at least occasionally—how often is impossible to determine. It may have been against the law, but the District Court of Colorado County never handed down an indictment for this crime until after emancipation.[21]

Only a few hints of these relations before the Civil War can be found in the remaining historical evidence. James Green, a slave in Colorado County, recalled years later that "after the war folks, white and black folks, looks down on white men and black women who had children together. Before we was free nobody thought nothing about it."[22]

Charles Tait wrote to his family about his own Colorado County slave: "Eunice will be delivered, in the course of a month or so, and as I judge from her conduct, of a mulatto." Two months later he wrote, "Nicey had a boy child on the 28th August, and white as I expected." The letters give no hint as to the identity of the father. However, the tone of Tait's letters indicates not only his disapproval of the act, but also that he blamed the slave woman. He ended the letter, "I have not yet sold same."[23]

According to reports of visitors to Colorado County, as early as 1833 the two Alley brothers lived with "a handsome black girl, who has several fine-looking partly colored children—specimens of the custom of some countries." This slave woman might have continued to live with William Alley as his mistress for years after. Two years after William's death three men and five women (along with their husbands) sued in probate court to administer William Alley's estate and have it descend to them as "the nearest of kin and the only heirs entitled to the estate." Further documents in the case reveal that the mother of the eight children, Caroline, had died in 1867; they claimed that she, although a slave, had lived with William Alley as his wife and borne his children. The eight ranged in age from eighteen to twenty-nine, thus putting their births at 1841 and forward—seven years after the first reported presence of a slave woman and mulatto children at the Alley residence. Walter Alley, the oldest of these children, might have been very light skinned, since he was listed on the 1870 census as white.[24]

Although William Alley never married anyone else, Alley's sister denied that he ever treated his slave Caroline as his mistress or wife. She reported: "in fact, previous to the death of said Alley and previous to the death of the mother of the plffs. the said Alley sold said mother and her children the plffs. to Geo L. Perry and Wm. Bridge and treated and considered them as his property not as his wife and children." The case went to district court, where in 1871 a jury of twelve men "could not agree on a verdict." After that, Walter Alley and his siblings asked for a change of venue (to try the case in another county). When this was denied, they allowed the matter to drop.[25]

The long-term nature of William Alley's relationship with his slave Caroline and the fact that he never married anyone else might have suggested more than merely a master taking advantage of a slave. According to at least one Texas historian, "black female concubinage, often an arrangement based on affection as well as convenience, was common on the early Texas frontier." However, Alley's sale of Caroline and her children, apparently sometime before 1860, shows how insecure such a relationship could be.[26]

Caroline's choices about her relationship with William Alley had been severely limited. There may indeed have been true emotion and love between the two, but even if there had been none on Caroline's part, she could not legally have made a substantially different decision. According to the former slave Jim Green, "the masters and the drivers takes all the nigger girls they want. One slave had four children right after the other with a white master. Their children was brown, but one of them was white as you is." Whether or not a slave woman loved or wanted a white man who had power over her, he could "take" her. The law recognized no such thing as rape of a slave.[27]

Undoubtedly slave women might consent or even seek out relationships with their white masters to get better treatment. James Green suggested that some might, but he did not believe this always helped them: "But [their children] was all slaves just the same, and the niggers that had children with the white men didn't get treated no better. She got no more away from work than the rest of them." Charles Tait's assumption that his slave woman Nicey was at fault for giving birth to a mulatto child, whether true in this individual case or not, followed the general belief of southerners that African American women were naturally promiscuous. It was believed that slave women either willingly had sex with white men or even seduced them. White men and women alike preferred to blame slave women as being lusty rather than truthfully evaluate the power relationships that allowed white men to use slave women.[28]

The unbalanced ratio of white males to white females during the frontier era made it especially tempting for white men to have relationships with black female slaves. Within the slave population, however, the ratio was reversed:

black women exceeded the number of black men. This ratio may have made it difficult for black women to find black husbands. Absolute numbers, however, were not necessarily the deciding factors in finding marriage partners or forming families. Again, because no law recognized the validity of black families, the laws or rules of the masters exerted enormous influence on the decisions slaves were given.[29]

Slave owners usually encouraged the formation of families (even if they did not always recognize them) because the children born of their female slaves symbolized an increase in the worth of their personal property holdings. Charles Tait looked for ways to "provide" his slaves with spouses. Charles wrote to his father hoping that his brother James would acquire "a suitable woman for a wife for [Charles's slave] King" before making the move to Texas. Charles felt that, "As we shall be so close together . . . an arrangement of that sort would do very well." Whether or not King would have a choice in the matter of taking a wife or which woman he might take for a wife is unclear. At least one other slave owner clearly did not allow his slaves marriage options. John Pinchback chose "the wife for every man on the place." According to James Green, "no one had no say as to who he was going to get for a wife. . . . Pinchback tried to get rid of women who didn't have children." Most slave owners probably did not go to this extreme but certainly encouraged their slaves to marry on the plantations.[30]

During the frontier era slaves' choices on their own plantations were rather limited. Although 91 percent of the Colorado County slaves lived in households with more than five slaves, over half of them lived on plantations of fewer than twenty. Marrying abroad, or marrying someone from a different plantation, required the permission of the master. John Pinchback certainly did not allow his slaves to marry abroad, but others gave such permission.[31]

In a frontier community such as Colorado County, marrying abroad was extremely risky. Small farmers took enormous risks to move to Texas, and many times those financial risks did not pay off, in which case they were forced to sell their slaves or pick up and move yet again. The high frontier death rate also meant that many slaves were divided among owners' children at the death of their masters. Not all these children lived in Colorado County, would remain in the county if they did, or even wanted to own slaves (and thus would sell them).[32]

Of the seventy-one slaveholders listed on the 1850 slave census, only a little over half (forty) were listed on the 1860 census. Nine of those who were not listed in 1860 had died in the intervening ten years, and their estates were distributed to heirs. Another two probably died as well, since their spouses were listed as owning slaves in 1860. The remaining twenty disappeared not only from the slave census but also from the free population schedule, indicating that they had moved out of the county. Of those who still remained in the county and owned slaves, four had fewer slaves in 1860 than in 1850. When slaves were sold or given as inheritance, or the slave owners moved, husbands and wives on different plantations were separated—often by such long distances that they never saw each other again.[33]

After the frontier era, as the white population boomed, so did the black population. The slave population in 1860 (3,558) was five times that of 1850 (723). Only a small portion of this was natural increase. The vast majority were moved to the county from other southern states, some of these moving as families. For instance, when John Crisp moved in 1856, he brought eighty slaves with him from his Mississippi plantation. Of the 284 slaveholders in 1860, 212 had not been listed on the free population schedule of the 1850 census. A little over half of the slaveholders who were new to the county owned five or fewer slaves, but forty-one (19 percent) owned twenty or more, and three claimed over one hundred slaves (only one person who had been listed on the 1850 census could claim this many in 1860).[34]

A journey overland to Colorado County, Texas, was a difficult one. James Williams Holt remembered that his family's slaves had traveled to Texas with them: "Our journey to Texas was any thing but pleasant. Twelve whites and about the same number of blacks made up the conveyance." If from the ten-year-old Holt's perspective, even in memory, the trip was difficult, it was even more so for the slaves. Holt remembered how "Joe Tooke, Allen Tooke, . . . poor old Nelse, a negro and old Hannah a negress, would put their shoulders to the wheel and up precipitous hills." Mrs. F. G. Mahon, remembering her childhood trip to Colorado County, thought that "the negroes singing as they traveled" meant that "they seemed to have no care in the world." More than likely, they sang as they did in the fields to help themselves cope with the difficult work and transition. The white family traveled overland in covered carriages while the slaves walked, and the family "sometimes camped on Saturday [so] that the negroes could do washing and some extra cooking."[35]

Besides the difficulty of making the journey, some slaves no doubt were mourning the loss of some family members. When all of a master's slaves made the trip together, fewer families were separated. But if any had families on other plantations, they were facing the very real probability of never seeing or hearing from them again. Making it illegal for slaves to read and write ensured that they would not be able to communicate with one another, and, of course, they were not free to return home to visit.[36]

The slaves who traveled with their masters to Colorado County, however, were luckier than the ones sold from other southern states and bought for slaveholders in Texas. For instance, slaves James Green and John Thompson never saw their families again after they moved to Texas. This type of slave migration was common as farmers and planters needed more and more slaves in Texas as cotton production increased and brought a much higher price. The slaveholders of 1850 who remained in 1860 had increased their holdings by 332 slaves collectively. Even plantation owners who, like John Crisp, had moved into the county since 1850 bought and transported more slaves to Colorado County after their arrival. While Crisp brought eighty slaves with him initially, by 1859 he had increased his holdings to 149, while his neighboring slaveholders had also increased theirs. Most of these slaves were bought and transported to Texas. Rarely were slaves sold in slave markets elsewhere and transported to Colorado County in complete families.[37]

Despite the obstacles and the high possibility of past and future heartbreaks due to separation, slaves continued to form families. The security of the slave family in Colorado County depended greatly upon the security of the master and the degree to which the slaveholder recognized and valued slave families. Some Colorado County masters recognized slave families and felt a moral obligation to keep them together. In his will William R. Turner asked that his personal property be divided among his heirs "and my slaves to remain in families as I am opposed to separating man and wife or families of Negroes."[38]

Other white Colorado County citizens at least recognized families of slaves, whether or not they insisted they be kept together. In a study of every sale, hiring out, probate, mortgage, or court case in which more than one slave was mentioned, 15 out of 199 records listed slaves in family units (husband, wife, and children). Seven more listed slaves as husband and wife. By far the most acknowledged slave relationship in these documents was that of the slave mother and her children. Mothers and their children were listed in eighty-three documents, 79 percent of the documents listing any relationship between slaves.[39]

Court records noted slave relationships more often in the antebellum and Civil War eras than during the frontier era. The documents filed during the Civil War indicated relationships in 74 percent of the documents, during the antebellum period in 55 percent, but during the frontier era in only 47 percent. One explanation for this is that with the larger plantations, larger slave populations, and larger concentration of slaves in areas, slaves had more time to form or have formed families in the years after 1852. On the other hand, these documents only indicate white recognition of slave families. As southern whites defended against increasing criticism and attacks on slavery from the North and the perceived threat of federal legislation on the issue of slavery, they argued that the peculiar institution was actually benign and bene-

fited slaves as well as masters. Part of this defense led at least some southerners to attempt to or desire to treat their slaves more humanely, thus recognizing slave families as having some claim to remaining intact.[40]

Even as slaves and their families became more notable to whites, most
slaveholders still put legal and financial interests ahead of the sanctity of slave
family ties. While husbands and wives were less recognized and more frequently separated, the most heart-wrenching separation was probably that of
a mother from her children. And while the sale of young children did not occur every day, it did occur with sometimes devastating effects on families.

Between 1837 and 1865 the ages of children were listed in 388 recorded
transfers of slaves from one party to another, either by sale, mortgage, or as
inherited property. Fifty-eight of these documents transferred ownership of
sixty-nine slaves under the age of eighteen without also transferring their parents. A person who was eighteen, of course, was not considered a child any-
more, but the separation no doubt was difficult even then. Slave mothers in
Colorado County, however, had to watch at least fifty children ages fourteen
and under separated from them by sale, gift, or as a result of the death of their
masters. Twenty-four children nine and younger were separated from their
parents; even children as young as age three were sold to other households.
Some of these sales or transfers might have occurred after or because the
mother had died, but many parents of young children separated can be ascertained still to have been living.[41]

When the probate court divided Susan Ann Gardner's estate, the slaves
went to four different heirs residing in different locations. Prince and Louisa
and their two small children, both under four years of age, descended to Robert Mosely in Fayette County. Clara, Clara's fifteen-year-old daughter (Sylvia),
and Clara's four-year-old son (Cyrus) went to Harrison Gregg in Colorado
County. However, J. Hamilton Stevenson in Colorado County took possession of Hannah (teenaged daughter of Prince and Louisa), Wallace (the three-
year-old son of Prince and Louisa), and Shade (the older and probably adult
son of Clara). Lucy and Caroline (the teenaged daughters of Prince and Louisa)
as well as Pamela (the six-year-old daughter of Clara) went with William
Stevenson, whose residence is unknown, although he was not living in Colorado County. The Colorado County records do not indicate what happened
to all the slaves at that point, but Harrison Gregg immediately sold Clara and
Cyrus to George Thatcher and sold Sylvia to W. R. Turner.[42]

No matter how considerate the masters or how much they might recognize
the family relationships in the slave communities, hard financial times and especially death could suddenly split slave families apart. Slave mothers lived
with the heart-wrenching possibility of never seeing their children again and

even faced the possibility that the children would not remember them. After emancipation, when former slaves desperately tried to reunite families torn apart during slavery, fathers and mothers relied on the Freedmen's Bureau to help them find and retrieve their children. On rare occasions the Freedmen's Bureau passed along the sad information that the children had no interest in returning to their parents. These children had grown up not knowing their parents and were happier to stay where they had called home.[43]

The social and legal expectations of white women in Colorado County were denied to slave women. White women fulfilled social expectations by marrying, remaining faithful to their marriages and husbands by bearing and raising children and by concentrating on the domestic duties necessary to make their families comfortable ones. Not only did white southern society have different expectations of slave women, but slave women were practically denied rights to many of these same actions.

Laws did not recognize slave marriages, and when separated from their husbands by circumstances, slave women were expected to marry again. The amount of faithfulness to their husbands depended in large part upon their masters' desire and ability not to separate husband and wife—and in some cases upon their masters' lack of desire to have particular slave women as mistresses. Although slave women had children, they could not be assured that they would be able to raise them. When they did remain with their children, they were not allowed to concentrate on the domestic duties for their families alone. Their children often went to the care of other slaves while they worked in the fields.

Slaves, and slave women in particular, valued marriage and children, but their familial and domestic roles came second to their "occupation" as workers for their master. Social ideals and laws made based on those social ideals constrained white women, but white women at least participated to a certain extent in the making and following of those ideals. Slave women had limited ability to shape the ideals and "rules" (made by southern white society and southern white masters, in particular) that defined their choices and actions.

CHAPTER 5

CIVIL WAR

If my sphere permitted me to go to the wars,
I should have taken delight in going some time ago,
and nothing could have prevented me from going.
—"HELEN," *COLORADO CITIZEN*,
SEPTEMBER 21, 1861

In February, 1861, Texas became the last of the Deep South states to secede from the Union. The *Colorado Citizen* headlines eight months earlier had proclaimed "Secessionists Rebuked!" in an extra edition covering a Columbus town meeting. After the election of Abraham Lincoln, the editors changed their tune: "May it be the proud boast of Texas, that she got out of the Union before Lincoln got into power!" In the election of secession convention delegates and in the secession referendum Colorado County citizens supported immediate secession. Only the predominantly German portions of the county opposed secession, but even those regions were not unanimous in their vote and were in any case too small numerically to affect the county's decision.[1]

Convention candidates, those who voted for them, and the editors of the newspaper that endorsed them were, of course, all men. Women's support from the beginning, however, was crucial to the cause of the Confederacy. According to the *Colorado Citizen:* "That cause can never perish which is sustained by the smiles and approval of our noble Southern women!" The newspaper consistently applauded the "powerful influence" of women at home, in the market, and with their decision-making husbands. The editors delighted in a story about a Williamson County, Texas, delegate who had voted against secession but asked permission to change his vote after he went home and "his wife wouldn't let him in at the front door."[2]

"Ladies" responded to the earnest requests of the *Citizen* to use their powerful influence to support all things southern and formed at least two organizations to support the war effort. The Ladies Military Association created committees to raise funds "for the purpose of equipping a company of volunteers from Colorado County, for the war." Another group of women made and presented a flag to the departing Company A, Fifth Regiment Texas Mounted Volunteers. Other women made or raised money for clothing and supplies for the "men." R. V. Cook, in supplying Captain Upton's company, "found the ladies everywhere filled with ardor and zeal and the cause of their country. None were unwilling to contribute." [3]

When women's support for the troops did not suffice to enlist all the young able-bodied men in the county, women used other powers of influence. At least one woman resorted to shame. A woman named Helen suggested that "all the young men that won't go to the wars, ought to put on hoops and long gowns." The article said that if these men thought they might "stay at home and marry while the choice young men are gone to the wars . . . they are much mistaken! A man that won't protect his country won't protect his wife." In a private letter John Shropshire asked his wife to "tell Georgia that if she had the pluck of our ancient mothers that she would hen peck Ben like the _____ if he did not leave soon for the wars." [4]

In the first year or so the war served to define gender roles further. Helen bemoaned that her sphere would not allow her to "go to the wars," since that public honor was reserved for men only. The support and influence of women, including the "henpecking," served to reinforce gender roles. The male heads of household left to protect their positions in southern society from the threats made by the Union armies. The women of Colorado County played the supportive and obedient role. Female tasks, such as knitting and sewing flags and uniforms, enabled men to pursue their honor on the battlefield. Women stoically sacrificed their men and boys to the fight, not complaining about their impending absence but instead encouraging them to enlist and defend southern society, including women's place in it. [5]

Men might have left their homes to fulfill their masculine roles in the war, but they had no plans to abdicate their places as heads of households. Men had often left their homes temporarily before the war, leaving overseers, male kin, or others to look after their household affairs or to assist their wives in these matters. Expecting a short war, southern men believed that their military duties would not interfere with their duties at home. In the first years of the war husbands and fathers continued to direct the activities at home. For instance, Capt. John Shropshire in letters in 1861 and early 1862 sent instructions to his wife Caroline about business with the expectation that she would forward them to her father. In January, 1862, Caroline was to "ask the Dr to have some cotton baled . . . and send it to Messrs Vance & Bro San Ant. and have it sold." John also included in his letter details of accounts that he held, debts that he owed, and those he wished to have paid first. All of this he expected her to relay to her father because, as John wrote, "I rely upon him entirely and feel satisfied that he will act entirely for the best."[6]

The Civil War, however, was no short affair. As the war dragged on for years, the men of Colorado County faced obstacles to their expectations of maintaining male authority over their households and over the community. Embroiled in battles or even surviving the boredom of camps where regiments saw little or no action, soldiers and officers faced new and different challenges that consumed their energies. Far removed from their farms, plantations, and businesses—which were facing new challenges because of the war—they comprehended less and less the difficulties there and less often had salient advice to give.[7]

As did most of Texas, Colorado County avoided the physical devastation that the war visited on much of the rest of the South. Union troops never invaded the interior of Texas, and many of the men who left joined home guards that did not see much fighting. Nevertheless, the war disrupted life in the county. Union blockades disrupted the cotton trade, decreasing the profits and livelihoods dependent upon the crop. The demands of the armies for food, clothing, and manufactured goods drove up civilian prices and led to scarcities. The flood of Confederate paper money caused inflation and confusion. With the men away from home, food and cotton production fell, making some families subject to hunger and general privation. Of course, many families felt the devastation of losing male family members in the units from Texas that did endure heavy casualties. As men in the armies understood less the circumstances faced by their households, those left behind had increasingly to use their own judgments in making decisions.[8]

The length of the war also demanded that many more men leave the county, increasing the number of women left behind to use their own judgments regarding household affairs. The patriotic zeal of the county's men and women led to the formation of at least four volunteer companies during the war. These companies enlisted a total of 424 men, an equivalent of 35 percent of the county's adult male population. By April, 1862, the Confederate Congress had enacted the conscription law, which demanded the enlistment of more men between the ages of eighteen and thirty-five and later was expanded to include ages seventeen through fifty. While some of the wealthy were able to hire substitutes, at least some of those substitutes were from Colorado County. The less wealthy could not afford the high price of a substitute and were drafted. In addition to the men who joined the Colorado County companies, evidence shows that many more enlisted in other regiments, although it is impossible to know precisely how many men left to fight for the Confederacy. In addition, at least a few German men from Colorado County fought for the Union army. By 1863, according to one man, "almost all the men in the county were drafted to the military service."[9]

Those remaining often determined that the shortage of men in the county meant that certain public activities could not continue. The three brothers who were editors of the *Colorado Citizen* complained in October, 1861, that "Columbus is now the dullest place perhaps, on the map." By the end of the year editors Ben, J. D., and Hicks Baker had all joined the army, leaving the county without a newspaper. The district judge for Colorado County, George W. Smith, did not enlist. However, with the large number of men enrolled and unavailable to answer suits and the legislative enactment of stay laws suspending the collection of debts, Smith canceled district court completely for the duration of the war.[10]

However, the citizens of Colorado County could not indefinitely postpone daily activities until the men returned to resume their public and head-of-household duties. Food and cotton crops still had to be raised and sold to support families, as well as to support the Confederacy. Other legal matters such as probating the estates of the men who died in and during the war could not wait. Although the men who remained guided both business and law in the county, women increasingly had to become actors in these public matters.[11]

Of all the changes wrought in gender expectations during the war, the most notable was the increase of married women's active participation in financial transactions. The antebellum laws of coverture had declared married women's business actions invalid without their husbands' express permission and signatures. However, husbands increasingly relied upon their wives, rather than other men, to take charge of the family plantations and businesses. As a result merchants and other men in the county abandoned their usual reluctance to conduct business with women.[12]

Although it is uncertain if Helen Le Tulle's husband Victor joined the army, he was absent during 1862 and 1863. During his absence Helen "acted in the capacity of agent for Le Tulle and Co.," her husband's business. When James Darby called on her with the intention of repaying a note Le Tulle and Co. held against him, she "examined the claims left with me by Le Tulle and Co. and failed to find any note." She then "received an am[oun]t of money in Confederate notes from James A. Darby and receipted to him for it." When her husband came home, Helen gave him the money and the accounts, and although the company no longer held the note, she reported that never "did her husband express any sorrow at my having received the money from Mr. Darby."[13]

Although she was a married woman, unable in normal circumstances to conduct her own business, much less that of her husband, Helen acted as her husband's agent in this and presumably other financial transactions during his absence. James Darby showed no reluctance at conducting business with this married woman and, in fact, insisted upon paying her money despite her hesitancy to take it when Helen could not find the note the company held against him. Her husband did not regret or challenge Helen's actions. Nor did anyone challenge her ability to act as her husband's agent during the court case that finally went to trial in 1868. The case against James Darby centered not on Helen's marital status, but on the fact that Le Tulle and Company had previously traded the note to another party.[14]

Victor Le Tulle never recorded any legal document giving his wife express permission to conduct his or her own business. He assumed that in the midst of the war Helen, although a married woman under the confines of coverture, naturally should serve as his agent. Other husbands, however, did attempt to leave legal documents giving their wives power to conduct business. Fanny Darden had spent her antebellum years protected from public activities, even in the seven district court cases before the war that disputed her separate property. William Darden had, as expected by society and law, acted as manager of Fanny's estate, handling the legal and financial aspects of protecting her property. Fanny had never even been required to sign a document in its defense or appear in court. By the time William entered the Confederate army as a substitute in mid 1862, the social proscription against wives conducting business in Colorado County had already been eased. Rather than try to run his and her business from the battlefield or turn matters over to another man who might subsequently leave for the war, William intended for Fanny to make the necessary decisions for their household. William recorded a power of attorney at the county courthouse appointing W. S. Delaney as his agent "in order to enable my wife Mrs. Fanny A. Darden . . . the better to manage and transact business during my absence in the wars." William intended for Fanny to make her own decisions, with Delaney instructed to sign his name "to any and all instruments of writing which my wife may think or deem necessary."[15]

At least one other husband attempted to enable his wife legally to take care of family financial matters. Michael McLemore registered a power of attorney in 1863. In this document duly recorded in the Colorado County Clerk's Office, McLemore appointed his wife Mary McLemore "to be my true and lawful attorney in fact to act for me and in my name, place and stead as agent to sell and convey any lands, houses and lots in the Town of Columbus or else where, or any negro slaves now belonging to either of us individually or owned by us as community property in as full and complete a manner as the same could be done if I were personally present and joined with her in making said conveyance."[16]

Mary McLemore had already begun conducting business in her own name before Michael left this power of attorney. In January, 1862, she had sold the family's piano to W. B. Dewees, taking a promissory note for $187. The power of attorney made it easier for Mary to conduct business of all kinds, but she did not use it for a major land transaction until nearly two years later. On March 20, 1865, she sold a plot of land for $1,200 to A. J. Folts. Ironically, even though she signed both her own and her husband's names, the county clerk conducted the married woman's separate examination to assure that her husband had not coerced her to sign the deed.[17]

While William Darden and Michael McLemore had the foresight to ensure that their wives had unquestionable legal ability to act upon their own financial decisions, few other husbands did so. Some husbands, however, still expected their wives to make such decisions and expected that the Colorado County community would accept them. While their wives did transact business, when land titles were in question, some wives had to resort to legal maneuvering to assuage the fears of purchasers that they alone could not effectively convey titles. When Martha Pankey wished to sell 160 acres of land to Robert Stafford in 1864, she enlisted John Hope to sign the deed on behalf of her husband Joseph Pankey. After the war Robert Stafford instituted a friendly (and uncontested) case in district court to clear the title of any doubt.[18]

If married women found ways of selling land without their husbands' express permission, they of course entered into sundry other transactions that were not as legally regulated. As described above, Helen Le Tulle conducted her husband's business. Another merchant and farmer, Samuel J. Redgate, left his wife Mary in "control" of his goods and merchandise. Mrs. Frances S. Chesley ran a hotel in 1865, signing leases and contracts without her husband. Numerous other married women carried on the business of farms and plantations, contracting with merchants for supplies, though the law allowed them to contract only for "family necessaries."[19]

Merchants and other businesspeople in Colorado County accepted the premise that married women acted as agents for husbands away during the war. These assumptions were widely held, and the exceptions made to laws during the war were upheld later in the Reconstruction era. The notes that Helen Le Tulle signed on behalf of her husband's company were accepted as valid by the courts, judges, and attorneys. The accounts, debts, and promissory notes signed by married women without their husbands also remained legally valid whenever they became aspects of litigation. No litigant during or after the war questioned the legality of a married woman's business transaction made during the Civil War. As law was reinterpreted during the war to allow women more responsibility and agency, social proscriptions fell away.

Women, married and single, left few wills (fourteen) between 1837 and 1873, and the drafting of wills by women did not necessarily increase during the Civil War. Only two women wrote wills dated during the war, and only one of those wills was probated during the war. During the frontier era the three married women who left wills gave everything they owned to their husbands, as did the three married women who wrote wills during the Reconstruction era. No married woman left a will during the antebellum years. Eliza Grace's Civil War–era will was unique in that for the first time a married woman took the opportunity provided by statute to leave her separate estate to someone other than her husband.[20]

During the Civil War, Eliza Grace took advantage of a right that had been allowed to married women since 1837 but never claimed. Shortly before she died in 1862 Eliza chose to bequeath all of her separate property to her children and none to her husband Thomas. The greater likelihood of her husband's death due to the war probably prompted Eliza to consider her children's best interests in case of the death of both parents. Her husband Thomas most likely consented to the provisions of the will before her death, or she believed he would after her death. She requested that he hold the property in trust for her minor children until they came of age, paying 10 percent interest on the proceeds to her children. The war years produced this unique instance in which a married woman chose to leave her property to someone other than her husband, although her husband's acceptance of the situation was probably crucial in Eliza's decision. Between 1837 and 1873 no other married woman in Colorado County made this kind of financial decision about how her property should be divided after her death.[21]

Married women were not the only ones to exhibit increased agency in public during the war. Most notably, the percentage of women taking active roles in probating the estates of deceased family members greatly increased. The percentage of widows acting as sole executors or administrators of their husbands' estates reached nearly the same level as that of the frontier period and was double that of the antebellum years. Of the twenty-four estates of married men probated during the Civil War, only 33 percent of the widows declined to administer, compared to nearly 59 percent who declined to administer during the antebellum years.

The most obvious reason that more women administered estates during the war than before was the shortage of men left in the county to conduct such business. The administration of estates in probate court, like the raising of food and cash crops, could not wait for men to return to fulfill their public responsibilities. Women, therefore, stepped into those male roles.

Seven widows found and chose to allow men to conduct the business of their deceased husbands' estates. Of the seven estates widows chose not to ad-

minister, five were administered by male relatives. One widow, Mary Bullington, apparently hired attorney John D. Gillmore to probate her deceased husband's estate on her behalf. Gillmore served as administrator for several estates
in Colorado County throughout his career. In J. C. Bullington's estate only
one action was necessary: to ask the court to set aside all the property to his
widow Mary.[22]

In each of two cases in which a widow chose to coadminister an estate, a
male relative helped with the administration. Sallie Windrow later complained
that although the probate court appointed her coadministrator, her brother
"Josiah F. Payne took the entire management of the said Estate collected and
disbursed the moneys of said Estate according to his own judgement in the
matters brought before the admr and admx. That the said Sallie A. as Admx
entrusted the entire business to the care and management of the said J. F.
Payne."[23]

From August, 1862, until September, 1865, when Josiah Payne resigned as
administrator, all petitions and actions in the probate court included Sallie's
name but not her signature. In late 1865 Sallie became sole administrator. She
discovered that she should have taken a greater role in the affairs of the estate
from the beginning, as she did not approve of Payne's handling of the estate.
Elvy Ann Carson coadministered her husband's estate with her son and apparently took a greater role than Sallie Windrow did. She appeared in court
and signed petitions and documents herself.[24]

The women who chose not to administer or coadminister each had a male
relative on which to rely, even if the relative did not always prove reliable. It
is not possible to determine with any certainty whether the widows who chose
to administer had the option of allowing male relatives to do so in their stead.
In several cases there clearly were no grown sons to take responsibility.[25] Wealth
seemed to be the greatest determinant in whether or not a widow would administer an estate herself. Half of the eight widows who acted as neither executor nor administrator had deceased husbands whose estates were valued in
the top quarter of the population. All but one estate was valued in the top half
or higher. The two widows who coadministered estates with male relatives dealt
with estates in the top tenth of the population in terms of wealth. The widows
who served as sole executors or administrators, on the other hand, administered less valuable estates. Of those fourteen estates, the value of ten can be
determined. Four fell in the bottom half of the population in terms of wealth,
while only one fell in the top quarter and none in the top tenth. Table 4 shows
the numbers of widows administering and declining administration of estates
as broken into categories of wealth.

The choice by widows not to administer the wealthiest estates contrasted

TABLE 4.

WIDOWS AND THEIR DECEASED HUSBANDS' ESTATES, BY WEALTH

Quarter of Wealth*	3	2	1	Top 10%	Total
Administrator or executor	4	5	1	0	10
Coadministrator	0	0	0	2	2
Declined administration	1	3	2	2	8
Total	5	8	3	4	20

*No estates were valued in the bottom quarter of wealth. The value of four estates of those widows who administered cannot be determined.

Source: Probate Records, CCCC; Schedule 1 (Free Inhabitants), Eighth Census of the United States (1860), Texas, Colorado County.

starkly with the antebellum management of estates. Before the war widows were more likely to administer or at least coadminister a high-valued estate themselves. But conscription laws favored exemptions for the wealthy by automatically excluding those who owned twenty or more slaves and by allowing the wealthy to hire substitutes. Older families were often wealthy, and some husbands, although not necessarily all, in this bracket were too old to fight in the army or be conscripted. As more men from wealthy families, for a variety of reasons, stayed home during the war than did those less wealthy, women within the wealthiest population bracket were more likely to have male relatives help them run their farms, plantations, and businesses than those in lower brackets. Therefore, those male relatives were available to take up administration of estates as well. The less wealthy widows were more likely to have male relatives, especially sons, participating in the war and were already in the position of taking care of family business. When their husbands died, they continued the businesses, even if great difficulties were involved. Maria Dungan complained to the district court after the war that she was unable to enforce a lease because she was "old and female" and the lessor declared "his intention of maintaining the property with the strong hand." Yet she continued the administration, neither remarrying nor turning it over to another male even after the war.[26]

Regardless of class, age, or ability, widows chose to rely on male relatives or their own efforts when it came to the administration of estates. This also contrasted starkly with the antebellum years, when half of the estates leaving widows had unrelated male administrators or executors. Antebellum women were less willing to enter a courtroom than to entrust their family estates to creditors or other men. Women in the Civil War years, however, had begun to take a more active role in their families' financial affairs. As more husbands left their wives to conduct business in their absence, the social prohibitions against women taking an active public role eased, making it not only possible but likely that women would exhibit more agency in the courtrooms.[27]

As the number of single women in the county increased, so did their activity in the public sphere. Women whose husbands had died in and during the war, as well as a few young unmarried women, often did not have the option to marry or remarry. Some, such as Helen of the *Colorado Citizen* editorial, perhaps chose not to marry men who would not protect their country. However, by 1862 the war had required so many men to leave for army duty that fewer women could find single men to marry. The number of marriages in 1861 reached an all-time high of fifty-two. The next year the number of marriages in Colorado County dropped to less than half that, with only twenty-one marriages taking place. In 1863 and 1864 the number of marriages barely increased to thirty and twenty-seven respectively.[28]

As a result single and widowed women, often already accustomed to taking care of family business in the absence of men, increasingly entered into business transactions. Mary Toland and Louisa Odom signed promissory notes to merchants for goods and farming supplies. Sarah E. Kuykendall, Elizabeth McAshan, and Julia Currie all loaned money or traded for notes during the war. Most frequently in order to make money, single women and married women alike rented out their slaves, sometimes taking promissory notes for payment. The estates of deceased women also indicated an increased amount of financial activity. Sarah Mason's estate showed that not only had she contracted debts during the war, but she had also lent money to merchants.[29]

Leonora Miller, barely twenty-one years old in 1864 and never married, became intricately involved in business dealings. William Harbert owed her $250 and had no money to pay. Instead of cash he offered her cotton, which at the time was not easily turned into currency because of Union blockades. Leonora accepted the cotton and hired John Taylor to use her wagon to take the load to Brownsville to be sold, presumably through the Mexican port city of Matamoros.[30]

The elderly widow Elizabeth K. Turner saw her sons leave for war and so entered into an agreement with Benjamin T. Ingram to jointly farm a portion of her land and split the proceeds. She furnished five of her slaves, "sufficient teams and farming tools," and food for the slaves and animals as well as the land. Benjamin furnished two slaves, teams, and farming supplies as well and agreed to oversee raising cotton, corn, and potatoes personally. The agreement did not work out as smoothly as planned. In addition to other problems, Benjamin was drafted into the army at the height of cotton picking season. "Being unable to have a man to take charge of the farm in his absence," Elizabeth lost the cotton in the field.[31]

Elizabeth Turner had other lands under cultivation at the time of her agreement with Benjamin Ingram. She decided that it would be in her best interest to remove her slaves to other projects than to allow them to work under only "such general supervision" as two male neighbors could provide. Women throughout the South had to make such decisions as they were left with the supervision of slaves. Some undertook this job vigorously, but with great difficulties. Without a white male nearby to make slaves work and with the hope of impending freedom in the air, women faced extraordinary difficulties. Some women chose to rent or sell their slaves rather than deal with overseeing and disciplining slaves when they could find no white men to help. Benjamin Ingram expected that only a man could properly take charge of the farms and hands. Yet obviously women, after nearly all the men in the county were drafted, provided at least on occasions some such supervision.[32]

Even poorer women who had no slaves continued to raise some crops without the assistance of their husbands or sons. Raising crops, entering contracts, making financial decisions, and relying on the few remaining men less and less, women increasingly took on male roles during the war. Yet the hardships of the war were more than some women could manage. Removing the male members of households, no matter how financially savvy the remaining women, created poverty for families who relied upon men for labor in the fields. Deprived of their male heads of household, destitute women (as well as elite women) turned to the government that had deprived them of their male providers either to release these males from service or to fill their place in providing at least minimal survival.[33]

Colorado County certainly did not face the extent of need or provide the same level of support as urban and war-torn areas of the South did. Even so, beginning in 1862 the Colorado County court commissioned a census of families of soldiers needing support. In January, 1863, some seventy families, almost exclusively married women and their dependents, received support from the county in amounts ranging from ten dollars to forty dollars. Nearly every month thereafter "widows, parents, and children" on a list were provided with some sustenance to curb starvation.[34]

With men at war, women faced economic hardships from starvation to difficulty managing slaves. As women took on unaccustomed male roles, and as the war loosened the restrictions placed on women to remain domestic, pure, pious, and submissive, tensions increased between husbands and wives. Many of these tensions related directly to the nature of war. War eased the normal restraints of courtship. Many young women, accepting the belief that women's goal was marriage, feared that the decreasing supply of men might doom them to spinsterhood. Some young couples married hastily in the excitement of war before young men went off to combat and then found that they had made a mistake.[35]

Martha Ivey at the age of thirteen had married Stephen Conner in 1860. When he joined the army, she lived with his mother where "she was treated with much unkindness." She appealed to her new husband to provide her with a new home, but "he disregarded her appeal." Stephen's absence from home while he was in the army surely complicated the possible success of this young marriage. In addition to the bonds of matrimony being tested by his mother's cruel treatment of her, Martha apparently had fallen in love with another man in his absence. After the war Stephen countersued and won a divorce when he produced a document proving that Martha had committed not only adultery but also bigamy by marrying another man.[36]

George Metz returned from two years in the army to find that his significantly younger wife had "formed a guilty and adulterous intimacy." Sarah "manifested no affection or welcome" to George when he returned home, and shortly after that George discovered the reason.[37]

Mike Scherer had lived in the Metz household to raise crops and tend the homestead after George joined the army. Mike, however, took more than just the business role of the husband in George's absence: Sarah Metz's "general conduct with Mike Scherer became so notorious for illicit conduct between the said Sarah and Scherer that the ladies of the neighborhood dropped her. They neither visited her nor encouraged her to visit them on account of her familiarity with said Mike Scherer and her indecent conduct towards the said Scherer unbecoming a married woman." [38]

Even after George's return home Mike Scherer refused to leave the house. He allegedly claimed "that he was bound to have communication with her, that there was 'a cord of love'(!) between him and the said Sarah which could not be severed until death." Before the war George and Sarah Metz had been upstanding members of their community. George had served as an elder in the Lutheran Church, while Sarah had been received in the company of some of the community's most elite ladies. Mike Scherer's reputation before the war is unknown; however, his brother served as minister of the same congregation to which George Metz had been elected elder. The young Sarah, who otherwise would have remained under the constant and watchful eye of her older husband, found an opportunity in the war to form an illicit relationship with a man closer to her age and apparently more to her liking.[39]

Although E. H. Blum was not a soldier, the war caused him to leave his home in 1861–62 to conduct business in Mexico. According to his petition, his wife "Emma[,] taking advantage of his absence[,] did . . . commit adultery with one John Duffy." Husbands had sued wives for adultery before the war as well, but the extended absences of husbands led to an increase in these cases. Many wives left to make their own decisions exercised not only financial independence but independence of affections. Other wives, unaccustomed to the difficulties of providing for themselves and their families (difficulties that increased because of wartime shortages), turned to other men when their husbands abandoned their duties as heads of household.[40]

Marriages that had been clearly unhappy before the war were strained by the tensions of the time. H. A. Tatum complained that his wife Jane had treated him cruelly before the war. After he returned from military duty, she "was incapable of returning his affection or of performing any of the duties of an affectionate wife." In his 1864 petition H. A. stressed his loyalty and his male duty to protect: "he entered in the military service of our country and remained with our army in Virginia until he was broken down in health and discharged from the service." Jane, on the other hand, "instead of contributing to the comfort and wants" of a patriotic and returning soldier, "was constantly leaving him alone, and engaging in frivolous amusements with noisy company."[41]

Jane Tatum countersued, producing reams of evidence that H. A. had been cruel and abusive even before the war. Like Martha Conner and Sarah Metz, Jane Tatum was significantly younger than her husband. At the time of the marriage Jane "was quite young, much younger than [H. A.] . . . so that [she] naturally looked up to [him] and instead of meeting with that reciprocity of affection which is due from one conjugal consort to the other, said advance and manifestations of affection were always repelled with sneers, or rebuffed with sarcasm, and often accompanied with oaths." Jane had separated from her husband before he joined the army; but on his return in 1863 he promised to reform his habits, so she agreed to return to him "in consideration of [his] just having returned from the war." Jane stressed her loyalty by forgiving the patriotic soldier. His service in the army, however, according to Jane, had merely increased his habits of drunkenness and cruelty, and she soon wanted a divorce.[42]

Ellen Lacy's husband too had been cruel, drunken, and abusive since their marriage in 1858. While serving in the army Beverly Lacy would come home on furlough "reeling drunk, and wholly inebriated . . . cursing and abusing" Ellen. When Beverly returned to their home after the war, Ellen made her first attempt to end their marriage through divorce.[43]

Although no divorce cases could be heard during the war, two men and four women submitted petitions for divorce anyway between April, 1861, and April, 1865. The first four who filed, after years of not having their cases heard, consented to dismissal of their cases when court resumed in 1866. Some who filed their petitions before the war did not have a hearing before 1861, so they could not extricate themselves from their marriages, and at least two dismissed their cases after waiting years for a hearing. Only two cases filed during the war were continued to a final hearing when the district court resumed functioning, and several more cases were filed after the war, although the separation and difficulties between the spouses had occurred during the war years.[44]

Although wartime traumas undoubtedly were not the only causes of difficulty between these couples, the absence of men did exacerbate marital problems. Women worried about their husbands' fidelity far away from home on the battlefield. Men worried about their wives at home. Some young women left alone for the first time exerted their newfound independence to find new lovers; other women turned to other men out of desperation. Some older women discovered that they would rather live without their husbands, in peace as in wartime, than continue in unhappy and abusive marriages.[45]

Colorado County citizens began the Civil War believing that militaristic adventures available only to men would further define gender roles and the assumptions about men and women. Men would fulfill their duties to "protect" their wives against the encroaching enemy, while women would wait at home keeping the domestic hearth burning. These southerners initially relied upon women merely to use their influence at home to encourage men to enlist, to support the war efforts, and to contribute domestically by making flags and clothing. However, as the war required more and more men to leave the county, women were forced to make contributions that challenged, rather than enhanced, gender roles and assumptions about women's abilities and nature.[46]

Women had to take over the duties on farms and in businesses. Married women who before the war had relied exclusively on their husbands to take care of the financial and public duties of the family stepped into these formerly male roles. Single women and newly widowed women, instead of looking to men in the county to protect them from public activities, increasingly took the burdens upon themselves because they could not find male relatives to do so. Some of these women alone and acting independently for the first time made choices that their husbands would not have approved, such as taking new lovers. Others decided that they were willing to make their own choices even when men returned. Overall, women in Colorado County, whether married or single, entered the public arena in large numbers during the Civil War and acted more independently of the men in their lives than ever before.

CHAPTER 6

LONG-AWAITED PEACE

Reconstructing Society

> Now I can write to you full of joy, since we have attained that
> so long awaited for "Peace." What the future will bring,
> time shall tell. You can very well imagine, how happy I am
> to have the chance to see all my children again.
> —HELEN RUHMANN TO EMMA RUHMANN, JUNE 5, 1865

Helen Ruhmann probably typified the reaction of Colorado County's women to the end of the Civil War. Exultant over reuniting her family, she also looked to the future with uncertainty.[1] And in June, 1865, the future of Colorado County, Texas, and the South was far from predictable. The Civil War, Confederate defeat, and the consequences of both shook the county's political, economic, and social structures to the core. In the eight and a half years following the Confederate surrender until Texas returned to southern Democratic rule, Colorado County and Texas sought to reestablish their society based on the new realities caused by the war and defeat.

The most public upheaval in the county, the state, and the South as a whole was the reorganization of the governments and politics in the defeated Confederate states. As in other southern counties, the Confederate-era leaders that Colorado County reelected to office under presidential Reconstruction were replaced by military appointees in 1867. In 1868 only those (white and black) who could take the "Iron-Clad" loyalty oath could vote or be elected to office. Because Colorado County had a large German population that was less likely to support the Confederacy, at least some of the postwar officeholders had political experience.[2]

Nonetheless, the disestablishment of the slaveholding planter aristocracy brought anger and frustration. Editors of the unreconstructed *Colorado Citizen* in 1869 expressed sympathy and admiration for the county officers "who have fallen under the political guillotine." In 1871 they expressed outrage that the governor had reappointed Charles Schmidt as sheriff despite his failure to post bond for office, "in utter defiance of law and decency, his only qualification being father-in-law to a Senator, so-called."[3]

Women exercised little power in the unfolding political events. During the war women had been encouraged to influence their husbands to support the Confederacy politically and militarily. During Reconstruction no such appeals for political activism went out to women from the Colorado County press. A *Colorado Citizen* front-page reprint of a story from the *Woman's Health Journal* suggested that women should "be made active and fruitful by interests and associations beyond the home." The suggestion was not that a woman enter politics, but that "she needs to care for her neighbors and for the welfare of the community." Nurturing, caring, and domesticity—women's proper roles according to antebellum social ideals—should be women's focus once again. Other editorials ridiculed the attempts of northern women to gain suffrage. White women's greatest contribution to the defeated and often demoralized South was to return to their proper relationships in society by deferring to their husbands, fathers, and brothers in business, law, and politics.[4]

Women in Colorado County most likely were much too involved in the other urgent matters brought about by the war and defeat to be worried about gaining a voice in politics. Texas escaped the large-scale physical devastation of buildings, animals, and crops that other southern states experienced. However, Colorado County had faced its share of scarcity and poverty during the war because depleted labor forces could not raise enough food for families at home and soldiers at the front. Additionally, the collapse of the Confederate monetary system bankrupted many in the county, even some of the wealthiest. Yeoman women especially, with their families, focused all their time and energy on merely rebuilding their livelihoods, trying to raise crops, and holding onto their land, as agricultural output decreased and land values declined.[5]

The most dramatic change in postwar Colorado County came with the emancipation of the slaves. For the slaveholding families this meant a drastic decrease in the amount of valuable assets and sometimes a complete bankrupting of their resources. In addition to their capital loss, former masters had to adapt to new labor relations with a free population. Formerly elite women could no longer depend completely on the service of slaves in their homes to perform the "servile toil" of the household.[6]

Of course, emancipation brought the greatest change for the former slaves. On June 19, 1865, Union commander Brev. Maj. Gen. Gordon Granger landed at Galveston, Texas, and declared all slaves free. Although some slaves in Texas, and possibly in Colorado County, did not learn of their freedom for months, the news was announced in the county on June 22. The former slaves received and reacted to the news in various ways. John Pinchback took nearly a week to announce to his 125 slaves that "all you niggers is free, just as damn free as I am." After the announcement he gave all the former slaves names and offered them wages to stay on his farm and work. As in many other places, once they had freedom to form their own destinies, half of Pinchback's slaves chose to leave while the others remained—at least for a time.[7]

African American women for the first time in Colorado County history were to be governed by virtually the same laws as Anglo and German women. "Black codes" passed by the Texas legislature shortly after emancipation abridged the rights of many. Even after radical Republicans repudiated the black codes, racism continued to prejudice the treatment they received in lawsuits and hearings. Yet many former slave women did have opportunity to enter the court as free women for the first time. At first African American women took their cases primarily to the Freedmen's Bureau, but as the bureau was discontinued and the Reconstruction era wore on, a few found themselves in the county's district court. All too often they were the targets of criminal prosecutions, but some were also plaintiffs, suing and being sued on matters of property, wages, rents, and divorce. Like most white women of the county in the Reconstruction era, black women focused mainly on economic necessity. White women helped their families rebuild lost fortunes; black women helped their families build new lives from nothing.

Economic necessity played an enormous role in the formation of gender roles and gender relationships in postwar Colorado County. "It is undeniable," editorialized the local county newspaper, "that a large proportion of the wives and mothers in our country are so absorbed in their daily round of duties that they cannot possibly give much attention to outside affairs." For southern white women, the daily round of duties encompassed much more than it had before the war, especially for elite women. Women, such as Ellen Lacy, "neither accustomed, nor used to it, was forced to servile labor." Cooking over a hot stove, scrubbing floors, ironing, washing clothes, mending, and sewing were time-consuming and difficult chores that some slaveholding women had never performed. The stress of postwar society and the new duties expected of women could cause conflicts between spouses. Ellen Lacy's husband, for instance, cussed her and "ridiculed her effort at cooking." The daily pressures of running plantations without the coerced help of slave labor forced women to work much harder at their traditional domestic duties.[8]

Many formerly elite simply could not afford to hire servants to take the place of their slaves. Economic devastation hit some wealthy families during the war and after, forcing them to economize. Servants hired by those households were first and foremost needed for field work. The wealthiest, of course, could still hire domestic servants and did. Yet, finding household and domestic servants on terms that former slaveholders could tolerate became extremely difficult in the postwar years. In claiming their freedom, many African American families chose to withdraw as many family members from labor as possible. Freed people hoped and tried to ensure that children went to school instead of to the fields. And African American women wanted and hoped to concentrate on their own families' domestic needs first and foremost.[9]

When freedwomen did take the jobs of household servants, they insisted that their positions be defined fundamentally differently than during slavery. Many refused to live in the household or be on call twenty-four hours a day, instead insisting upon some time to concentrate on their own families' needs. White expectations of docile servants clashed with black claims to true freedom, leading to a high turnover rate in household servant positions. Freedwomen refused to accept long hours, mistreatment, or low wages and left their positions. White women dismissed workers to save money or because they found them to be unlike the docile slaves to which they were accustomed. Elizabeth Turner, for instance, for reasons unknown, drove Sarah Hartfield out of her house after just three months and refused to pay her.[10]

While many former slaveholding women struggled over daily chores in order to economize and help their families in the postwar economic stress, other women were forced to or chose to assist their families' income in other ways. In both elite and less-than-elite white families, working—even the earning of wages—became necessary in the economic struggles during Reconstruction. Women became increasingly visible in vocations only a few had performed during the war. Women increased the ranks of teachers, a traditionally acceptable position even for a lady, as the availability of education increased in the county and the South as a whole. Advertisements and announcements of new female-taught schools proliferated in the county's newspapers. "Mrs. Kate Oakes, one of our most estimable and worthy ladies, is now teaching a private school at the Seminary in our town. We understand she has a good school, and we know there is no lady in our State better qualified to teach than Mrs. Oakes." This announcement, like others, highlighted the entrance of married "ladies" into the paid workforce. Although this occupation paid below subsistence wages, teaching allowed both married and single women to make some type of living or contribute to their families' income.[11]

Teaching in freedmen's schools also provided a source of income. Probably most teachers in freedmen's schools in Colorado County came from outside the county, but a few women already residing in the county chose to pursue this occupation, whether out of charity or economic necessity. Mrs. Eliza A. Grace, from Georgia, had "resided in the county for sometime and . . . [was]

very well calculated to teach primary branches." Mrs. Mary Matthews taught freedmen in the county for several months before being officially appointed as a teacher by the Freedmen's Bureau.[12]

Several other women ran boardinghouses. A widow, Mrs. Arnold, provided "good board, good rooms, pleasantly situated, and in a quiet delightful portion of our city, with a pleasant, and, affable family." Another widow, Mrs. B. Foote, kept "a hotel in the town of Columbus for the support of herself and family." Other women who did not advertise hotels or run boardinghouses might take in boarders for extra money. Ann Guy received ten dollars from the county treasury "for one month board of Blind Woman." Mrs. E. Haskell, "a widow, with three little children to support," wrote that she was "entirely dependent upon my boarders for a support for myself and children." Even women who did not run boardinghouses or hotels of their own contributed valuable work to the families that did. "The nicest dinner" that the editors of the *Colorado Citizen* attributed to "Mr. N. Bonds of the Colorado House, upon reopening" was undoubtedly cooked by his wife, Malissa.[13]

Two widows took over the management of their deceased husbands' stores. Beetha Bryan ran the grocery store her husband John had begun in Columbus. Elizabeth Rhode "managed" the dry goods store in Frelsburg where her husband Adolph had previously been a merchant. A. Doregan apparently sold some dry good items on account, perhaps also running a store. Even single women who did not engage in any obvious occupation left evidence of conducting business for their support. Jane Greer engaged in some type of financial enterprise that earned her promissory notes and allowed her to trade those notes in the community. S. E. Kuykendall went to the Justice of the Peace Court ten times regarding notes and accounts due her.[14]

Of course, single white women during Reconstruction—as during previous periods—farmed or otherwise made livings off their land. Mary Taylor and Samuel B. Dehart entered a partnership to farm 32.5 acres together. Julia A. Currie listed her occupation as a farmer, making agreements with workers black and white alike to raise her crops. The Freedmen's Bureau frequently cited women farmers to answer complaints of their workers.[15]

White single women who continued to farm were often aided by older sons still at home. Thirty-eight percent of the white female-headed households in 1870 had sons eighteen or older still living and working at home. Sixty-four percent had sons thirteen or older. Depressed economic conditions most likely contributed to a rise in the number of sons who stayed at home during the Reconstruction era and enabled many women to continue as heads of households, as a higher percentage of all white families had sons eighteen or older living at home than in 1860. All but three white women heading households who listed farmer or farming as their occupation (twenty-four total) had sons at least thirteen years old at home. The three women who continued farming without older sons were all German women who had financial resources placing them within the top quarter of the population in terms of wealth. These women could afford to hire labor if they could find it. One German woman's daughter, eighteen-year-old Verona Wessch, listed her occupation as farm laborer, the only white woman to do so in the 1870 census.[16]

Women became more involved in moneymaking ventures in the Reconstruction era. The 1870 census, however, did not reflect this reality. No matter what other moneymaking enterprises they undertook, row after row of women had their occupations listed as "keeping house" or "at home." Only six white women listed occupations other than farming or keeping house: two schoolteachers, one "keeping hotel," one domestic servant, one farm laborer, and one who listed her occupation as "pedler" as did her son. All six of these women were single. Two were heads of households, two still lived with their parents, and two others lived in the households of other families. Only 3 percent of the adult white women in the county listed occupations other than keeping house or at home, whereas 6 percent of antebellum white women had listed occupations.[17]

The 1870 census in Colorado County, as in the rest of the South, was the first to recognize "keeping house" as an "occupation." A few single women might have listed occupations in 1850 and 1860, but the occupation category next to married women always remained blank. In the 1870 census white married women listed occupations, but all either kept house or were at home. Forty-seven single white female heads of household also claimed keeping house or at home as their occupations. Even of the twenty-four white women who listed "farmer" or "farming" as their occupation, seven added "and keeping house." This recognition of white women's occupations came as a result of women entering wage-earning and work areas more often during Reconstruction. White women, however, for several reasons listed keeping house above all else they might be engaged in. It probably fulfilled the expectation of the census taker, who would make that assumption first of white women and ask about other work later. White women and men alike also wanted to return to and maintain the ideals of womanhood that had been threatened by the war and by women's increased need to engage in moneymaking enterprises in the financially troubled era.[18]

Perhaps most likely, however, the whites of Colorado County wanted to emphasize the domestic nature of white women's occupations in contrast to work of African American women. In the struggle to declare their independence and capitalize on their freed status, African American families after emancipation had withdrawn women as much as possible from the work force so that they, like white women, could concentrate on their families' domestic duties. Whites, however, motivated by both racism and the labor shortage, continued to see black women's proper place as workers.[19]

Economic necessity, contracts that bound entire families' labor, and the rise of sharecropping all increased the pressure on African American women to perform occupations besides keeping house. By 1870 these tensions were reflected in the occupations listed for black women in the census. While 538 black women indicated keeping house as their occupation (and two other female heads of household over seventy years old were "at home"), almost as many African American women (503) listed other occupations. Only one black woman listed the skilled occupation of teacher, while others were domestic servants, washers, or cooks. The vast majority (356) of those who listed occupations were farm laborers or day laborers. Despite the hopes of black families that women might be mothers and wives first, 150 married women with children had occupations outside the home.[20]

The war, economic devastation, and especially the emancipation of slaves all contributed to changing the types of work women in Colorado County performed during the era of Reconstruction. While elite white women performed more work in their own homes, many white women from all classes, but especially the poorest, found themselves seeking new ways to contribute to their families' income. Women teaching, taking in boarders, washing, farming, running businesses, or even laboring in the fields helped some families hold onto their land and recoup the losses of the war. Many African American women continued to labor on farms and in homes, but under a new social structure that allowed them a certain amount of freedom in what jobs they chose. And many African American women chose a position denied them before the war: that of housekeeper.

Despite the changing realities of women's work, the ideals of women's proper place in society did not change. As former slaves were declared free by the government and as they claimed their rights as freed people, former slaveholders found their ideas of independence and dependency being challenged. Before emancipation, slaveholders derived their public and political power from the private power that they exercised as heads of household over many dependents: their wives, their children, and their slaves. When slaves were no longer dependents in their households, and in fact set up households and claims to public power, white southern men found it increasingly important to solidify their claims of power over the remaining dependents. In an effort to return to the ideals of prewar society, whites tried to force freed people into dependent relations once again. While these sets of relations were being negotiated and challenged, white men could not afford to brook any challenge to their control over the other dependents.[21]

White women not only accepted this resumption of control but reinforced it by upholding gender ideals. Women, married and single, had learned during the Civil War that they were capable of performing those duties of business and law for which antebellum ideals had deemed them unsuitable. Yet the Colorado County women who could, did indeed return to a focus on the domestic tasks to which they believed women were destined by nature.

Some historians have argued that throughout the South the legacy of women's independence during the Civil War and the lack of available husbands after the war enabled many women to find a new sense of confidence in their financial and legal abilities.[22] Most women in the South probably did not find that the occupations open to them, with their poverty-level wages, gave them confident, independent lives or increased their individual senses of confidence. If indeed more women remained independent and single, it had more to do with the gender imbalance caused by the destruction of prime-aged males during the war, which gave women fewer chances to marry and remarry.

Colorado County differed from many other places in the South because fewer men died during the war, and by 1870 males still outnumbered females (2,413 males, 2,224 females) and adult white men still outnumbered adult white women (1,114 men, 933 women). Whatever changes the war wrought in the self-esteem of women, after the war most women given the chance to marry did not choose to remain single. The percentage of single white women in the county rose by two percentage points between 1860 and 1870, but this was not nearly as high as the rise in percentage of adult white women in the county: seven percentage points. Although during the war the number of marriages per year had dropped off significantly, after the war the number increased above the prewar levels. According to the 1870 Colorado County census, 80 percent of adult white females lived in what appeared to be households with their husbands. Colorado County did not experience a "generation of women without men." The white women of Colorado County were able to return much more quickly to marriage. In addition, given the opportunity to do so, they also retired from the public world, deferring to their husbands and other male family members in matters of business, law, and politics.[23]

Like the new constitutions and laws of other readmitted Confederate states, Texas' 1869 constitution and laws did not recognize women's wartime roles and abilities. One Texas law in Reconstruction expanded married women's rights. This November, 1871, law gave married women who were appointed administrators of estates the right to post bonds using their separate property as security even when their husbands refused to join. No married woman in

Colorado County availed herself of this new provision in the Reconstruction era. Otherwise, the laws of Texas remained firmly committed to the patriarchal order that required a married woman's property, and therefore her business interests, to be controlled by her husband.[24]

The cases that came before the district court in Colorado County showed that the community experienced some confusion about the role married women were to play after the war. A few married women still sought to carry on business independent of their husbands. Mrs. N. B. Murray signed a five-year contract in 1868 renting a cotton plantation from Joel Shrewsbury, without her husband's signature or permission. When Shrewsbury sold the land to W. J. Jones a few months later, Jones sued in the Justice of the Peace Court to eject Mrs. Murray from the plantation. The court, however, ignoring the fact that Mrs. Murray had signed the lease, subpoenaed James H. Murray, and not his wife, to answer the suit. A jury decided to evict Mrs. Murray, and she appealed to the district court but had to be joined pro forma with her husband to pursue her case, which was eventually settled out of court.[25]

Another married woman in 1869 signed her husband's name to a promissory note, an act common during the war. However, the complainant suing to recover the amount of the note was forced to drop his case when Mary Kussatz's husband answered that "he did not make or deliver the promissory note mentioned in the plaintiff's petition and that the name thereunto signed is not his signature but was written wholly without his knowledge consent or authority." While upholding the business transactions women had made during the Civil War, the court nevertheless resisted attempts to hold married women, or their husbands, accountable for the acts married women made after the war.[26]

Most married women, however, did not attempt to act independently of their husbands in public business. Most often married women's property came into dispute when husbands or others tried to shelter the families by keeping some property in their wives' names. In the uncertain and financially troubled postwar years, the number of gifts or nominal sales to married women increased substantially. Nine husbands recorded deeds of gift to their wives during Reconstruction, and twenty-two other deeds granted separate property to married women from other friends or relatives. Of these thirty-one deeds, only two gave the wives any ability to control their own property. John Prude transferred all his work animals and an ambulance to his wife Amanda. Although the animals and ambulance were items John probably used every day in pursuing his livelihood, the deed purportedly gave them to Amanda "free from any claim or control" by him. This provision no doubt gave John Prude greater protection from creditors and perhaps others who would sue him for negligence or accidents. Charles Schultz's deed of property to his wife Charlotte, however, seemed much more sincere in its protestations that she have "full power to sell and convey the same for valuable consideration." He signed the deed just before he left the county to work on frontier forts so that his wife could conduct the business necessary for family survival.[27]

These gifts and deeds to wives and other relatives often resulted in lawsuits alleging fraud. The district court found that Sion Bostick had transferred his only property to his children in fraud of his creditors and vacated the deeds. D. D. Claiborne and Thomas Garner sued to keep P. E. Waddell from transferring any more of his property after Waddell gave his married daughter a "gift" of one town lot against which Claiborne had a lien. Garner's petition outlined the problems that such a gift caused: Waddell's daughter and son-in-law moved onto the lot and claimed the "same as their homestead exempt from execution or forced sale." With the couple claiming it as a homestead, it created "a cloud upon the vendor's lien," making it impossible for Garner to foreclose upon the land should the mortgage not be paid. In all but one of the nine cases instituted after transferring property to married women, either the gifts were found to defraud the creditors, or defendants offered cash value to the plaintiffs in settlement.[28]

Except for the one deed from Charles Schultz to his wife Charlotte, most grants of property to married women were not intended to give married women more financial power or independent abilities. Instead, husbands retained the right to control their wives' property while placing that property beyond the reach of their or their families' creditors. The vast majority of district court cases involving married women in actuality only involved their separate property that their husbands controlled. Husbands overwhelmingly acted as the sole agents for both their own and their wives' property. In eighty-nine of ninety-nine cases involving married women, only husbands' actions were found in the court records.

Yet the Colorado County District Court recognized some leeway. Since 1848 a married woman could sue in her name alone on behalf of her separate property if her husband refused to join the suit. No married woman had ever chosen to do so until Emeline Cherry sued to recover two bales of cotton that she and her husband had raised in 1872. In her petition she stated that her husband Albert had abandoned her earlier in the year "and now fails and neglects to join her in this suit."[29]

The lack of a separate acknowledgment to a deed of land was the key issue in the only other case where a Colorado County married woman attempted to sue in her name alone before the end of the Reconstruction era. Texas law still required that whenever a married woman's separate property or the homestead was sold, she was required to sign the deed and be examined "separate and apart" from her husband. This law, passed in 1840, had become so well known by Reconstruction that very few deeds made it into records without the wife's acknowledgment; and most buyers knew that without it, their titles were invalid.[30]

In the case of *Ernestine Illg v. William Burford,* the purchaser was a freedman misled by Ernestine's husband into believing his title was legitimate. Ernestine Illg first complained in September, 1870, that William Burford had taken possession of part of her homestead over three years earlier. According to Ernestine, Burford claimed the property "under some pretended conveyance from her said husband Jacob Illg and . . . that if such conveyance exists it was made without her consent and is in violation of her rights." Assuming that the property was indeed part of the homestead, the law was in Ernestine's favor, but only if she publicly declared that her husband had fraudulently conveyed the property. She had to state in her petition or in court that she disagreed with her husband's managing of their property and that she was asserting her own rights against the wishes of her husband. Ernestine would not declare that her husband refused to join her in the suit. The court sustained William Burford's demurrer that Ernestine did not "show any legal reasons entitling her to sue alone" and dismissed the case.[31]

A few months later Ernestine Illg again sued William Burford for the property, in her name alone. Although this seemed to be quite a defiant act of independence by a married woman, again she would not say that her husband refused to join her in the suit. In the defendant's answer William Burford expressed doubt that the suit was Ernestine's idea at all. He claimed that it was an attempt to defraud him of the property, "instigated thereby by her husband who lays back and induces his wife to do what he is ashamed to do himself . . . whilst it is well known that her husband is the real mover and inciter in the whole business."[32]

Events seemed to bear out his claim. According to Burford, Jacob Illg had assured him that he had the right to sell the property without his wife's permission. If Jacob Illg had joined the suit, he would have been required to testify and lie about his representations to Burford. The case remained unresolved on the dockets for almost two years. Then Burford died. At the next term of the court Jacob Illg made himself a party to the suit, claiming that he had told Burford the "deed would be of no value without the signature of [his] wife."[33]

When the case finally went to trial in October, 1874, the jury found that the deed was null and void without Ernestine Illg's signature, thus upholding a married woman's right to be consulted before her husband transferred a family's homestead. William Burford's widow and two sons thus were evicted from the home they had built and lived in for seven years. The jury did not require that the Illgs reimburse the Burfords for the improvements made upon the property but did render a judgment against Jacob Illg for the two hundred dollars plus interest that William Burford had paid him for the land. Jacob Illg was insolvent, and at least two years later the judgment still had not been paid.[34]

Ernestine Illg had not filed her suit bolstered by a newfound confidence in her abilities fostered during the war. Instead, like the vast majority of white married women in Colorado County, Ernestine allowed her husband to manage and control the financial and legal aspects of their lives, even while using her name. Jacob Illg took advantage of laws that seemed liberating to Texas women in order to control his own family's affairs and also to cheat a family of freedmen of their home and financial assets.

This one freed family battled hard to maintain the right to this plot of land not only because it was morally, if not legally, theirs but also because their chances of acquiring any other land were small. Few former slaves in Colorado County were able to acquire land or property. Some, such as the Burfords, were cheated of the land they could acquire. As in other parts of the South, Texans generally refused to sell or rent land to African Americans. Racism, of course, played a large role in this discrimination, as did the desire to keep blacks propertyless and therefore working as cheap laborers for white families. As sharecropping established itself in the county and African Americans became embroiled in a web of debt, few freed people could raise enough money to buy land even if it were for sale. Only thirty-one registered deeds before 1874 reflected sales made to freedmen, and all the purchasers were men.[35]

Few former slaveholders offered land to those who had worked for them. From his home in New York City, Swante M. Swenson divided an entire league of land among his nineteen former slaves who had "worked" for him in Fort Bend County. He dictated that six women and thirteen men receive forty acres each. A portion of the league was designated as a common area for the building of schools, churches, and other public buildings. In this idealistic act Swenson paid fifty dollars to survey the land he had acquired many years earlier and never cultivated. The subassistant commander of the Freedmen's Bureau in Columbus "advised the colored people not to take the land because of its being so poor." These freedmen, like many others who saw true freedom in the chance to own their own land, were, however, "determined to have it." Owning land was extremely important to these freed people and they took it, even though virtually none was able to keep it because the land was not fertile enough to support a family.[36]

Therefore, few African Americans owned land in Colorado County before 1874, and those few who did were men who had recently acquired it. As a result, neither black married women nor their husbands on their behalf ever appeared in district court to protect "separate" property. What little property a married African American woman might have in Colorado County was almost exclusively community property or not of high enough value to place it in the district court.

In addition to owning little land, freed people found the costs of bringing suit beyond their reach. Economic considerations and not the dictates of society therefore kept married African American women away from the district court. Women did appear in cases before the Freedmen's Bureau, however. The marital status of African American women was rarely noted in these cases. When it was noted, as with a white married woman, a black married woman often appeared in complaints only as the "wife" under which her husband sued. "George Williams f. m. c. and wife et al." filed a complaint against George Thatcher of Eagle Lake "for arrearages of wages due wife." Other men listed formal complaints on behalf of themselves "and family." One married woman noted in the records as such, however, took her complaint to the bureau herself: Jane Wright, "wife of Robert Wright," sued W. E. Wall for her 1867 wages.[37]

Married African American women had little opportunity to exert their independence in financial matters in places where such independence might be recorded. The few records, those of the Freedmen's Bureau, indicate that most black women followed the southern ideal by which wives deferred to their husbands' control and management of their finances. However, African American women were at least somewhat less likely to marry or live in traditional marriage arrangements than their Anglo and German counterparts.

Between the years 1869 (when freed people were officially given the legal right to marry) and 1873 only 153, or 22 percent, of the 683 marriages recorded in Colorado County were between African Americans, although blacks made up 44 percent of the population. This number does not necessarily signify a desire by black women or men to remain single. Reconstruction Texas generally and Colorado County particularly placed many impediments in the way of formal marriages between African Americans. As slaves, they had not been allowed legally to marry at all. Even though many slaves saw their marriages as permanent and significant, they were still informal, continued only at the desire and financial ability of the master to keep the family together and not reinforced by any legal codes whatsoever as free white marriages were. After emancipation the Texas legislature, and Texans themselves, were slow to recognize the marriages formed during slavery and even slower to permit former slaves to claim the right of legal marriage. Only in 1869 did the new state constitution allow and require African Americans to marry on the same standing as whites.

Even after the 1869 constitution took effect, blacks were discouraged by the southern whites from marrying. Black ministers had difficulty getting the ordination required to perform the ceremonies, and not all white ministers would do so. The white county clerk could intimidate and make difficult the process of getting a license. The license cost ten dollars, a hefty sum of money for former slaves with virtually no property and income. And when a license was obtained, at least in Colorado County, a marriage of African Americans was recorded in a separate book in some attempt to maintain its difference, and lesser significance, from a marriage between whites.[38]

Whether or not they could legally marry, the vast majority of black women lived in family units that probably included men they considered husbands. The 1870 census showed only 30 percent of adult black women living in households without husbands. This was a higher percentage than the 20 percent of adult white women who had no husbands residing with them. A partial explanation of this fact is that black women outnumbered black men in the county. Whereas 47 percent of adult whites were women, 51 percent of adult blacks were. Another possible explanation for part of the difference is that some African American married women may have continued to live with the white families for whom they worked instead of with their husbands, therefore not being obviously married in the analysis of the census.[39]

In the Reconstruction era, therefore, black women likely placed the same kind of importance upon marriage as white women did, whether or not they legalized their marriages. Economic necessity forced black women into work more often than white women. But in the few places and cases where married black women could exert their independence from their husbands (such as the Freedmen's Bureau), their actions did not differ remarkably from those of married white women.

Women, black and white, preferred to marry and allow their husbands to shoulder the legal and primary financial responsibilities of the household. If the Civil War had any lasting impact upon women's confidence in Colorado County, it can be seen in the actions of single white women. When husbands died, deserted, or were otherwise absent, single white women acted much differently than they had during the antebellum years. Forced in many circumstances to work both during marriage and after, widows and a few young single women learned during the war and in the troubled era of Reconstruction to rely more upon themselves.

The number of single women involved in lawsuits as plaintiffs or defendants during the Reconstruction era rose to thirty-six, compared to only ten during the antebellum era (a 260 percent increase). This number, of course, reflected a slightly increased number of white women in the population (295, or 15 percent more in 1870 than in 1860) as well as a greater litigiousness in the county as many defaulted on loans and forfeited mortgages in the financial devastation and reorganization following the war (an approximately 28 percent increase in cases). However, these factors alone do not account for women's greater appearance in court. Single women simply became more involved in financial matters and acted more on their own behalf after the war than they had during the antebellum era.[40]

Widows, in particular, took active roles in their own financial and legal affairs during Reconstruction. Of the twenty-six estates of men leaving widows and requiring administration, nineteen widows (73 percent) chose to administer or coadminister. Of the twelve wills left by men, eight widows (67 percent) executed the provisions. Not only did this represent a vast increase in participation by widows in estates over the antebellum period, it was also an increase from the Civil War era probating of estates by widows (see appendix A).

Even the widows who chose not to administer their husbands' estates themselves took more active roles in the activities than in previous eras. For instance, Martha Tobin "declined to administer" in May, 1866, but requested that the court appoint her father and another man in her stead. A few months later Martha Tobin again appeared in court to request that the court set aside property to her in lieu of a homestead, as she had "a very large and helpless family some eight children who have to be educated, clothed, and fed." A suit filed much later in the district court alleged that Martha Tobin had connived to "appropriate and absorb all the valuable property of the estate," aided and assisted by the administrators. Another widow who took an active role was Julia Anna Stalle, who appeared in court to request that M. Malsch, the attorney she had hired, be granted letters "as your Petitioner is not able herself to attend to the administration." Both Julia Ann Stalle and Martha Tobin explained that they could not administer their husbands' estates because of the pressures of a large family. Another widow, Agnes Roever, insisted that "the affairs of said Est. are in a confused condition requiring the service of a business man." Although these widows felt themselves unsuited for the large responsibilities, they took active, not passive steps, to insure that appropriate persons guarded their financial and legal interests.[41]

Susan B. Harbert did not administer her husband's estate, but at the public sale of the estate's furniture she appeared and purchased several important personal items. Of the seven widows who declined to administer estates, five widows chose persons to execute in their stead. Two hired people to do so. Each of these five also appealed to the court on at least one other occasion. Only one widow who declined to administer did not show some active involvement in the estate. Elizabeth Summerlatte was "absent or had already abandoned the homestead," and even she wrote the court agreeing to the sale.[42]

TABLE 5.

RECONSTRUCTION WIDOWS ADMINISTERING ESTATES
OR EXECUTING PROVISIONS OF WILLS, BY WEALTH

Quarter of Wealth*	3	2	1	Top 10%	Total
Administrator	4	5	3	2	14
Coadministrator		1	1	2	4
Executor	2	1	3	1	7
Declined administration	1	2	3	1	7
Declined or not appointed executor		1	3		4
Total	7	10	13	6	36

*No estate probated fell into the bottom quarter of wealth. Wealth can be determined for only thirty-six of the thirty-nine estates probated.

Source: Probate Recores, CCCC; Schedule 1 (Free Inhabitants), Eighth Census of the United States (1860), Texas, Colorado County.

Two of the four widows who coadministered estates were actively involved in the business and legal matters of the estates. Mary Ann Crenshaw, after her initial petition, allowed her coadministrator, Don Payne, to handle all the matters before the probate court until 1871 when Payne died. Thereafter Mary Crenshaw acted as the sole administrator. While Virginia Patterson supposedly administered jointly with W. Daniels, only she transacted the small amount of business on the estate before the court.[43]

The two other widows to coadminister estates both did so with their new husbands, and in both cases the husbands assumed full responsibility for the legal transactions in probate court. While the probate court provided the opportunity for many single women to act for themselves and an 1871 law allowed married women more freedom to act as administrators with or without their husbands, married women in Colorado County still chose to turn over the responsibilities to their husbands.[44]

As seen in table 5, wealth did not play the largest role in widows' decisions about whether or not to administer estates. Widows were just as likely to administer estates valued in the bottom half of the population as those in the top 10 percent (86 percent in the bottom half administered; 83 percent in the top decile did so). In the top quarter (but not the top decile) and the second quarter of wealth, widows were slightly more likely to decline to administer.

Age also seemingly played no role in widows' decisions on administration. Widows ranging from sixteen to fifty-five years old chose to administer estates, while widows as young as twenty-four and as old as fifty-three chose not to administer. The average age of widows administering, coadministering, or executing the provisions of wills in estates was forty years old. The average age of widows not taking the legal roles was only slightly less at thirty-six years old.

German and Anglo women made different choices about probating their deceased husbands' estates. Ten of the eighteen German widows chose to administer estates solely, while only three Anglo women made that choice. Overall, German widows took some responsibility for their husbands' estates 78 percent of the time, Anglo women only 56 percent of the time. German men were more likely to appoint their wives executors of their estates. The three wills left by German husbands appointed their wives executors, and the widows chose to act on the appointments in every case. Anglo widows were appointed sole executors by their husbands' wills only four out of nine times, coexecutors twice. One Anglo widow appointed executor of her husband's will declined to act.

The difference between German and Anglo women's involvement in administration did not necessarily reflect wealth or class differences. The Germans and Anglos who left estates did so roughly in the same categories of wealth, and overall, wealth did not seem to encourage or deter widows of either ethnicity from conducting business. Of course, because blacks in Colorado County remained property-poor, considerations of wealth played the largest role in African American widows' lives. Before 1873 not one black man leaving a widow had an estate probated in Colorado County's court. African American widows did not have the opportunity to choose whether or not to take on the legal responsibilities left behind by their husbands, and there is no evidence to show that they did so outside of the courts.

Widows' decisions to become involved in matters before the probate court, therefore, seem to have been influenced by individual and private concerns. Overall, Reconstruction-era widows chose to be much more active in their late husbands' financial and legal affairs than widows had since the frontier era. As in the frontier era, the financial difficulties of Reconstruction led many wives to become more involved in contributing not just to the work of the family but also to the family income. Although married women, even in probate court, overwhelmingly allowed their husbands to act for them, most single women acted for themselves. Women's experiences during the Civil War had loosened social restrictions and contributed to a belief that women could make financial decisions when necessary. After the war, while married women attempted to return to the prewar roles of deferring to their husbands, single women took a more active interest in their own financial and legal affairs.

Women in Colorado County after the Civil War did not face a dearth of men and had the option to marry and remarry. Most of these women chose to do so, and the percentage of single white women increased only slightly during the years of Reconstruction. Even as widows increased their active participation in public and financial matters at this time, 39 percent chose to remarry and turn over those responsibilities to their husbands. Marriage, domesticity, and dependency remained the ideals for women in Colorado County during Reconstruction. However, many more women than in any previous period decided that although marriage in the abstract might be the ideal, their particular marriages were not. Twenty-three white women filed for divorce before the end of 1873, exceeding the number (nineteen) filed by women in the antebellum period and the number (thirteen) during the frontier period (see appendix B).

Wives' grounds for divorce also expanded, and they sued for and received divorces on all the grounds available to them: cruelty, adultery, and abandonment. The disruptions of the war and the economic uncertainty of Reconstruction made it somewhat easier and even desirable for husbands to leave their wives. Six white women charged their husbands with desertion in divorce petitions. Four of those husbands had left their wives either during the Civil War or shortly afterward, and three of the four marriages had taken place right before or during the war. At least some men upon returning home from fighting apparently regretted the commitments they had made in the midst of the excitement. Of course, long separations during the war made it possible for husbands and wives simply to grow apart and find one another intolerable upon their return.[45]

Abandonment during Reconstruction did not occur locally as it had during the antebellum years. The war expanded the geographical horizons of many men who went to war, and the social upheavals and dislocations made it as easy in some cases to relocate as to rebuild lives. While many antebellum wives who charged abandonment knew where their husbands were, most Reconstruction wives clearly indicated that they did not. Elizabeth Jackson had "not heard one word" from her husband in over four years when she filed for divorce. Daniel C. Holliday had "left the State of Texas with a common prostitute" and had "been gone 3 years and . . . never been heard from." Anna Bridge's husband Augustus never returned nor communicated with her after November 9, 1863, when "he secretly left the house where they were residing." Three of the six women who filed for divorce on the grounds of abandonment dropped their cases before going to trial, but the three who pursued the cases won their divorces.[46]

Social disruptions and wartime dislocations may have made it easier for men to leave their wives, but they also increased the opportunities for women to leave their husbands. Two husbands sued for and received divorces for abandonment by their wives during Reconstruction. While Henry Boone knew where his wife had gone, Henry Nelson claimed that his wife "took up with Strangers and shamefully abandoned Petitioner and left to parts unknown." Other husbands who filed for divorce on different grounds also lost track of their wives' whereabouts. George Metz came home from the Civil War to find his wife engaged in an adulterous relationship with another man. By the time his suit for divorce reached a jury, Sarah Metz had abandoned the county, causing George to fear that his "children will be clandestinely abducted and carried beyond jurisdiction." Whether or not women had left for parts unknown, most of the Reconstruction-era adultery divorces filed by men went unchallenged in court—five of the seven accused wives defaulted.[47]

Men continued successfully to sue their wives for abandonment and adultery, as they had in earlier periods in Colorado County. Women, however, for the first time began successfully suing their husbands for adultery. While adultery served as a popular grounds for divorce for men from the frontier-era through Reconstruction, no woman received a divorce for the adultery of her husband until the November term of the court in 1870. Only four women before the Reconstruction era filed petitions alleging that their husbands committed adultery, and none of those four received a divorce. After the Civil War, however, the court granted divorces to four white women on the grounds of adultery, nearly as many as those granted to men (five). Wives during Reconstruction exerted their prerogative to file for divorce on the grounds of adultery and pursued it in court even when their husbands fought the action (three of the five husbands filed answers).[48]

Perhaps with the disruptions of the war more men abandoned their wives to live in adultery with other women. Just as likely, women became more willing to risk scandal and publicly charge their husbands. After the war women availed themselves of all the grounds possible for divorce. However, most petitions filed by women (twelve of twenty-three) still cited cruelty as the primary reason for wanting to end the marriages.[49]

Wives wanting divorces on the grounds of cruelty, though, had much more difficulty pursuing their cases, but not necessarily because the court discouraged them. Eight of the twelve suits filed were dropped by the wives before going to trial. Ellen Lacy filed two of those eight suits that were dismissed by agreement of the parties. She filed for divorce three times before finally pursuing it to the jury. She filed first in September, 1865, but less than two months later agreed to drop the suit when her husband Beverly "had apparently reformed his habits [and] made such protestations of affection for petitioner and their two children." Ellen "soon found to her sorrow that the intentions of the Defendant [Beverly] were still of the most base character and that his object was only to deceive [her] and if possible more deeply to degrade her." Four years later she filed for divorce again, and when Beverly, "pretending to be penitent and promising [her] to reform his life and do better in the future," asked for a reconciliation, "she was induced for the sake of her children to withdraw her suit and try still to live with him in the marital state." Two years later Ellen sued for divorce one last time. The jury found her allegations of abuse to be true, and the judge granted her divorce more than seven years after her initial filing.[50]

As Ellen Lacy's case shows, wives in the economic uncertainties of Reconstruction might attempt to endure a certain amount of cruelty, even physical abuse, in order to remain in their marriages. Cases of adultery and abandonment—when husbands had already essentially ended the marriages—made easier women's decisions to become legally single again. The increase in women's petitions for divorce in the Reconstruction era, however, still indicates that at least some married women were not afraid to become self-sufficient.

District court was one of the few places where African American women appeared with any frequency to handle public or legal matters. African American women and men could file for and receive divorces on the same grounds as white men and women could. In the Reconstruction era eight blacks filed for divorce and six were granted. However, in stark contrast to white divorces, which involved men filing in at least a third of the cases, no African American man filed for divorce from his wife. All eight divorce suits were brought by African American women.[51]

African American women faced several obstacles to obtaining divorces. Like white women, black women had to prove that their husbands had committed adultery, abandoned them, or treated them cruelly enough to warrant divorce. Unlike white women, many African American women also had to prove that they were indeed married to the men they sought to divorce. Marriages under slavery had been informal matters and never legally recognized. After emancipation, as former slaves throughout the South sought to have their marriages recognized, different states enacted different procedures to deal with the problem. In Texas the 1869 state constitution declared that slaves living together as husband and wife during slavery and continuing to live together as of 1869 would be considered legally married.[52]

While some petitioners for divorce had married after emancipation, those involved in slave marriages often used the language of the state constitution or cited it directly when averring that they had been married. Cornelia Johnson claimed that in 1864 "she was living with the said Jack Johnson as his wife and continued so to live until the 1st day of March A.D. 1871." Alcey Holmes and Isaac Holmes, according to their divorce petition, were legally married "by section twenty-seven article twelfth of the Constitution of this state." Hiram Harris, in answering the petition for divorce, "specially denies that he was ever married to the defendant or that he ever lived with or recognized her as his wife."[53]

Overwhelmingly, African American women for economic reasons went to the trouble of proving that they were married in order to obtain divorces. Although they were freed in 1865, they began to marry legally in Colorado County in 1869, and their previous marriages were recognized by the state constitution in 1869, the first suit for divorce by an African American woman was not filed in the Colorado County District Court until 1871. While the Freedmen's Bureau had operated in the county, some freedwomen took their marital problems there. The subassistant commander heard Fanny Walker's case against David Walker not for divorce but for "the support of child." However, when Louisa Davis complained to the bureau that her husband had "taken up with another woman," the bureau agent "directed her to go before the grand jury." If she did so, Tate Davis was never indicted, nor did Louisa ever bring a civil suit against him for divorce.[54]

Most African Americans immediately after emancipation probably continued informal dissolutions of their marriages. Only after a period of time had elapsed in which marriages legally performed had gone sour or a few families had accumulated enough wealth over which to argue were the first divorces filed. Of those who filed eight divorces in the Reconstruction era, Alcey Thomas and John Thomas were legally married in 1869, Charity Whitley and Dennis Whitley in 1871, Mary Susan Tatum and Frank Tatum in 1869. Martha Harris filed for divorce when Hiram Harris by "some pretended legal proceedings" before the justice of the peace tried to evict her from their homestead. Alcey Holmes sought division of community property she held with her husband Isaac Holmes, including oxen, wagons, mules, cows, furniture, and a set of blacksmith's tools. Fanny Smith wanted to finish paying for the fraction of the town lot her husband had bought and take the title in her name. Rachel Virginia did not originally seek a divorce; she just sought to divest her husband of his interest in a promissory note so that she could buy a homestead. Only one petition out of the eight sought to dissolve without mention of property a marriage formed during slavery.[55]

While property considerations played a larger role in inducing African American women to seek legal divorces than they did for white women, the grounds for divorce charged by African American women were similar to those of white women. Although the total numbers are small for comparison purposes, it is illuminating that the percentages of African American women charging adultery, abandonment, or cruelty were close to the same as those of white women on each grounds (see table 6).

TABLE 6.

**PERCENTAGES OF GROUNDS ALLEGED
IN PETITIONS BY WOMEN**

	White	African American
Abandonment	26%	13%
Adultery	22%	25%
Cruelty	52%	62%

African American women were much more likely to pursue their divorce cases and win than were white women. Only one black woman dropped her case after reaching an agreement with her husband, compared to twelve white women's cases that were either dropped or reached agreement (13 percent black women, 52 percent white women). When one African American pursued her case, the jury found her allegations of abuse not true. The other six black wives who filed, however, received divorces.[56]

Divorces granted by juries in district court allowed women, black and white, legally to end marriages that had often already ended in actuality. Three of the six African American women granted divorces can be determined to have remarried, while only two of the white women who filed and received divorces can be determined to have done so. Although marriage remained the ideal for black and white women, the higher number of petitions filed by women in the Reconstruction era, the much larger number successfully pursued, and the smaller percentage of divorcees remarrying reflected some confidence by women that they could support themselves. White women had a more difficult time pursuing divorces against husbands who were still around but were less than ideal mates. However, the number of wives who believed that no marriage was a better option than a bad one increased.[57]

Although more women pursued divorce in the postwar era and single women showed greater assertiveness in traditional male realms, the vast majority of women clung to the ideals of marriage and domesticity, leaving their husbands unchallenged as heads of households. The Civil War in Colorado County did not leave a generation of women without men and asserting their independence and enjoying their liberty. The statistical impact on the county was such that women still had ample ability to find husbands or new husbands after being widowed or divorced. Given the chance to marry or remarry, Colorado County women did so. Married women, active in business and law in their husbands' absence during the war, quickly abandoned these duties to their husbands when they returned home. Social expectations, court actions, and even census takers reinforced a return to the antebellum ideals for men and women. A husband's proper place in the family, it was assumed, was to take care of his family financially, politically, and legally. A wife's proper role was to take care of the family's domestic concerns, including "keeping house."

While whites assumed that this arrangement accommodated the "natural" abilities of white men and women, they refused to recognize black women's attempts to adhere to this ideal. Whites tried to force as many black women as possible back to laboring for them through the development of sharecropping and labor contracts. Black women resisted the effort somewhat successfully, as over half of the black married women were somehow able to stay "at home" and "keep house."

Even as husbands insisted on resuming their proper place as heads of household, they relied on the labor and skills of their wives during Reconstruction much more than ever. White women, married and single, increased the amount of work they did and, even in this rural southern county, increasingly entered into wage-earning situations in order to help support their families. Black women, although retiring from the fields whenever they could, also contributed income and work to their families, and they did so much more often than white women did.

The entrance of women into moneymaking occupations did not necessarily threaten the patriarchal order of the family, as married women still deferred to their husbands in financial and legal matters. However, the social recognition of women's abilities that occurred during the war, as well as women's increased ability to earn incomes without social disapproval, led to an increase in single women's activities in the financial and legal worlds previously reserved for men.

The emotional and physical toll of the war, economic devastation, and the emancipation of slaves required Colorado County men and women to rebuild their society, community, and social relations. As men returned, women shifted the burdens they had undertaken in the war back to their husbands. Although undertaking many new responsibilities during the Reconstruction era, women willingly relinquished control of the "male" duties to their husbands whenever possible. In their efforts to rebuild their society and reassert white supremacy in race relations, women were willing to resume the patriarchal order of the household that had existed before the war, despite their demonstrated capabilities and newfound talents.

EPILOGUE

Died on the 3d day of October at 9 A.M. . . . Mrs. Teresa E. Ivey.
She . . . was a remarkable woman for energy, perseverance,
and industry. Was a friend to the orphans and hospitable to those
who visited her. She was a member of the Baptist church here,
and loved to entertain her pastors. . . . A large concourse of friends
and neighbors followed the remains to their last resting place.
—*WEIMAR MERCURY, OCTOBER 11, 1890*

Teresa E. Wooldridge was born in Georgia around 1814 to a planter household. When she was young her family moved west to Mississippi, as had many
other southern families. Sometime before 1844 Teresa married Jesse Ivey, a
planter on a nearby farm across the border in Alabama. She and Jesse were
raising at least one girl when something went wrong in their marriage. The
evidence is extremely unclear, but Teresa apparently returned to her parents'
home to live in 1852. Shortly thereafter Jesse indicated the permanent nature
of the separation by signing over a large amount of property to Teresa, naming her brother Augustus B. Wooldridge as trustee of the property.[1]

When Augustus and his wife Caroline decided to move to Texas, Teresa
chose to accompany them. Leaving behind the child or children she had been
raising, Teresa tried to begin a new life in Colorado County, Texas, in November of 1853. Teresa retained her married name of Mrs. Teresa E. Ivey but
apparently worked hard to keep the people of her new community from finding out that she had left a husband and a failed marriage in Alabama. Years
later another citizen referred to their arrival in the county as that of "a brother
and a widowed sister." Teresa's brother continued to manage her extensive
wealth, including fine carriages, china, furniture, and approximately twenty
thousand dollars in slave chattel. This probably allowed her to live a relatively
leisured life without becoming a burden on her brother's family.[2]

Teresa's life changed dramatically when in October, 1856, her brother Augustus died. Caroline Wooldridge remarried less than a year later, and Teresa

found herself living in the household of a stranger. Because, obviously, Augustus could no longer act as her trustee, the legal management and control of her property became a problem. As a married woman she legally had no control over her own property. Since the community assumed that she was a widow and not a married woman, Teresa probably took over the management of "hiring out" her slaves for an income. Yet her legal position was, at best, tenuous.[3]

About the same time that Caroline remarried, a distant cousin died in the county, leaving his widow, Mary M. B. Smith, to face enormous legal and financial difficulties. Teresa tried to assist her by posting a bond for Mary so that she could administer her husband's estate. Creditors of Alfred Smith, in fear of losing substantial amounts of money and property, had already been mounting an intense battle to administer the estate instead of allowing Mary to do so. When Teresa posted the bond, it removed one impediment to Mary's assumption of the administration, and the creditors moved quickly to find a way to discredit the bond. Somehow the creditors discovered that Teresa, "at the time of signing" the bond for security, was "a married woman, and could not legally sign said bond."[4]

Between her brother's death and the challenge to her ability to use her own property, Teresa's life became more complicated. Whether she asked her husband to do so or the timing was just fortuitous, that year Jesse Ivey filed for and received a divorce from Teresa in Alabama. Once divorced, Teresa had legal control of her property and moved quickly to take control of her destiny as well. She moved out of her sister-in-law's house and bought a block of town lots in a small fledgling town called Prairie Point. She began working vigorously to build up the town, selling her lots for profit.[5]

After setting up her own home Teresa decided to bring the children she had been raising in Alabama to Colorado County to live with her. Although both of the girls were probably her own children, a supposed "widow" could not suddenly show up with two daughters, so Teresa claimed that they were her nieces and then officially adopted them as her daughters and heirs.[6]

When the Civil War broke out, Teresa's oldest daughter, Martha, was only thirteen years old. In the heady excitement of soldiers enlisting and leaving for the "battlefront," Martha married soon-to-be soldier Stephen Conner. Because of war and separation, not to mention the youth of both parties, Martha's marriage turned sour (see chapter 5). Ironically enough, Teresa had told her daughter so little about her own life that Martha did not understand the need to end a marriage legally. Without the benefit of a divorce, Martha married another man, David Calhoun, and thus unwittingly became a bigamist. Whereas Martha might have benefited from her mother's experience, her mother had kept her secret not only from most of the community but from her own daughters as well.[7]

EPILOGUE

Teresa never remarried. She lived through the Civil War, the emancipation of her slaves, and Reconstruction, and she died in October, 1890. Through the years Teresa tenaciously protected her social image through charitable gifts of property, raising children, and active membership in her church. Her obituary reflected her success by describing Teresa in terms suitable for a southern lady and as mourned by many friends and neighbors.[8]

Teresa E. Wooldridge Ivey was far from a typical southern lady; nor was she typical of the women of Colorado County, Texas. What Teresa held in common with most other southern women, however, were the social ideals regarding the roles of women, the legal constraints placed upon women, and the very nature of her life in the rural South. Clearly, Teresa's choices were limited by the law. She could not even control her own property as a married woman despite her clear independence and physical and emotional separation from her husband. Only a divorce gave her the true freedom to act on her own behalf. Teresa's options were limited by being a single woman in the rural South. Although she owned slaves, she could hardly buy land and attempt to oversee a plantation without a male to control the slaves and act as caretaker of her business. Instead, Teresa chose to hire out her slaves and invest her time and money in an urban setting—even if she had to build the tiny town herself.

Teresa was also limited by the social ideals to which she adhered. In order to be accepted as a "lady," she could not or would not admit to her divorce. Although her masquerade as a widow gave her a socially acceptable position in society, she went well beyond this pretense in proving herself to be a true southern lady: she raised children, participated in her church activities, and was a friend to the poor and orphaned. At the same time she acted shrewdly in business to support herself, she worked to live up to the ideals of womanhood: piety, purity, domesticity, and submissiveness.

Neither Teresa's life nor the individual and collective lives of the other women in Colorado County can be said to typify the lives of all southern women. The examination of these many lives at the local level, however, sheds new historical light on the ways that the physical limitations of the rural South, the legal disabilities of women, and social ideals interacted to shape the actions and reactions of women in the South. The collective study of the choices and options available to women in places such as Colorado County helps clarify widespread historical trends. For instance, it becomes clearer why feminism did not appeal to the women of the South. When Teresa divorced her husband and decided to live an independent life (only after her brother died and she was left without family in Texas), she did not strike out against the system of marriage or the social ideals of women's place in society. She sought to relieve herself of her own bad marriage. When Emeline Cherry sought to sell her bales of cotton without her husband's permission (see chapter 6), she did not claim the right to do so because married women should have that right, but because her husband had abandoned her and refused to do so. These women did not argue that the ideal had failed, but that their husbands had failed to live up to the ideal. The courts of Colorado County agreed and reinforced the ideals when they recognized the exceptions.

When women took on traditional male duties after the men had gone to war, they were not striking out for more economic freedom for themselves. Instead, they considered themselves dependent, but economically productive, members of households that needed their temporary assistance in matters they usually deferred to their husbands. And when their husbands returned, women were as anxious as the men were to rebuild their lives amidst the many challenges that the Reconstruction era posed. Before the war women had found stability within the household. After the war they hoped that return to households as economic units where both women and men contributed their different but complementary skills would restore that stability. They sought to reestablish their own power and privilege through their association with men of their race and class. Their increased involvement in financial and legal enterprises, therefore, does not reflect the demand for more individual power and autonomy for themselves that feminists in the North sought. Their individual efforts promoted the financial and social gains of their families.

In the end, each individual woman in Colorado County, Texas, as well as in the South, made individual decisions based upon individual circumstances. Yet their choices were confined by the social, legal, and physical contexts in which they lived. An understanding of the ways these contexts affected the lives and decisions of the women of Colorado County, Texas, is but one crucial piece to understanding the women of the South as a whole.

WIDOWS *and* ADMINISTRATION

	Frontier	Antebellum	Civil War	Reconstruction	Totals
Sole administrator	23 (54%)	6 (18%)	11 (46%)	15 (40%)	55 (40%)
Coadministrator	11 (26%)	3 (9%)	2 (8%)	4 (11%)	20 (14%)
Sole executor	4 (9%)	4 (12%)	3 (13%)	8 (21%)	19 (14%)
Coexecutor	0 (0%)	2 (6%)	0 (0%)	0 (0%)	2 (1%)
Declined administration	5 (12%)	12 (35%)	7 (29%)	7 (18%)	31 (22%)
Declined or not appointed executor	0 (0%)	7 (21%)	1 (4%)	4 (11%)	12 (9%)
Total	43 (101%*)	34 (101%*)	24 (100%)	38 (101%*)	139 (100%)

*Totals do not add up to 100 because of rounding.

DIVORCES FILED *and* GRANTED *by* GENDER *and* ERA

	Frontier	Antebellum	Civil War	Reconstruction	Totals
Filed by men	9	14	2	12	37
Filed by women	13	19	4	31	67
Granted to men	8	7	1	8	24
Granted to women	6	8	1	18	33
Success of men	89%	50%	50%	67%	65%
Success of women	46%	42%	25%	58%	49%

GROUNDS *for* DIVORCE *by* GENDER *and* ERA

		Frontier	Antebellum	Civil War	Reconstruction
Abandonment	H	3/2	3/2[a]		2/2
	W	3/1	5/1		7/4
Adultery	H	2/1	10/4[b]	1/0	7/5
	W	1/1[c]	2/0	2/0	7/6
Cruelty	H	4/4	1/1	1/0[d]	3/1[e]
	W	9/4[f]	12/6	1/0[g]	17/7[h]
Total	H	9/7	14/7	2/0	12/8
	W	13/6	19/7	3/0	31/17

Note: x/y where x is the number of divorces filed and y is the number granted.

[a]One other divorce granted to wife on cross suit.

[b]Includes two suits by same two petitioners.

[c]Actually marriage annulled for bigamy, not adultery.

[d]One divorce granted to wife on cross suit.

[e]One other divorce granted to wife on cross suit.

[f]One other divorce granted to husband on cross suit.

[g]One divorce granted to husband on cross suit.

[h]Includes three suits filed by same petitioner.

NOTES

INTRODUCTION

1. Petition, *Adelade Lewis v. Wm Walker alias Lewis,* July 25, 1873, Docket File No. 2970, Colorado County District Clerk's Office, Columbus, Texas (hereinafter referred to as CCDC).

2. Elizabeth Fox-Genovese, *Within the Plantation Household: Black and White Women of the Old South,* pp. 38–39, 77–78, 101–109; Richard G. Lowe and Randolph B. Campbell, *Planters and Plain Folk,* pp. 1–9; Peter W. Bardaglio, *Reconstructing the Household: Families, Sex, and the Law in the Nineteenth-Century South,* pp. xiv, 23–27; Victoria Bynum, *Unruly Women: The Politics of Social and Sexual Control in the Old South,* pp. 2–8, 71; Jane Turner Censer, *North Carolina Planters and Their Children, 1800–1860,* p. 72; Stephanie McCurry, *Masters of Small Worlds: Yeoman Households, Gender Relations, and the Political Culture of the Antebellum South Carolina Low Country,* p. 74.

3. Bardaglio, *Reconstructing the Household,* pp. 23–28; McCurry, *Masters of Small Worlds,* p. 97; Laura F. Edwards, *Gendered Strife and Confusion: The Political Culture of Reconstruction,* pp. 6–7, 24–30.

4. Answer, *Charlotte Cherry v. Thomas Cherry,* Nov. 4, 1857, Docket File No. 1203, CCDC.

5. Fox-Genovese, *Within the Plantation Household,* pp. 116, 195; Catherine Clinton, *The Plantation Mistress: Woman's World in the Old South,* pp. 23–28, 50, 165.

6. D. Harland Hagler, "Down from the Pedestal: The Role of Women in the Antebellum South," in Candace M. Volz and LeRoy Johnson, Jr., eds., *Texana II: Cultural Heritage of the Plantation South,* The *Revised* Proceedings of a Humanities Forum Held at Jefferson, Texas, June 4–6, 1981, pp. 56–62; George C. Rable, *Civil Wars: Women and the Crisis of Southern Nationalism,* pp. 5–8; Fox-Genovese, *Within the Plantation Household,* pp. 116, 195; Clinton, *Plantation Mistress,* pp. 23–28, 50, 165; Brenda E. Stevenson, *Life in Black and White: Family and Community in the Slave South,* pp. 39–40; Anne Firor Scott, *The Southern Lady: From Pedestal to Politics, 1830–1930.*

7. Barbara Welter, "The Cult of True Womanhood: 1820–1860," *American Quarterly* 18 (summer, 1966): pp. 151–74. The most classic discussion of the development of separate spheres or cult of domesticity ideology in New England is found in Nancy F. Cott, *The Bonds of Womanhood: "Woman's Sphere" in New England, 1780–1835.* For a historiographical discussion of the use of separate spheres and the ideal of true womanhood as an analytical tool, see Linda K. Kerber, "Separate Spheres, Female Worlds, Woman's Place: The Rhetoric of Women's History," *Journal of American History* 65 (June, 1988): 9–39. Kerber points to a "third stage in the development of the metaphor of separate spheres" where the "sphere was socially constructed both *for* and *by* women" (p. 18).

8. Fox-Genovese, *Within the Plantation Household,* pp. 8 – 20, 79, 109 – 10, 142, 195; Bynum, *Unruly Women,* pp. 2 – 8; Bardaglio, *Reconstructing the Household,* pp. xiv, 23 – 28; Censer, *North Carolina Planters,* p. 72; Clinton, *Plantation Mistress,* pp. 6, 20 – 30, 50; McCurry, *Masters of Small Worlds,* pp. 74 – 88; Sandra L. Myres, *Westering Women and the Frontier Experience, 1800 – 1915,* p. 172.

9. Harriette Andreadis researched women's diaries in nineteenth-century Texas and found that Texas women brought the ideals of female behavior with them from their homes in the South or the East. Texas women accepted the prevailing ideas of separate spheres and tried to live up to the model of the cult of true womanhood; see Harriette Andreadis, "True Womanhood Revisited: Women's Private Writing in Nineteenth-Century Texas," *Journal of the Southwest* 31 (summer, 1989): 179 – 204. Newspapers and magazines exerted great influence on Texans; Max S. Lale, in "The Influence of the Press on Nineteenth-Century Texans: Robert W. Loughery and the Marshall *Texas Republican,*" in Candace M. Volz and LeRoy Johnson, Jr., eds., *Texana II: Cultural Heritage of the Plantation South,* The *Revised* Proceedings of a Humanities Forum Held at Jefferson, Texas, June 4 – 6, 1981, pp. 22 – 26, discusses the influence of the press on the decision to secede. Other historians who argue that these ideals also influenced southern women's ideas about themselves include Scott, *The Southern Lady;* Sally G. McMillen, *Southern Women: Black and White in the Old South;* and Elizabeth Hayes Turner, *Women, Culture, and Community: Religion and Reform in Galveston, 1880 – 1920.*

10. Bardaglio, *Reconstructing the Household,* p. xiv; Censer, *North Carolina Planters,* pp. 46 – 55, 106 – 10; Fox-Genovese, *Within the Plantation Household,* pp. 108 – 13; McCurry, *Masters of Small Worlds,* pp. 88, 177.

11. Bardaglio, *Reconstructing the Household,* p. xiv; Fox- Genovese, *Within the Plantation Household,* pp. 100 – 101, 133 – 41.

12. Bardaglio, *Reconstructing the Household,* pp. xiv, 23; LeeAnn Whites, *The Civil War as a Crisis in Gender: Augusta, Georgia, 1860 – 1890;* Bynum, *Unruly Women;* Jacqueline Dowd Hall, "Partial Truths: Writing Southern Women's History," in Virginia Bernhard, Betty Brandon, Elizabeth Fox-Genovese, and Theda Perdue, eds., *Southern Women: Histories and Identities,* p. 16; Fox-Genovese, *Within the Plantation Household;* Jean E. Friedman, *The Enclosed Garden: Women and Community in the Evangelical South, 1830 – 1900;* Bynum, *Unruly Women;* McCurry, *Masters of Small Worlds;* Nancy Isenberg, *Sex and Citizenship in Antebellum America,* p. 108; Clinton, *Plantation Mistress,* p. 6.

13. Bardaglio, *Reconstructing the Household,* pp. xvi–xvii; Bynum, *Unruly Women,* pp. 4 – 5.

14. Williamson S. Oldham and George W. White, comps., *A Digest of the General Statute Laws of the State of Texas . . . ,* p. 312; Kathleen Elizabeth Lazarou, "Concealed under Petticoats: Married Women's Property and the Law of Texas, 1840 – 1913," Ph.D. diss., Rice University, May, 1980, pp. 195 – 96; Ocie Speer, *A Treatise on the Law of Marital Rights in Texas,* p. 195; Linda E. Speth, "The Married Women's Property Acts, 1839 – 1865: Reform, Reaction, or Revolution?," in D. Kelly Weisberg, ed., *Women and the Law: A Social Historical Perspective,* vol. 2, p. 74, of *Property, Family and the Legal Profession;* Peggy A. Rabkin, *Fathers to Daughters: The Legal Foundations of Female Emancipation,* p. 22. See also Suzanne Lebsock, *The Free Women of Petersburg: Status and Culture in a Southern Town, 1784 – 1860,* p. 84; John Bell, "Powers of Married Woman in Texas Aside from Statutes," *Texas Law Review* 6 (June, 1928): 516; and Isenberg, *Sex and Citizenship,* pp. 7, 176 – 79.

15. Bardaglio, *Reconstructing the Household,* pp. xvi–xvii; Bynum, *Unruly Women,* p. 61;

Fox-Genovese, *Within the Plantation Household,* pp. 63–64, 203; McCurry, *Masters of Small Worlds,* p. 89.

16. Lebsock's *Free Women of Petersburg* was probably the most groundbreaking work in the use of public records to illuminate women's lives. Other fine local studies of women include Bynum, *Unruly Women;* Edwards, *Gendered Strife and Confusion;* and Whites, *Civil War as a Crisis in Gender.*

17. Suzanne Lebsock's study has been criticized harshly for taking as its subject the urban environment of Petersburg, Virginia, the sixth-largest city in the South. Although recognizing that her book is vastly informative, historians such as Elizabeth Fox-Genovese argue that the urban women's lives Lebsock uncovered in Petersburg were atypical of women in the predominantly rural South; see Fox-Genovese, *Within the Plantation Household,* p. 70.

18. Walter Prescott Webb et al., eds., *The Handbook of Texas,* vol. 1, pp. 379, 382.

19. The settled portion of Texas (the eastern three-fifths of the state) as a whole exhibited these southern characteristics. See Randolph B. Campbell, *An Empire for Slavery: The Peculiar Institution in Texas, 1821–1865,* pp. 209, 258; Lowe and Campbell, *Planters and Plain Folks,* pp. 3–19, 44, 69, 182.

20. Webb, *The Handbook of Texas,* pp. 378–79; Bill Stein, "Consider the Lily: The Ungilded History of Colorado County, Texas, Part 5," *Nesbitt Memorial Library Journal* 7 (Jan., 1997): 45; Slave Schedule, Seventh Census of the United States (1850), Colorado County, Texas; Lowe and Campbell, *Planters and Plain Folks,* pp. 209, 258.

21. Slave and Population Schedule, Seventh and Eighth Censuses of the United States (1850 and 1860), Texas, Colorado County; 214 percent increase in Texas as a whole. See Randolph Campbell, "Reconstruction in Colorado County, Texas, 1865–1876," *Nesbitt Memorial Library Journal* 5 (Jan., 1995): 7; Campbell, *An Empire for Slavery,* p. 191; Lowe and Campbell, *Planters and Plain Folks,* pp. 158, 182. Even though the vast majority of whites were not slaveholders, their commitment to the institution has been documented in many ways. See, for instance, Randolph Campbell, "The Slave Hire System in Texas," *American Historical Review* 93 (Feb., 1988): 107–14; *State of Texas v. Richard Putney,* Oct. 30, 1860, District Court Minutes, Book C2, p. 200, CCDC.

22. Schedule 1 (Free Inhabitants), Seventh and Eighth Censuses of the United States (1850 and 1860), Texas, Colorado County; Lowe and Campbell, *Planters and Plain Folks,* pp. 44, 179; Myres, *Westering Women,* p. 96.

23. Schedule 2 (Slave Inhabitants), Seventh and Eighth Censuses of the United States (1850), Texas, Colorado County; Glen E. Lich, *The German Texans,* pp. 68–85; Rudolph Leopold Biesele, *The History of the German Settlements in Texas, 1831–1861,* pp. 42, 51–55; Terry G. Jordan, *German Seed in Texas Soil: Immigrant Farmers in Nineteenth-Century Texas,* esp. pp. 8, 194; Campbell, *An Empire for Slavery,* pp. 191, 215–17; Walter Struve, *Germans and Texans: Commerce, Migration, and Culture in the Days of the Lone Star Republic,* pp. 75–76.

24. Stein, "Consider the Lily . . . , Part 5," p. 49.

CHAPTER 1. WOMEN, WORK, FAMILY, AND LAW ON THE FRONTIER

1. Letter of Cordelia Simmons, *Weimar Mercury,* Apr. 16, 1915, repr. in "Documents, Letters, Reminiscences, Etc.," *Nesbitt Memorial Library Journal* 6 (Jan., 1996): 54.

2. Bill Stein, "Consider the Lily: The Ungilded History of Colorado County, Texas,

Part 2," *Nesbitt Memorial Library Journal* 6 (Jan., 1996): 44–51; and Bill Stein, "Consider the Lily: The Ungilded History of Colorado County Texas, Part 3," *Nesbitt Memorial Library Journal* 6 (May, 1996): 63. For a discussion of what constitutes the end of a frontier and the justification for choosing 1852 as the end of the Colorado County frontier, see chap. 3.

3. Andrew F. Muir, *Texas in 1837,* quoted in Colorado County Historical Commission, comp., *Colorado County Chronicles: From the Beginning to 1923,* vol. 1, p. 52; Dr. Ferdinand Roemer, *Texas,* trans. Oswald Mueller (San Antonio: Standard Printing Company, 1935), p. 81; Schedule 1 (Free Inhabitants), Seventh Census of the United States (1850), Texas, Colorado County.

4. Campbell, *An Empire for Slavery,* pp. 191–201, 258; Lowe and Campbell, *Planters and Plain Folks,* p. 44.

5. Census Report, Dec. 31, 1825, summarized and reprinted in Bill Stein, "Consider the Lily: The Ungilded History of Colorado County, Texas, Part 1," *Nesbitt Memorial Library Journal* 6 (Jan., 1996): 32–33; Schedule 1, Seventh Census of the United States (1850), Texas, Colorado County; Myres, *Westering Women,* p. 168.

6. Petition, *Mary M. B. Smith v. Henderson and Tooke,* Dec. 19, 1856, Docket File No. 1221, CCDC; Myres, *Westering Women,* p. 168; Joan E. Cashin, *A Family Venture: Men and Women on the Southern Frontier,* p. 44.

7. James W. Paulsen, "Remember the Alamo[ny]! The Unique Texas Ban on Permanent Alimony and the Development of Community Property Law," *Law and Contemporary Problems* 56 (spring, 1993): 7–70.

8. Petition, *James Dickson v. Hetty Dickson,* May 8, 1843, Docket File No. 227; and Petition, *Richard Insall v. Caroline Insall,* Jan. 27, 1851, Docket File No. 690, CCDC. Rusha Hope's husband John still received the divorce but on the grounds of cruelty, not abandonment. She, however, remained in Colorado County and remarried. Petition, Nov. 23, 1840, and Jury Findings, *John Hope v. Rusha Hope,* Mar. 6, 1843, Docket File No. 137, CCDC; Marriage Records, Book B, p. 52, 1844, Colorado County, Office of the County Clerk, in the Colorado County Courthouse, Columbus, Texas (hereinafter CCCC). When confronted by his latest wife William Dunlap "confessed that he had been married three times before and that his wife was still living." How many wives were still living remains unclear. Petition, *Joannah Dunlap v. William Dunlap,* Feb. 10, 1840, Docket File No. 138, CCDC.

9. Letter of James W. Holt, *Weimar Mercury,* May 14, 1915, repr. in "Documents, Letters, Reminiscences, Etc.," *Nesbitt Memorial Library Journal* 6 (Jan., 1996): 56. For description of some southern women's reluctance to move west, see Cashin, *A Family Venture;* Myres, *Westering Women;* and Clinton, *Plantation Mistress,* pp. 101–103, 166.

10. Cashin, *A Family Venture,* pp. 48, 57; Lowe and Campbell, *Planters and Plain Folks,* p. 11; Myres, *Westering Women.*

11. "Reminiscences of James Williams Holt," *Nesbitt Memorial Library Journal* 6 (Sept., 1996): 152–54; Myres, *Westering Women.*

12. Myres, *Westering Women,* pp. 6–7, 146–59; Bynum, *Unruly Women,* p. 72; Clinton, *Plantation Mistress,* pp. 23–28; McCurry, *Masters of Small Worlds,* p. 78; Cashin, *A Family Venture,* p. 69.

13. Letter of James W. Holt, in "Documents, Letters, Reminiscences, Etc.," p. 56; Letter of Cordelia Simmons, in "Documents, Letters, Reminiscences, Etc.," p. 54; Letter of Seaborn Trumbul Stapleton, *Weimar Mercury,* Apr. 30, 1915, repr. in "Documents, Letters, Reminiscences, Etc.," p. 55; Myres, *Westering Women,* pp. 140–50; Cashin, *A Family Venture,* pp. 66–67.

14. Letter of Cordelia Simmons, in "Documents, Letters, Reminiscences, Etc.," p. 54; Stapleton received his first pair of pants in 1845 or 1846. See Letter of Seaborn Trumbul Stapleton, in "Documents, Letters, Reminiscences, Etc.," p. 55; Julie Roy Jeffrey, *Frontier Women: The Trans-Mississippi West, 1840–1880,* p. 59; Myres, *Westering Women,* pp. 160–64.

15. Myres, *Westering Women,* pp. 7, 130; Cashin, *A Family Venture,* p. 69.

16. Petition, *David Wade v. John Townsend et al.,* July 5, 1837, Docket File No. 1, CCDC. David Wade claimed that the men had "carried away by force" his daughter Sarah. Although the description sounds like a kidnapping, it might possibly have been a seduction instead.

17. Bardaglio, *Reconstructing the Household,* p. 31; Myres, *Westering Women,* esp. pp. 6, 174, 241; Linda Kerber and Jane Sherron DeHart, eds., *Women's American Refocusing the Past,* 5th ed., p. 28. Frontier southern states such as Tennessee and North Carolina generally had more liberal divorce laws than did the older established southern states. See McMillen, *Southern Women,* p. 46; and Lawrence B. Goodheart, Neil Hanks, and Elizabeth Johnson, "'An Act for the Relief of Females . . .': Divorce and the Changing Legal Status of Women in Tennessee, 1796–1860, Part I," *Tennessee Historical Quarterly* 44:3 (1985): 320. Jones shows in a later period in the western United States that the more liberal laws and frontier regions did not necessarily lead to an increase in divorce; see Mary Somerville Jones, *An Historical Geography of the Changing Divorce Law in the United States,* pp. 30–31, 166–71.

18. John C. Townes, "Sketch of the Development of the Judicial System of Texas. I," *Quarterly of the Texas State Historical Association* 2 (July, 1898): 29–53, esp. 30; "The Constitution of the Republic of Texas, Mar. 17, 1836," in Ernest Wallace, ed., *Documents of Texas History,* pp. 102–103; Campbell, *An Empire for Slavery,* pp. 191–201, 258; Lowe and Campbell, *Planters and Plain Folks,* p. 44.

19. Lazarou, "Concealed under Petticoats," pp. 49–51, 59–62, 83; Oldham and White, *Digest of General Statute Laws,* p. 700. Historians disagree on the amount of control a married woman wielded over her separate property under Spanish law in Texas. Nina Nichols Pugh claims that under Spanish civil law in Louisiana the wife's ability to administer her own property was nearly complete; she could turn over administration to her husband, but even then the courts assumed that she was responsible for his mismanagement and the capacity to control it; see Nina Nichols Pugh, "The Spanish Community of Gains in 1803: *Sociedad de Gananciales,*" *Louisiana Law Review* 30 (Dec., 1969): 3–6, 12–15. Other historians have assumed that this was also the case in Texas; see Joseph W. McKnight, "Texas Community Property Law: Conservative Attitudes, Reluctant Change," *Law and Contemporary Problems* 56 (spring, 1993): 71; Suzanne Reynolds, "Increases in Separate Property and the Evolving Marital Partnership," *Wake Forest Law Review* 24 (summer, 1989): 255. Jean Stuntz, in a study of married women's property under Spanish, English, and Texas Republic law, found that married women had much less control over their separate property. They could control it with special permission from the court based on their husbands' abandonment or rascality, but not as a general rule; see Jean Stuntz, "Three Flags over Texas: Marital Property under Spanish, English, and Republic of Texas Law," paper in possession of author, 1996. See also Bea Ann Smith, "The Partnership Theory of Marriage: A Borrowed Solution Fails," *Texas Law Review* 68 (Mar., 1990): 689–735.

20. McKnight, "Texas Community Property Law," p. 79; William Ransom Hogan, *The Texas Republic: A Social and Economic History,* p. 245. The Texas Congress set up district courts to replace and take over the functions of the Mexican alcalde courts, including jurisdiction in pending cases. The legislature gave county courts and district courts overlapping original jurisdiction in civil cases, but the district courts alone could hear cases in-

volving land. The county courts served also as the probate courts. See *Laws of the Republic of Texas, In Two Volumes,* vol. 1, p. 153.

21. Colorado County Historical Commission, comp., *Colorado County Chronicles,* vol. 1, p. 50; Hogan, *The Texas Republic,* pp. 251, 256. Of course, all states issued and had conflicting court opinions.

22. Bonds and Deeds Transcribed, Book A, p. 151, Oct. 2, 1837, CCCC; Petition, *Aldridge & Davis v. Martha Bostick,* Mar. 5, 1839, Docket File No. 36, CCDC; Summons, *Wm. B. Dewees v. Martha Bostick,* July 12, 1839, Docket File No. 63, CCDC; Petition for injunction, *Martha Bronson v. David Wade as sheriff in favor of David Smith,* Sept. 28, 1839, Docket File No. 60, CCDC; *W. B. Dewees v. Martha Bostick,* Oct. 3, 1839, Docket File No. 6, County Court Minutes, Book A-1840, p. 7, CCCC; *Solon and Stevenson and others v. Martha Bostick and others,* Nov. 14, 1839, Docket File No. 50, District Court Minutes, Book AB, p. 29, CCDC; Reynolds, "Increases in Separate Property," p. 249.

23. Petition, *Nathan D. Barr on behalf of Rachel Barr v. Jacob Lynch,* Dec. 24, 1838, Docket File No. 49, CCDC.

24. Petition and Answer, Oct. 9, 1839, *Rachel Barr (late Rachel Newman) and Andrew Rabb, guardians of Andrew Newman (minor heir of Joseph Newman decd) v. David Wade as sheriff in favor of Jacob Lynch,* Docket File No. 66, CCDC; Nov. 14, 1839, District Court Minutes, Book AB, p. 28, CCDC. According to Pugh in "The Spanish Community of Gains": "Even when she administered her separate assets herself, it was still necessary for her husband to authorize most of her contracts and all of her appearances in court in regard to her patrimony; but this requirement of authorization seems to have been a mere formality, easily obtained by court order, if the husband appeared reluctant to give it" (p. 15).

25. McKnight, "Texas Community Property Law," p. 83; Lebsock, *The Free Women of Petersburg,* p. 24; Oldham and White, *Digest of General Statute Laws,* p. 700.

26. Estate of Robert Gray Cummings, May 4, 1839, Probate Minutes, Book A, p. 21, CCCC.

27. Lebsock, *The Free Women of Petersburg,* p. 56. In 1840 the legislature made it clear that "the court shall, in the first instance, endeavor to try each cause by the rules and principles of law. Should the cause more properly belong to equity jurisdiction, the court shall, without delay, proceed to try the same according to the principles of equity"; see Townes, "Sketch of the Development of the Judicial System of Texas," p. 37.

28. Norma Basch, *In the Eyes of the Law: Women, Marriage, and Property in Nineteenth-Century New York,* p. 20; Marylynn Salmon, *Women and the Law of Property in Early America,* pp. 11, 41–57, 81–119.

29. Lebsock, *The Free Women of Petersburg,* pp. 79–84; Rabkin, *Fathers to Daughters,* p. 22. See also Speth, "The Married Women's Property Acts," p. 74; Bertram Wyatt-Brown, *Southern Honor: Ethics and Behavior in the Old South,* p. 263.

30. Hogan, *The Texas Republic,* pp. 245–46; Joseph W. McKnight and William A. Reppy, Jr., *Texas Matrimonial Property Law (Provisional Second Edition),* pp. 4–5; Oldham and White, *Digest of General Statute Laws,* p. 729; Bea Ann Smith, "The Partnership Theory of Marriage," pp. 702–703. When the framers of the Texas state constitution of 1845 wrote the married women's property rights into the constitution, they did so similarly to other southern states. A writer for the *Louisiana Picayune* even claimed that it was a copy of Louisiana's measures. See Frederic L. Paxson, "The Constitution of Texas, 1845," *Southwestern Historical Quarterly* 18 (Apr., 1915): 388.

31. Oldham and White, *Digest of General Statute Laws,* p. 696.

32. Of fourteen deeds before 1840, one transferred community property and one transferred the separate property interest of a husband but contained his wife's relinquishment. See Bond and Deed Records, Book A, pp. 5, 47, 61, 89, 162, 164, 172, 205, 257, and 286; Bond and Mortgage Records, Book B, p. 123; Deed Records Transcribed, Book B, pp. 144, 413; and Deed Records Transcribed, Book C, p. 3—all in CCCC.

33. Fifteen deeds conveyed a married woman's interest in property in 1841. Eight contained no judge's verification of separate exams at all. Three married women were examined by judges three and four years after the deed was enacted. Two deeds were recorded indicating married women were examined by judges in other counties in 1841. One deed conveyed a wife's power of attorney without her husband's signature or consent. One wife was examined by Kidder Walker, the chief justice of Colorado County. See Deed Records Transcribed, Book C, p. 151, Dec. 27, 1841, CCCC. See also Deed Records Transcribed, Books C, D, E, and I; Bond and Mortgage Records, Book B, esp. p. 288, Feb. 25, 1842, CCCC.

34. Oldham and White, *Digest of General Statute Laws,* p. 72.

35. See also Lazarou, "Concealed under Petticoats," pp. 1–2.

36. Lazarou, "Concealed under Petticoats," pp. 9 (first quote), 19, 50 (second quote); Bardaglio, *Reconstructing the Household,* pp. 117, 134–35; Bynum, *Unruly Women,* p. 67; Cashin, *A Family Venture,* p. 109; Fox-Genovese, *Within the Plantation Household,* p. 203; Isenberg, *Sex and Citizenship,* pp. 172–79; Speth, "The Married Women's Property Acts," pp. 74–75.

37. Donna Sedevie convincingly argues that the married women's property act in Mississippi came near the end in and partially as a result of a series of legal advancements for women in Mississippi; see Donna Sedevie, "Women and the Law of Property in the Old Southwest: The Antecedents of the Mississippi Married Woman's Law, 1798–1839," pp. 84–88. Other scholars dismiss the possibility that these acts represented a change in society's attitudes toward women's legal rights and view them primarily or solely as debtor relief acts; see Norma Basch, "Equity v. Equality: Emerging Concepts of Women's Political Status in the Age of Jackson," *Journal of the Early Republic* 3 (fall, 1983): 311–18; Sandra Moncrief, "The Mississippi Married Women's Property Act of 1839," *Journal of Mississippi History* 47 (May, 1985): 110–16; Richard H. Chused, "Late Nineteenth Century Married Women's Property Law: Reception of the Early Married Women's Property Acts by Courts and Legislatures," *American Journal of Legal History* 29 (Jan., 1985): 34–35; Lazarou, "Concealed under Petticoats," pp. 1–7; McKnight and Reppy, *Texas Matrimonial Property Law,* p. 3; Bea Ann Smith, "The Partnership Theory of Marriage," p. 702; Cashin, *A Family Venture;* Bynum, *Unruly Women;* and Clinton, *Plantation Mistress.*

38. Bonds and Deeds, Book A; Transcribed Deed Records, Books B–Q; Bond and Mortgage Records, Books B–F—all in CCCC. See also Bynum, *Unruly Women,* p. 66.

39. Abner Lipscomb quoted in Lazarou, "Concealed under Petticoats," p. 198; Wyatt-Brown, *Southern Honor,* p. 268; Cashin, *A Family Venture,* pp. 109–11; Bynum, *Unruly Women,* p. 66. Despite the Texas Supreme Court's concern about coercive husbands, Jane Turner Censer argues that separate property was rarely used as a way of punishing sons-in-law or protecting wives against profligate husbands. Instead, husbands and fathers worked together to provide a buffer for the family; see Censer, *North Carolina Planters,* p. 117.

40. See Bond and Deed Records, Book A; Bond and Mortgage Records, Books B, C, D; and Deed Records Transcribed, Books B, C, D, E, F, G, H, I, J, K, L—all in CCCC. See also Oldham and White, *Digest of General Statute Laws,* p. 72. The percentage of married women in the population being examined separately per year was figured with the estimated

239 married women on the 1850 census and assuming that the number was the same every year of the frontier era (which undoubtedly was much less in the early 1840s). In the period from Jan. 1, 1841, to Dec. 31, 1852, 302 deeds contained a wife's relinquishment, averaging about 25 deeds per year, or 10.6 percent of 239.

41. Bertram Wyatt-Brown suggests that these types of legal protections were nearly useless, as "husbands did what they liked with their wives' property regardless of the law"; see Wyatt-Brown, *Southern Honor,* p. 268. See also Bonds and Deeds, Book A; Transcribed Deed Records, Books B–Q; and Bond and Mortgage Records, Books B–F—all in CCCC. See also Censer, *North Carolina Planters,* p. 117; and Clinton, *Plantation Mistress,* p. 71.

42. Answer, *Alexander Brown v. Robert Stevenson & Susan Ann Stevenson,* Mar. 4, 1844, Docket File No. 282, CCDC.

43. *Alexander Brown v. Robert Stevenson and Susan Stevenson,* Sept. 3, 1845, District Court Minutes, Book AB, pp. 278–79, CCDC. Married women could sue in their names only if the unauthorized act of their husbands caused the necessity of suing a third party to recover the separate property of the wife. See Oldham and White, *Digest of General Statute Laws,* pp. 313–14. See also Clinton, *Plantation Mistress,* p. 117.

44. These include any case in which a married woman was named in the suit because of her interest in the property, whether separate or community. It does not include cases in which married women were serving as the administrators of others' estates. Docket numbers for these district court cases are 134, 183, 210, 211, 225, 226, 248, 275, 348, 366, 399, 407, 435, 436, 510, 742 and 761. See Lazarou, "Concealed under Petticoats," pp. 195–96; Bynum, *Unruly Women,* pp. 61–66; Speer, *Treatise on the Law of Marital Rights,* p. 195. See also Bell, "Powers of Married Woman in Texas," p. 516.

45. The case in question involved partitioning of the estate of John H. Dabney. Elizabeth Pace and Margaret Ramsey were among the heirs, and their husbands Dempsey and Martin accepted service of the suit on their behalf. The court hopefully would have been more strenuous in its notification had the married women's property involved been in jeopardy because of some action of the husbands, and not settling a question of heirship. See Back of Petition, *Wylie Jones, gdn of Randel Jones v. Eliza Dabney et al., heirs of Jno H. Dabney, decd.,* Mar. 4, 1846, Docket File No. 436, CCDC (petition dated Mar. 4, 1846, service waived Oct. 8, 1846); *Joannah Tipps v. Martin D. Ramsey,* Oct. 4, 1847, District Court Minutes, Book AB, p. 362, CCDC; Petition, *James M. Caller, next friend of Catherine Tinkler v. Saml. J. Redgate and George B. Halyard,* Feb. 17, 1844, Docket File No. 275, CCDC. A "next friend" is someone who has legal standing and who files suit on behalf of a person who does not, such as a minor or a *feme covert.*

46. Oldham and White, *Digest of General Statute Laws,* p. 313.

47. Petition, *Joannah Dunlap v. William Dunlap,* Feb. 10, 1840, Docket File No. 138; Petition, *Samuel Mixon v. Jacob Tipps and Joanah Tipps,* Nov. 5, 1840, Docket File No. 134; Petition, *Alfred Kelso v. Jacob Tipps and Joanah Tipps,* Nov. 10, 1841, Docket File No. 183— all in CCDC (hereinafter cited as *Mixon v. Tipps* and *Kelso v. Tipps,* respectively). See Speer, *Treatise on the Law of Marital Rights,* p. 195; Bell, "Powers of Married Woman in Texas," p. 516; and D. Edward Greer, "A Legal Anachronism: The Married Woman's Separate Acknowledgement to Deeds," *Texas Law Review* 1 (June, 1923): 409.

48. Petition, *Mixon v. Tipps.* The due date on one promissory note was June 9, 1841, and on the other, June 9, 1842. The timing of Mixon's suit is curious; the due dates had not yet passed. Perhaps Joannah's marriage prompted Mixon to attempt to legally clarify his position; see *Joanah Dunlap v. W. Dunlap,* Apr. 27, 1840, District Court Minutes, Book AB,

pp. 40, 46, 56, CCDC. Joanah McCrabb married Jacob Tipps on May 20, 1840; see Marriage Records, Book B, CCCC. Joanah reverted to her maiden name, McCrabb, at some time in 1840 and was listed in the 1840 tax roles under this name; see Colorado County, Republic of Texas Tax lists, 1840, Nesbitt Memorial Library, Columbus, Texas.

49. Basch, *In the Eyes of the Law*, p. 51; Rabkin, *Fathers to Daughters*, p. 129.

50. For example, "Wherefore he prays the court . . . ," Filing, Dec. 1, 1840, *Mixon v. Tipps.*

51. Injunction, Dec. 4, 1840, and Judgement, Dec. 2, 1841, *Mixon v. Tipps.*

52. Bond and Deed Records, Book B, pp. 197–99, CCCC; *Scire facias*, Nov. 11, 1843, *Mixon v. Tipps;* Statements of Fact, Spring Term, 1843, *Kelso v. Tipps;* Filing, Dec. 2, 1841, *Kelso v. Tipps;* Petition, Oct. 21, 1842, *Kelso v. Tipps;* Papers, *Kelso v. Tipps;* and District Court Minutes, Book AB, p. 160, CCDC.

53. Filing, Mar. 9, 1843, *Kelso v. Tipps.*

54. The 1911 statute allowed a woman to become a merchant or trader only with the permission of her husband or upon his desertion; see Speer, *Treatise on the Law of Marital Rights*, p. 323. The common law in England, however, had allowed for women to contract with their husbands to achieve *feme sole* powers as early as 1783; see Hendrik Hartog, "Marital Exits and Marital Expectations in Nineteenth Century America," *Georgetown Law Journal* 80 (Oct., 1991): 99. The colonial courts and statutes sometimes allowed wives to appeal for status of *femes sole,* but usually after their husbands had deserted them for a number of years; see Marlene Stein Wortman, ed., *Women in American Law, Volume I: From Colonial Times to the New Deal,* p. 17. See also Charles O'Brien, "The Growth in Pennsylvania of the Property Rights of Married Women," *University of Pennsylvania Law Review* 49 (Sept., 1901): 525–26. Throughout the nineteenth century desertion was the primary reason for granting married women this status; see Basch, *In the Eyes of the Law,* p. 93. Some states began passing statutes in the early to mid nineteenth century allowing married women, with the consent of their husbands, to apply to either the judiciary or legislature to be a "sole trader" or "free trader." Ely and Bodenhamer claim that southern states were more progressive in granting sole trader status and encouraged women in business by eliminating imprisonment for debt; see James W. Ely, Jr., and David J. Bodenhamer, "Regionalism and American Legal History: The Southern Experience," *Vanderbilt Law Review* 39 (Apr., 1986): 563; Eleanor M. Boatwright, "The Political and Civil Status of Women in Georgia, 1783–1860," *Georgia Historical Quarterly* 25 (Dec., 1941): 311. These women exercised legal capacities equal to single women but only if engaged in merchandising, trade, or other employment. Therefore, in Texas by 1844 English common law had prepared the courts to consider cases of married women acting as *femes sole.* By 1853 the Texas Supreme Court recognized the right of a wife abandoned for six years to convey her property and contract as a *feme sole.* See Bell, "Powers of Married Woman in Texas," p. 517; and Oldham and White, *Digest of General Statute Laws,* p. 313.

55. Bond and Deed Records, Book A, pp. 197, 199, CCCC; Tax lists, 1840; *Joannah Dunlap v. W. Dunlap,* District Court Minutes, Book AB, pp. 40, 46, 55, CCDC.

56. *Kelso v. Tipps,* Mar. 7, 1844, District Court Minutes, Book AB, p. 211, CCDC.

57. District Court Minutes, Book AB; and Agreement of Parties, Aug. 11, 1845, *Kelso v. Tipps,* CCDC. According to the Bond and Deed Records, the agreement signed on Aug. 11, 1845, was that Alfred Kelso pay $500 to Jacob and Joannah Tipps, and they in turn signed over all their rights to the two pieces of property in question. Samuel Mixon and John Toliver (the holders of the lien on the property) also signed over their claims on the same lots

to Kelso for the sum of $1,000. The settlement for the Tippses was hardly a victory. Joannah lost all claims to title on the two lots and received only $500 reimbursement, while she had paid $775. See Bond and Deed Records, Book E, CCCC; Execution in District Court, Fall Term, 1844, *Mixon v. Tipps*. Stephanie McCurry found women who successfully acted as *feme sole* traders and then pleaded coverture to escape debts; see McCurry, *Masters of Small Worlds*, p. 90.

58. Bardaglio, *Reconstructing the Household*, pp. 28, 117.

59. Petition, *Charles Kesler v. Abel Beeson and Dolores Beeson*, Dec. 14, 1852, Docket File No. 761; Apr. 14, 1853, District Court Minutes, Book C, p. 738, CCDC. See Myres, *Westering Women*, p. 171; and Fox-Genovese, *Within the Plantation Household*, pp. 13—20.

60. Appeal Bond, Judgment, and Summons, *Johanna Tipps v. M. D. Ramsey*, July 28, 1845, Aug. 5, 1845, July 20, 1847, Docket File No. 435; Oct. 4, 1847, District Court Minutes, Book AB, p. 362, CCDC.

CHAPTER 2. TO FIND A NEW HUSBAND

1. Lizzie Thatcher to Fannie Thatcher, Eagle Lake, Aug. 20, 1852, printed in Dorothy Elkins Cox, comp., *Pioneer Texans: Montgomery and Thatcher Families and Their Descendants* (N.p., n.d), p. 172.

2. McCurry, *Masters of Small Worlds*, p. 9; Cashin, *A Family Venture*, p. 48; Myres, *Westering Women*, pp. 6—7, 162; Clinton, *Plantation Mistress*, p. 78; Bynum, *Unruly Women*, p. 7.

3. "Reminiscences of James Williams Holt," pp. 152—54; Schedule 1 (Free Inhabitants), Seventh Census of the United States (1850), Texas, Colorado County. No other woman, German or Anglo, let herself be listed on the census as a laborer until 1870 when the predominant occupation for women that year was "farm labor," and this was primarily made up of the freed black population. Even in 1870 only three German women and no Anglo women considered themselves laborers, farm or otherwise. See Schedule 1 (Free Inhabitants), Eighth and Ninth Censuses of the United States (1860 and 1870), Texas, Colorado County. For the restrictions on women's occupations, especially teaching, see Rable, *Civil Wars*, pp. 26—29.

4. McCurry, *Masters of Small Worlds*, p. 78; Myres, *Westering Women*, pp. 6, 162—67; Fox-Genovese, *Within the Plantation Household*, pp. 109, 193.

5. Schedule 1 (Free Inhabitants), Seventh Census of the United States (1850), Texas, Colorado County; Fox-Genovese, *Within the Plantation Household*, pp. 203—205.

6. Schedule 1 (Free Inhabitants), Seventh Census of the United States (1850), Texas, Colorado County; McCurry, *Masters of Small Worlds*, p. 123; Fox-Genovese, *Within the Plantation Household*, pp. 203—206.

7. Bynum, *Unruly Women*, p. 77; Fox-Genovese, *Within the Plantation Household*, pp. 11, 203—206; Cashin, *A Family Venture*, p. 111.

8. Clinton, *Plantation Mistress*, pp. 9, 22, 165, 176; Fox- Genovese, *Within the Plantation Household*, pp. 98, 210; McCurry, *Masters of Small Worlds*, p. 121; Cashin, *A Family Venture*, pp. 15, 84.

9. Of forty-four widows, thirty-seven can be traced a year later, usually within Colorado or surrounding counties. Six married before administration, thirteen married one or fewer years after, eight married within two years, four within three, and two within four. One widow did not marry for seven years. Of the three widows who did not marry, one, Judith

Callaway, died less than two years later, while Eliza Hopson and Jane Naill remained *feme sole* for many years before disappearing from the records. Seven other widows were present when letters of administration were taken out on their husbands but did not reappear in court or court records again, nor can they be found anywhere in the county after that. See Probate Records, Marriage Records, County Court Minutes, CCCC; District Court Records, CCDC. See also Myres, *Westering Women,* p. 168; Clinton, *Plantation Mistress,* p. 78.

10. *State of Texas v. Thomas Bateman,* Criminal Docket File No. 140; *Elizabeth Bateman v. Thomas Bateman and A. J. Wicker,* Docket File No. 802; *Elizabeth Bateman v. G. T. Jamison,* Docket File No. 962—all in CCDC.

11. Sue Dunlavy McIlveen, comp., *Footprints: The Dunlavys and Related Families,* pp. 23–26; Robert L. Hunter, comp., "Hunter & Combs-Dunlavy Bible Records," *Stirpes* 4 (Sept., 1964): 93–95; *Joannah Dunlap v. William Dunlap,* Feb. 10, 1840, through Apr. 27, 1840, Docket File No. 138, CCDC. See Censer, *North Carolina Planters;* Fox-Genovese, *Within the Plantation Household;* Steven M. Stowe, *Intimacy and Power in the Old South: Ritual in the Lives of the Planters;* Daniel Blake Smith, *Inside the Great House: Planter Family Life in Eighteenth-Century Chesapeake Society;* Stevenson, *Life in Black and White,* pp. 37–62.

12. Lizzie Thatcher to Fannie Thatcher, Eagle Lake, Aug. 20, 1852, and Sarah Mirah Thatcher to Fannie Thatcher, Eagle Lake, Aug. 25, 1852, in Cox, comp., *Pioneer Texans,* p. 173. In addition to wars, Indian battles, and disease, the frontier was probably an even more violent place than the rest of the South, as it was noted for violence leading to premature deaths. See Cashin, *A Family Venture,* p. 102; Myres, *Westering Women,* pp. 22, 210; and Clinton, *Plantation Mistress,* p. 105.

13. Lizzie Thatcher to Fannie Thatcher, Eagle Lake, June, 1852, and Aug. 20, 1852, in Cox, comp., *Pioneer Texans,* pp. 175 (first and second quotes), 177 (third and fourth quotes); Sarah Mirah Thatcher to Fannie Thatcher, Eagle Lake, Aug. 25, 1852, in Cox, comp., *Pioneer Texans,* p. 174. Although "ornamental" values were stressed by wealthy southern families, at least some girls received broader and more practical educations as well. See Censer, *North Carolina Planters,* pp. 46–55; Fox-Genovese, *Within the Plantation Household,* pp. 196–202.

14. Oldham and White, *Digest of General Statute Laws,* pp. 120, 200, 260. In order for a deposition to be accepted instead of appearance in court, the only stipulation for women was "where the witness is a female." This was followed in all the courts and its practice recognized by statute for the Justice of the Peace and county courts as well as the district courts. Quote from Petition, *William J. Jones and Angus McNeill and Rebecca his wife v. Peter Cass and Elizabeth his wife and Henry Haly and Olive E. his wife,* Aug. 28, 1849, Docket File No. 611, CCDC. See Estate of William Watts, July 25, 1847, Probate Minutes, Book C, p. 66, CCCC; Amended Petition, *Robert Robson v. Isam Tooke Admr of estate of Wm Watts, decd.,* Aug. 20, 1855, Docket File No. 872, CCDC. Women were not often involved in filing suits in probate court either. Of seventy-six suits filed in cases involving women, four were filed by women solely and sixteen were filed by husbands on behalf of or joined by their wives.

15. Estate of John Shelby McNeill, Dec. 27, 1852, Probate Minutes, Book D, p. 111, and Probate Final Record, Book D, p. 590; Probate Records and Minutes—all in CCCC.

16. Estates of Bernard Beimer, James Dickson, George William Brown, and James M. Caller, Probate Minutes and Probate Final Records, CCCC. James Dickson appointed two men to coexecute the will with his widow, Ellender.

17. Oliver C. Hartley, *A Digest of the Laws of Texas . . . ,* pp. 325–40. In her study of widows administering estates in Virginia, Suzanne Lebsock points out that "there was nothing

inherently satisfying, after all, in chasing debtors, in instigating litigation, or in any of the other chores that came with settling an estate"; see Lebsock, *The Free Women of Petersburg,* pp. 37, 123.

18. Estates of Charles Jesse, Walton Harvey, Jorge Cherry, and John Mallet, Probate Minutes, CCCC.

19. Estate of Robert Stevenson, Jan. 29, 1844, and Feb. 6, 1844, Probate Minutes, Book B; May 26, 1845, and June 30, 1845, Probate Minutes, Book C; Final Probate Record, Book B, pp. 344–46, 423, 438, 449—all in CCCC. Clinton suggests that widowhood was difficult because planters kept notoriously bad records and had much of their capital tied up in slaves and land; see Clinton, *Plantation Mistress,* p. 77.

20. Estate of William Earp, June 27, 1842, Aug. 30, 1842, Dec. 26, 1842, Dec. 27, 1842, Feb. 2, 1843, May 29, 1843, July 31, 1843, Sept. 23, 1843, Oct. 30, 1843, Nov. 27, 1843, and June 24, 1844, Probate Minutes, Book B, p. 128, and Final Probate Record, Book B, p. 209.

21. Docket File Nos. 633, 863, 927, 929, 930, 1332, 1436, 1437, 1524, CCDC; Estate of Joseph Adair, May 31, 1841, Probate Minutes, Book B, p. 11, CCCC; Petition, *Elizabeth Adare v. Isabella Cummins alias Adare,* Mar. 20, 1841, Docket File No. 203, CCDC.

22. Hartley, *Digest of the Laws of Texas,* p. 337; Lebsock, *The Free Women of Petersburg,* pp. 37, 123; Estate of Robert Stevenson, Jan. 29, 1844, Final Probate Record, Book B, pp. 344–45, CCCC.

23. Estate of Joseph Adair, Dec. 12, 1840, Probate Minutes, Book B, p. 1; Estate of William Colwell, Dec. 26, 1842, Probate Minutes, Book B, p. 75; Estate of William Wright, Mar. 25, 1850, Probate Minutes, Book C, p. 240—all in CCCC; Hartley, *Digest of the Laws of Texas,* p. 407.

24. Dec. 12, 1840, Dec. 26, 1842, July 31, 1843, and Feb. 6, 1844, in Minutes of the Probate Court, Book B; Estate of Robert Stevenson, Jan. 14, 1844, Final Probate Record, Book B, pp. 333, 344–45; June 30, 1845, Probate Minutes, Book C, p. 13—all in CCCC.

25. Estate of Noah Zumwalt, Sept. 28, 1840–Apr. 24, 1843, Probate Minutes, Book A, p. 40; Probate Minutes, Book B, pp. 22, 25, 86; Final Probate Record, Book B, p. 75—all in CCCC. The other estates were Naham Mixon, John McCrosky, Gabriel Strawschneider, and Robert G. Cummings. Robert H. Kuykendall also died leaving a widow, and although a partition of his estate was heard in probate court, apparently no letters of administration were granted. See Estate of Francis Kuster, Dec. 4, Dec. 29, 1851, Final Probate Record, Book D, pp. 343–45, CCCC.

26. Jamima Bartlett, Jane A. Naill, Nancy Colwell, Judith Callaway, and Anna Clara Kleykamp Snider served with nonrelatives; Mary Thompson Thomas, Catherine Schimmer Moeller, G. M. Damke Meier, and Elizabeth Pieper served with their new husbands; Isabella Cummings served with a relative, while Susan A. Shepherd served with her son-in-law. See Probate Files, Probate Minutes, and Probate Final Records; Estate of Robert Gray Cummings, Mar. 25, 1839, Probate Minutes, Book A, p. 17, Jan. 25, 1841, Probate Minutes, Book B, p. 5; Estate of Joseph Adair, Dec. 12, 1840, Probate Minutes, Book B, p. 1—all in CCCC. Isabella's two estates were in the court minutes on twenty-two separate occasions.

27. While a female of fifteen was technically a minor, once she married she was considered of majority, and statute specifically protected a spouse's right to administer the estate of a spouse even when under twenty-one, "provided, however, that such letters may be granted to a surviving husband or wife who may be under twenty-one years of age"; see Oldham and White, *Digest of General Statute Laws,* p. 166. Only two women served as administrator while under twenty-one.

28. To determine the approximate wealth of estates, I have used bond amounts, inventory estimates, and/or census figures for those probated by widows. Then I used the census to figure the estates' approximate position of wealth in Colorado County. See Probate Records, CCCC and 1850 Census. Fox-Genovese argues that planter women might have inherited households but always turned the management over to men; see Fox-Genovese, *Within the Plantation Household,* p. 203.

29. The rough figure is based on all identifiable German decedents whose estates required a bond. Seven of thirty-four active widows whose ethnicity can be verified were German: Rebecca Kuster, Sophia L. Jesse, Catherine Elizabeth Ketterman Beimer, Catherine Schimmer (also Moeller), G. M. Damke (also Meier), Elizabeth Simon (also Pieper), and Anna Clara Kleykamp (also Snider). See Probate Records, CCCC and Schedule 1, Seventh Census of the United States (1850), Texas, Colorado County.

30. At least one of the widows, Catherine Schimmer Miller, did not know how to sign her own name; she marked instead of signing the required bond. See Estate of Bernard Schimmer, May 26, 1850, Probate Final Record, Book D, pp. 392–93, CCCC. Some eighteen years later she still marked her legal documents. See Bond and Mortgage Records, Book F, p. 440, Sept. 9, 1868, CCCC. See also Dona Reeves-Marquardt, "Tales of the Grandmothers: Women as Purveyors of German-Texan Culture," in Theodore Gish and Richard Spuler, eds., *Eagle in the New World: German Immigration to Texas and America.*

31. Colorado County widows might have been more reluctant than other southern women to administer estates. Suzanne Lebsock found in antebellum Petersburg, Virginia, that most women given a choice accepted the administration; see Lebsock, *The Free Women of Petersburg,* pp. 120–22. In eighteenth-century Virginia, according to Gunderson and Gampel, widows "rarely refused" their first right to administer an intestate husband's estate; see Joan R. Gunderson and Gwen Victor Gampel, "Married Women's Legal Status in Eighteenth-Century New York and Virginia," *William and Mary Quarterly* 3d series, 39 (Jan., 1982): 119. However, in Colorado County, with the exception of the frontier period, a large number of widows refused to administer.

32. Sarah Mirah Thatcher to Fannie Thatcher, Eagle Lake, Aug. 25, 1852, in Cox, comp., *Pioneer Texans,* p. 174; Marriage Records, Probate Records, CCCC; Myres, *Westering Women,* p. 172.

33. Probate Records and Marriage Records, CCCC.

34. According to McKnight, the Spanish law system appealed to Texans for the very reason that it allowed a wife to become co-owner of property acquired during marriage "and comported with the realities of frontier conditions under which both spouses stood together against natural and human forces"; see McKnight, "Texas Community Property Law," p. 79.

35. Oldham and White, *Digest of General Statute Laws,* p. 172 (emphasis added).

36. Estate of John P. Thompson, May 4, 1839, Probate Minutes, Book A, p. 22; Estate of Kaspar Simon, Aug. 27, 1849, Probate Minutes, Book C, p. 195—both in CCCC.

37. Estate of Bernard Schimmer, June 30, 1851, Probate Minutes, Book D, p. 18, CCCC.

38. Estate of Bernard Schimmer, June 30, 1851, Final Probate Record, Book D, pp. 392–93, CCCC.

39. Estate of Robert Gray Cummings, Mar. 25, 1839, Apr. 29, 1844, and other dates, Probate Final Record, Book B, p. 368; Estate of Thomas Slaughter, Sept. 5, 1838, Aug. 15, 1840, and other dates, Probate Minutes, Book A, pp. 11, 38—all in CCCC.

40. Estate of Benjamin F. Stockton, Jan. 24, 1852, Mar. 28, 1853, Probate Final Record, Book D, p. 411, Probate Minutes, Book D, p. 137, CCCC.

41. Petition, Feb. 10, 1840, *Joannah Dunlap v. William Dunlap,* Docket File No. 138, CCDC.

42. Petition, *Louisa Muller v. Frederick Muller,* Aug. 16, 1843, Docket File No. 240, CCDC.

43. *Alfred Kelso v. Jacob Tipps and Joannah Tipps,* Mar. 7, 1844, District Court Minutes, Book AB, p. 211, CCDC.

44. Petition, *Joannah Dunlap v. William Dunlap,* Feb. 10, 1840, Docket File No. 138; and *Joannah Dunlap v. William Dunlap,* Apr. 27, 1840, District Court Minutes, Book AB, p. 55, CCDC; Marriage Records, Book B, p. 18, CCCC. See also Bynum, *Unruly Women,* p. 77; and Cashin, *A Family Venture,* p. 111.

45. *Joannah Dunlap v. William Dunlap,* Apr. 27, 1840, *Caroline Kahnd v. Jacob Kahnd,* Oct. 19, 1848, *Louisa Muller v. Frederick Muller,* Sept. 5, 1843, *Julia Shoemaker v. James Shoemaker,* Oct. 4, 1846, *Virgillia Woolsey v. Abner Woolsey,* Sept. 1, 1845, District Court Minutes, Book AB, pp. 55, 402, 194, 290, 276, respectively, CCDC.

46. Petitions, *Elvira W. Perkins v. Jasper Perkins,* Oct. 20, 1848, and Apr. 2, 1850, Docket File No. 546; Oct. 20, 1848, District Court Minutes, Book AB, p. 409; Apr. 2, 1850, District Court Minutes, Book C, p. 771, CCDC; Oldham and White, *Digest of General Statute Laws,* p. 149. Historians have described how divorce statutes elsewhere were passed to benefit women; see Jane Turner Censer, "'Smiling through Her Tears': Ante-Bellum Southern Women and Divorce," *American Journal of Legal History* 25 (Jan., 1981): 27; Goodheart, Hanks, and Johnson, "An Act for the Relief of Females," pp. 322–23; McMillen, *Southern Women;* Rable, *Civil Wars,* p. 11; Robert L. Griswold, "The Evolution of the Doctrine of Mental Cruelty in Victorian American Divorce, 1790–1900," *Journal of Social History* 20 (fall, 1986): 127; Norma Basch, "Relief in the Premises: Divorce as a Woman's Remedy in New York and Indiana, 1815–1870," *Law and History Review* 8 (spring, 1990): 1–24.

47. Petition, *Jesse Robinson v. Sarah alias Sally Robinson,* Feb. 1, 1843, and Jury Finding, Mar. 8, 1843, Docket File No. 220; District Court Minutes, Book AB, Mar. 8, 1843, pp. 161–62, CCDC.

48. J. Frank Dobie, "A School Teacher in Alpine," *Southwest Review* 47 (autumn, 1962): 273–74, quoted in Dan Kilgore, "Two Sixshooters and a Sunbonnet: The Story of Sally Skull," in Francis Edward Abernethy, ed., *Legendary Ladies of Texas,* p. 70 (first quote); Texas Historical Marker dedicated to Sally Scull, repr. in Kilgore, "Two Sixshooters and a Sunbonnet," p. 57 (second and fourth quotes); Petition, *Jesse Robinson v. Sarah alias Sally Robinson,* Feb. 1, 1843, Docket File No. 220, CCDC (third quote). See Answer, Mar. 8, 1843, *Jesse Robinson v. Sarah alias Sally Robinson,* Docket File No. 220, CCDC. For examples of women divorced for failing to be true women, see also Goodheart, Hanks, and Johnson, "An Act for the Relief of Females," p. 332. For explanations of the gendered acceptability of violence and temper in the South and in the frontier period, see Fox-Genovese, *Within the Plantation Household,* pp. 109, 196–202, 238; Clinton, *Plantation Mistress,* pp. 97–105; Cashin, *A Family Venture,* p. 102; Myres, *Westering Women,* pp. 22, 210.

49. Petition, Nov. 23, 1840, Amended Petition, Apr. 28, 1841, *John Hope v. Rusha Hope,* Docket File No. 137, CCDC.

50. Petition, Nov. 23, 1840, and Amended Petition, Apr. 28, 1841, *John Hope v. Rusha Hope,* Docket File No. 137, CCDC. Marriage Record, Book B, p. 23, CCCC. Rusha Hope hired an attorney to fight the divorce; see Writ of Scira Facias, Aug. 6, 1844, *A. M. Lewis v. Rusha Ware and Thomas Ware,* Docket File No. 137. She remained in the county after the divorce was decreed and married Thomas Ware on Feb. 29, 1844; see Marriage Record, Book B, p. 52, CCCC.

51. Petition, May 8, 1843, Interrogatories, May 16 and Aug. 1, 1843, *James Dickson v. Hetty Dickson,* Docket File No. 227, CCDC; *James Dickson v. Hetty Dickson,* Sept. 5, 1843, District Court Minutes, Book AB, 176, CCDC; H. P. N. Gammel, comp., *The Laws of Texas, 1822–1897,* vol. 7, pp. 483–86; Marriage Record, Book B, p. 47, CCCC.

52. District Court Docket Files.

53. Amended petition, Aug. 24, 1844, and Petition, Aug. 4, 1843, *Margaret Pinchback v. James Pinchback,* Docket File No. 322; Amended Petition, Apr. 16, 1852, and Petition, Oct. 23, 1850, *Mary Dresler v. Henry Dresler,* Docket File No. 739; *Margaret Pinchback v. James Pinchback,* Sept. 5, 1843, and Sept. 3, 1844, District Court Minutes, Book AB, pp. 191 and 232, and *Mary Dresler v. Henry Dresler,* Apr. 13, 1853, District Court Minutes, Book C, p. 934, CCDC.

54. Petition, *Caroline Kahnd v. Jacob Kahnd,* Oct. 19, 1848, Docket File No. 541, CCDC.

55. Petition, *Louisa Muller v. Frederick Muller,* Aug. 16, 1843, Docket File No. 240, CCDC.

56. Petition, *Virgillia Woolsey v. Abner W. Woolsey,* May 22, 1845, Docket File No. 381; Petition, *Susan Bostick v. Sion Bostick,* Oct. 17, 1851, Docket File No. 709; District Court Minutes, Book C, Mar. 30, 1852, p. 878—all in CCDC. The court records do not specifically state why these cases were dismissed. When a plaintiff decided to pursue a case no longer, a notation to that effect was made. When the parties reached agreements, this also was noted in the records.

57. Only one divorce action brought by a wife, contested by the husband, was won. In that case she charged physical abuse of herself and of her daughter. For evidence of the husband's contesting of the divorce see Petition for Continuance, *Mary Dresler v. Henry Dresler,* Apr. 13, 1853, and Answer, Apr. 14, 1853, Docket File No. 739, CCDC.

58. Griswold, "The Evolution of the Doctrine of Mental Cruelty," p. 130; Censer, "Smiling through Her Tears," pp. 28–29, 34–35. Griswold maintains that in the 1840s cruelty was considered by judges to mean just physical cruelty and that thereafter it gradually came under attack. In Texas, lower courts had the ability to interpret cruelty as mental suffering until the Supreme Court guided them to do so no longer, which it did in 1848. Later, cruelty was broadened by the Texas Supreme Court in a way that favored women much more than the local district court did, i.e., by allowing a false charge of adultery to be considered cruelty. See Petition, *Reuben Bonds v. Darcas Bonds,* Apr. 1, 1850, Docket File No. 650; Petition, *Moses Townsend v. Rebecca C. Townsend,* Sept. 26, 1857, Docket File No. 1267; Petition, *Thadeus W. Hunter v. Tempie J. Hunter,* Sept. 16, 1873, Docket File No. 2995—all in CCDC.

59. Petition, *John Hope v. Rusha Hope,* Nov. 23, 1840, Docket File No. 137; Petition, *James Dickson v. Hetty Dickson,* May 8, 1843, Docket File No. 227; Petition, *Joesh Otto v. Geshe Otto,* Oct. 23, 1850, Docket File No. 666; Petition, *Richard Insall v. Caroline Insall,* Jan. 27, 1851, Docket File No. 690; Petition, *Wingate W. Woodley v. Elizabeth Woodley,* Apr. 22, 1842, Docket File No. 204—all in CCDC.

60. Petition, *Polly Reels v. Patrick Reels,* Aug. 29, 1843, Docket File No. 245; Petition, *Margaret Zimmerschitte v. Fredrick Zimmerschitte,* May 24, 1848, Docket File No. 538—both in CCDC.

61. *Margaret Zimmerschitte v. Frederick Zimmerschitte,* District Court Minutes, Book C, Apr. 6, 1850, p. 782, CCDC; Margaret Zimmerschitte to Josephine Leyendecker, Jan. 1, 1857, anonymous translation, Leyendecker Family Papers, Center for American History, University of Texas (hereinafter Leyendecker Family Papers).

62. Petition, *Margaret Zimmerschitte v. Fredrick Zimmerschitte,* May 24, 1848, Docket

File No. 538, CCDC (quote); Jan. 1, 1857, anonymous translation, Leyendecker Family Papers; "Suit dismissed by agreement," *Polly Reels v. Patrick Reels,* Sept. 3, 1844, District Court Minutes, Book AB, p. 233; Execution of Judgment, *Polly Reels v. Patrick Reels,* Nov. 6, 1844, Docket File No. 245, CCDC.

63. Oldham and White, *Digest of General Statute Laws,* p. 313.

CHAPTER 3. SETTLING UP

1. The population grew from 1,534 white persons in 1850 to over 4,325 in 1860. See Schedule 1 (Free Inhabitants), Seventh and Eighth Censuses of the United States (1850 and 1860), Texas, Colorado County; Jordan, *German Seed in Texas Soil,* pp. 26–27; Letter of James W. Holt, in "Documents, Letters, Reminiscences, Etc.," p. 56; Lizzie Lookup Thatcher to Fanny Thatcher, Eagle Lake, Aug. 15, 1852, printed in Cox, comp., *Pioneer Texans,* pp. 169–70.

2. Letter of Seaborn Trumbul Stapleton, in "Documents, Letters, Reminiscences, Etc.," p. 55; Tax Rolls, 1849–54, Colorado County, Texas, on microfilm at Nesbitt Memorial Library, Columbus, Texas. The number of deeds involving women increased from 1852 to 1853. While the number of deeds per year in my database of deeds involving women remained at about 80 in 1850–52, 104 deeds were recorded in 1853. The number remained at about 100 deeds per year for 1853–55 and climbed steadily thereafter. See Bond and Mortgage Records, Books D and E; Deed Records Transcribed, Books G–O.

3. "The Town of Columbus," *La Grange Texas Monument,* Feb. 11, 1852, p. 2; "Sketches of Travel in Western Texas," *La Grange Texas Monument,* Mar. 17, 1852, p. 2.

4. The number of households increased from 273 in 1850 to 801 in 1860. See Schedule 1 (Free Inhabitants), Seventh Census of the United States (1850) and Eighth Census of the United States (1860), Texas, Colorado County; Charles William Tait to Brother Robt. Tait, May 14, 1854, Columbus, Charles William Tait Papers, Center for American History, University of Texas (hereinafter Tait Papers).

5. Tax Rolls, 1849–54, Colorado County, Texas, on microfilm at Nesbitt Memorial Library, Columbus, Texas; Letter of Seaborn Trumbul Stapleton, in "Documents, Letters, Reminiscences, Etc.," p. 55. Julie Roy Jeffrey enumerates the common threads of life for frontier women: crude living conditions and housing with little privacy; a shortage of capital and labor; small diversified farming; the arduous preparation of food; the threat of violence, particularly from Indians; isolation from other white women; and a sexual imbalance. See Jeffrey, *Frontier Women,* pp. 53–58.

6. Colorado County Historical Commission, comp., *Colorado County Chronicles,* vol.1, p. 78.

7. Cashin, *A Family Venture,* pp. 81–82; Colorado County Historical Commission, comp., *Colorado County Chronicles,* vol. 1, p. 74; Charles William Tait to father, Aug. 24, 1854, Tait Papers.

8. Schedule 1 (Free Inhabitants), Eighth Census of the United States (1860), Texas, Colorado County; Charles William Tait letters, Tait Papers.

9. Schedule 1 (Free Inhabitants), Eighth Census of the United States (1860), Texas, Colorado County.

10. Saint Peter and Paul Catholic Church, Frelsburg, Feb., 1854, although Fr. F. A. Jacobs was first resident pastor who baptized the child in Apr., 1847; Trinity Lutheran Church,

Frelsburg, June 5, 1855; First Methodist Church, Columbus, 1848; Saint John's Episcopal Church, Columbus, Apr. 14, 1856; Stein, "Consider the Lily . . . , Part 5," p. 130; *The Record Book of Luther Chapel,* Columbus, Center for American History, University of Texas.

11. Excerpt from the diary of Fannie Darden, repr. in *History of Saint John's Episcopal Church,* Columbus, Texas, Apr. 14, 1856–Apr. 14, 1956, p. 4. Fannie Darden's original diary has unfortunately been lost. See Colorado County Historical Commission, comp., *Colorado County Chronicles,* vol. 1, p. 72.

12. Bond and Mortgage Records, Book D, p. 518, July 4, 1854, CCCC; Stein, "Consider the Lily . . . , Part 5," p. 131. Although women became increasingly involved in church or charitable societies, there is no evidence that this led to a separate "women's culture" or that it had the direct link to feminist activities that it did in the North. See Rable, *Civil Wars,* p. 17.

13. Lich, *The German Texans,* pp. 124–25; Jordan, *German Seed in Texas Soil,* pp. 194–95; Biesele, *The History of the German Settlements in Texas,* pp. 51–55, 211. See Glen E. Lich, "Rural Hill Country: Man, Nature, and the Ecological Perspective," p. 38; Reeves-Marquardt, "Tales of the Grandmothers," p. 202; and Ingeborg Ruberg McCoy, "Tales of the Grandmothers, II," pp. 212–20—all in Gish and Spuler, eds., *Eagle in the New World.*

14. Jordan, *German Seed in Texas Soil,* p. 8; Schedule 1 (Free Inhabitants), Eighth Census of the United States (1860), Texas, Colorado County.

15. Schedule 1 (Free Inhabitants), Eighth Census of the United States (1860), Texas, Colorado County; Colorado County Historical Commission, comp., *Colorado County Chronicles,* vol. 1, p. 95; Letter of Seaborn Trumbul Stapleton, in "Documents, Letters, Reminiscences, Etc.," p. 55. For discussions of women's limited occupational choices and especially the reasons why few women in the South became teachers, see Rable, *Civil Wars,* p. 29.

16. In addition to teaching herself, Mrs. E. C. Crawford employed Judge Cooper at her school for "the instruction of the youth hereabout," *Colorado Citizen,* Jan. 9, 1858, pp. 2, 3. Mrs. C. A. Connelly, who had thirty years teaching experience elsewhere, opened a school in 1860 "in the new School-room near her dwelling"; see *Colorado Citizen,* July 21, 1860, p. 2. Nannie and Carrie Martin were the assistant teacher in the literary department and the music teacher at the Columbus Female Seminary, respectively, in Feb., 1860; see *Colorado Citizen,* Feb. 18, 1860, p. 4. Mrs. Blackshear was a music teacher at the Eaton Institute; see *Colorado Citizen,* Sept. 18, 1858, p. 2. See Schedule 1 (Free Inhabitants), Eighth Census of the United States (1860), Texas, Colorado County; Colorado County Historical Commission, comp., *Colorado County Chronicles,* vol. 1, p. 159; Bill Stein, "Consider the Lily: The Ungilded History of Colorado County Texas, Part 4," *Nesbitt Memorial Library Journal* 6 (Sept., 1996): 134. See also County Court Minutes, Book 2, p. 183, Feb. 10, 1856, CCCC; Deposition, *Goode and Sons v. Josiah Kuykendahl,* Apr. 30, 1858, Docket File No. 1348, CCDC. Arthur and Mary Sherrill ran a Hotel; see Petition, *John Hope and A. J. Bonds v. Arthur Sherrill,* Mar. 21, 1856, Docket File No. 1136, CCDC. Mr. G. Good ran a boardinghouse in 1858, had a wife named Julia (according to the 1860 census), and had four boarders; see Deposition, *Goode and Sons v. Josiah Kuykendahl,* Apr. 30, 1858, Docket File No. 1348, CCDC. These women might or might not have been intimately acquainted with their husbands' businesses, but they certainly worked for them. Suzanne Lebsock found systematic analysis of women's gainful employment in Petersburg nearly impossible. Women's money-making ventures were rarely recorded, although in Petersburg, as in Colorado County, in addition to census returns, the "odd deed, will, letter, diary entry, legislative petition, and court report" gives clues to women's active employment. Petersburg women who took in boarders partic-

ularly eluded notice unless they advertised. No Colorado County women advertised in the Columbus newspaper; see Lebsock, *The Free Women of Petersburg*, pp. 167–69. McCurry argues that even when women participated in wage-earning activities or production, they allowed the men to conduct the exchanges; see McCurry, *Masters of Small Worlds*, p. 123.

17. Seventy-one percent of heads of households (male and female) in 1860 listed an occupation directly relating to farming, including farmer, farm renter, farming, and farm manager. Of 764 families, 117 had sons eighteen or older, and 233 had sons thirteen or older. This was an increase of 3 percent and 4 percent, respectively, over 1850. In 1860 there were 156 farm laborers and 55 farm managers out of 1,250 people listing occupations (17 percent). In 1850 only 23 people listed laborer as their occupation out of 453 listing occupations (5 percent). See Schedule 1 (Free Inhabitants), Seventh Census of the United States (1850), Texas, Colorado County; Schedule 1 (Free Inhabitants), Eighth Census of the United States (1860), Texas, Colorado County. See also Campbell, *An Empire for Slavery*, p. 264.

18. Schedules 1 and 2 (Free Inhabitants and Slaves), Seventh and Eighth Censuses of the United States (1850 and 1860), Texas, Colorado County; Stein, "Consider the Lily . . . , Part 5," pp. 51–59. Thirty-one percent of women slaveholders and thirty-one percent of slaveholders overall owned twenty or more slaves.

19. Schedule 1 (Free Inhabitants), Eighth Census of the United States (1860), Texas, Colorado County; Estate of William R. Turner, Dec. 12, 1857, Final Probate Record, Book E, p. 632, Aug. 19, 1859, Probate Minutes, Book E, p. 94, and Estate of Abel Grace, May 30, 1859, Probate Minutes, Book E, p. 77, all in CCCC. Teresa E. Ivey's participation in farming is a great mystery. She listed her occupation as farming and owned twenty-one slaves but controlled virtually no land of her own. Her brother's widow remarried, and the census indicates that E. B. and Caroline Fowlkes lived in the household next to Ivey with about seven hundred improved acres on two different plantations. The next household listed a "farm manager" and his family who might have taken care of the Ivey and Fowlkes properties and slaves. That they transacted business with one another is clear; in 1861 E. B. Fowlkes loaned Ivey over $1,300. See Stein, "Consider the Lily . . . , Part 5," pp. 51–53; Schedule 1 (Free Inhabitants), Petition, *E. B. Fowlkes v. Teresa Ivey*, Aug. 22, 1865, Docket File No. 1809, CCDC. Fox-Genovese found that planter women almost always turned over plantation business to men; see Fox-Genovese, *Within the Plantation Household*, pp. 203–206.

20. Only Susan Shepherd did not win the entire amount for which she sued. See Petition, Amended Answer and Replication, Deposition, and Charge of the Court, *Susan A. Shepherd v. G. G. Loomis*, Oct. 24, 1859, May 7, 1860, Oct. 30, 1860, and Oct. 31, 1860, Docket File No. 1484; Petition, *Ann Upton v. J. J. and M. M. Sherer*, Oct. 10, 1860, Docket File No. 1568; Petition, *E. Y. Hopson v. D. B. Rhodes*, Mar. 13, 1856, Docket File No. 1124—all in CCDC.

21. Papers, *Elizabeth Earl v. Asa Smith, Shff. and Securities on his official bond*, Jan. 9, 1855, through Dec. 1, 1858, Docket File No. 958, CCDC. Single women were plaintiffs or defendants eight times in sixteen years in the frontier era. Ten antebellum cases in eight and a half years involved single women on their own behalf. Considering the vast differences in the number of single women in the population (40 in 1850, 142 in 1860), this represented a decrease in the percentage of single women suing or being sued (1.3 percent of the single population in the frontier period might file a suit in court, while in the antebellum era .83 percent would).

22. Deposition, *George Turner v. Gabriel Abrams*, Dec. 4, 1860, Docket File No. 1481; Deposition, *Nelson P. Smith v. Alfred Smith and A. B. Wooldridge*, Nov. 7, 1857, Docket File

No. 1126; Deposition, *C. Mitterzwei v. J. G. Mackel*, May 6, 1857, Docket File No. 1226—all in CCDC.

23. Deposition, *Isam Tooke v. A. Smith, shff and his securities*, May 4, 1857, District Court Docket File No. 1182; Deposition, *Weissberg and Hoffmann v. A. H. and R. L. Davidson*, Apr. 9, 1861, Docket File No. 1618, CCDC.

24. For instance, see Depositions, *Ann Fisher et al. v. Wm. J. Jones*, Sept. 9, 1859, Docket File No. 1259; Deposition, *Goode and Sons v. Josiah Kuykendall*, Apr. 30, 1858, Docket File No. 1348; Deposition, *William Bauer v. Julia Bauer*, May 4, 1860, Docket File No. 1472; Deposition, *Jacob Illg v. Sophia Illg*, Oct. 26, 1859, Docket File No. 1466; Deposition, *Elizabeth Hahn v. Jacob Hahn*, Apr. 23, 1860, Docket File No. 1459—all in CCDC.

25. Interrogatories, *John C. Baker v. Wm. M. Byars*, Apr. 28, 1860, Docket File No. 429; Depositions, *Watkins L. Smith v. Wm H. Strahan and others*, Oct. 18, 1854, Docket File No. 806—all in CCDC.

26. Deposition, *George Turner v. Gabriel Abrams*, Dec. 4, 1860, Docket File No. 1481; Deposition, *Goode and Sons v. Josiah Kuykendall*, Apr. 30, 1858, Docket File No. 1348—both in CCDC.

27. In the eight and a half years of the antebellum period 580 married women executed deeds, averaging about 10 percent of married women every year. It was unnecessary to examine 14 (9 were executed by couples acting as coadministrators, and 5 were signed by husbands who had their wives' power of attorney). Of the 566 that required examination, 551 were examined apart. Four of fifteen incomplete deeds were recorded by James and Francis Montgomery conveying property to their children. By law, Francis Montgomery should have been examined, but she was unlikely to challenge gifts to her children. Three other conveyances involved bonds or mortgages, and another three involved out-of-state couples. These six wives were unlikely to mount challenges, and the county clerks probably overlooked their deficiencies. See Bond and Mortgage Records and Deeds Transcribed Records, CCCC. About 11 percent of frontier married women executed deeds every year in the frontier period.

28. *Colorado Citizen*, Aug. 17, 1860, p. 4.

29. Oldham and White, *Digest of General Statute Laws*, p. 729 (first quote); Petition, *John Williams v. Darden and wife*, Feb. 18, 1858, Docket File No. 1307, CCDC (other quotes). According to law, the husband and wife could be jointly sued for debts "contracted *by the wife*, for necessaries furnished herself or children, and for all expenses which may have been incurred *by the wife* for the benefit of her separate property"; see Oldham and White, *Digest of General Statute Laws*, p. 313 (emphasis added).

30. Stein, "Consider the Lily . . . , Part 5," pp. 17, 42. See also Bond and Mortgage Records, Book D, p. 212, May 24, 1853, CCCC; Amended Petition, *L. M. Newsom v. William J. Darden and wife*, Nov. 5, 1856, Docket File No. 1173; Amended Petition, *L. M. Newsom v. William J. Darden and wife*, Nov. 12, 1857, Docket File No. 1173; Petition, *Thomas J. Neavitt v. W. J. Darden and wife*, Apr. 18, 1857, Docket File No. 1224; Petition, *John Williams v. Darden and wife*, Feb. 18, 1858, Docket File No. 1307; Petition, *Woodson Coffee v. W. J. Darden*, Apr. 19, 1858, Docket File No. 1356; Petition, *Charles Schmidt v. W. J. Darden and F. A. Darden*, Mar. 14, 1861, Docket File No. 1645—all in CCDC. See also Oldham and White, *Digest of General Statute Laws*, p. 313. According to *Black's Law Dictionary*, 6th ed. (Saint Paul, Minn.: West Publishing Company, 1990): "Necessaries consist of food, drink, clothing, medical attention, and a suitable place of residence, and they are regarded as necessaries in the absolute sense of the word. However, liability for necessaries is not limited to articles re-

quired to sustain life; it extends to articles which would ordinarily be necessary and suitable, in view of the rank, position, fortune, earning capacity, and mode of living of the individual involved" (p. 1029).

31. *Blum and Mayblum v. W. J. Darden et al.,* May 6, 1859, District Court Minutes, Book C, p. 53; Answer, *Blum and Mayblum v. W. J. Darden et al.,* May 6, 1859, Docket File No. 1425; Petition, Answer, and Amended Petition, *Blum and Mayblum v. W. J. Darden et al.,* Jan. 28, 1860, Nov. 2, 1860 (quote), and Nov. 10, 1860, Docket File No. 1493; *Blum and Mayblum v. W. J. Darden et al.,* Nov. 10, 1860, District Court Minutes, Book C2, p. 245; Petition and Application for Writ of Garnishment, *Charles Schmidt v. W. J. Darden and F. A. Darden,* Mar. 14, 1861, and July 9, 1870, Docket File No. 1645; Nov. 3, 1865, District Court Minutes, Book C2, p. 442—all in CCDC. For the two settled cases, see Amended Petition, *L. M. Newsom v. William J. Darden and wife,* Nov. 5, 1856, Docket File No. 1173; Petition, *Thomas J. Neavitt v. W. J. Darden and wife,* Apr. 18, 1857, Docket File No. 1224—both in CCDC.

32. Petition, *John Williams v. Darden and wife,* Feb. 18, 1858, Docket File No. 1307; Writ of Execution, *John Williams v. Darden and wife,* Sept. 13, 1860, Docket File No. 1307; Petition, *Woodson Coffee v. W. J. Darden,* Apr. 19, 1858, District Court Docket File No. 1356; *Woodson Coffee v. W. J. Darden,* District Court Minutes, Book C, p. 1359—all in CCDC. Neither Fannie nor William Darden owned land or a plantation; they owned town lots. Most likely the plantation was rented.

33. Petition and Motion for New Trial, *Charles Harrison v. George C. Hatch and Mary Hatch,* June 21, 1854, and Apr. 2, 1856, Docket File No. 878, CCDC.

34. Petition, *Logue and Whitfield v. M. T. Hawkins and Agnes Hawkins,* Apr. 22, 1859, Docket File No. 1454, CCDC.

35. Amended Answer, *Logue and Whitfield v. M. T. Hawkins and Agnes Hawkins,* May 11, 1859, Docket File No. 1454, CCDC.

36. Amended Petition, *Logue and Whitfield v. M. T. Hawkins and Agnes Hawkins,* May 11, 1859, Docket File No. 1454, CCDC.

37. Petition, *Logue and Whitfield v. M. T. Hawkins and Agnes Hawkins,* Apr. 22, 1859, Docket File No. 1454, CCDC.

38. *Logue and Whitfield v. M. T. Hawkins and Agnes Hawkins,* May 12, 1859, District Court Minutes, Book C2, p. 63, CCDC.

39. Petition and Writ of Execution, *W. H. Secrest v. A. McNeill and wife,* Oct. 8, 1853, and Jan. 22, 1855, Docket File No. 824; Oct. 27, 1854, District Court Minutes, Book C, p. 1046—both in CCDC.

40. Affidavit, *Mahala Smith v. C. R. Perry and J. Kauffmann,* Apr. 3, 1855, District Court Docket File No. 907, CCDC; Oldham and White, *Digest of General Statute Laws,* p. 313.

41. *Joseph C. Megginson v. George Fisher and wife,* Nov. 5, 1856, District Court Minutes, Book C, p. 1221, CCDC.

42. Exceptions, *Richard Putney v. T. S. Anderson and wife,* Nov. 3, 1860, Docket File No. 1570, CCDC.

43. Articles in the *Colorado Citizen* often discussed the natural intellectual superiority of males and the moral superiority of females. The Columbus Debating Society at one meeting in 1858 took up the question "Is man superior, intellectually, to woman?," although the conclusion, according to the *Citizen* editors, was foregone. The debaters decided that men indeed were women's intellectual superiors and that women were men's moral superiors. The debate spawned several public addresses by attorney R. V. Cook, in which he explained

the importance of maintaining these "natural" distinctions to the happiness of married couples. Even at a young age boys were considered superior intellectually to girls. One article argued for the education of boys and girls together because of these biologically determined attributes: "It is impossible to raise the girls as high, intellectually, without the boys as with them; and it is impossible to raise boys morally as high without girls. The girls morally elevate the boys, and the boys intellectually elevate the girls"; see *Colorado Citizen,* Apr. 17, 1858, p. 1; Mar. 27, 1858, p. 2; and Mar. 26, 1859, p. 2.

44. Dianah Miller Obenhaus, Anna Margaretha Botard, Caroline F. Wooldridge, Elizabeth Moller, and Barbara Heimann all remarried within a year of the probate of their husbands' estates. Sarah E. Berry, Elizabeth Brandt Suhr, Louisa Ficken, and Matilda McDonald Volkey remarried within two years. Anna Kaiser, Sarah Lee, and Mary Robson remarried within three to five years. Martha Logue waited for fourteen years. Sarah Mercer, Maria Hallenberg, Martha Hersperger, Elizabeth Simon Pieper, Margaret M. McMillan, Louisa Townsend, Rebecca Beeson, Eliza Secrest, Lucinda Miller, Susan E. Rivers, P. A. E. Bonds, Sophie Ernest, Rebecca C. Grace, and Maria Leipscher did not remarry or else remarried outside the county after a significant period of time. See Probate Records, Marriage Records, County Court Records, Deed Records, CCCC; District Court Records, CCDC.

45. See Probate Records, CCCC.

46. Barbara Heimann, Anna Margaretha Botard, and Sophia Ernst were appointed sole executors in their husbands' wills and chose to serve. Virginia D. Moore and Elizabeth K. Turner were appointed coexecutors and chose to serve. Elvira Walker was appointed by her husband but declined to act as executor. The husbands of Rebecca Beeson and Elizabeth Brandt named no executor in their wills. Beeson chose to serve as executor, while Brandt declined. See Estate of Casper Heimann, Jan. 28, 1856, p. 214; Estate of William H. Moore, Oct. 3, 1856, pp. 312–13; Estate of William R. Turner, July 27, 1857, pp. 401–402; Estate of Leander Beeson, Jan. 25, 1858, pp. 679–80; Estate of John B. Botard, May 30, 1859, pp. 99–100—all in Probate Final Record, Book E, CCCC. See also Estate of Ferdinand Brandt, Oct. 13, 1859, pp. 375–79; Estate of F. K. Walker, Jan. 13, 1860, p. 275; Estate of Max Ernst, Apr. 4, 1860, pp. 365–66—all in Probate Final Record, Book F, CCCC.

47. Probate Records, CCCC.

48. Estate of Alfred Smith, May 14, 1857, Final Probate Record, Book F, p. 119; Estate of John G. Logue, Jan. 5, 1861, Final Probate Record, Book F, p. 437—both in CCCC.

49. The petitions often stated the relation of the person applying for letters, and sometimes relations can be ascertained from other sources.

50. Twenty-six percent of those accepting were German, 30 percent of those declining. Of the eleven Anglo widows who accepted, nine were southern, and of the fourteen who declined, twelve were southern.

51. Estate of John G. Logue, Dec. 21, 1860, Jan. 5, 1861, and other dates, Probate Final Record, Book F, p. 437, and July 28, 1867, and other dates, Probate Final Record, Book G, pp. 740–97, CCCC. See also Clinton, *Plantation Mistress,* pp. 33, 77.

52. Estate of Alfred Smith, July 14, 1856, Final Probate Record, Book E, pp. 346–57, CCCC. See Docket File Nos. 1126, 1144, 1190, 1221, 1222, 1242, 1258, 1260, 1274, 1276, 1305, 1313, 1314, 1315, 1316, 1317, 1358, and 1374, CCDC. See also Estate of Robert Jones Rivers, Jan. 29, 1855, Probate Minutes, Book D, p. 281, CCCC; and Docket File Nos. 865, 1062, 1259, 1354, 1657, 1658, 1722, 1952, 1962, 1963, 2059, 2117, 2124, and 2125, CCDC. In addition to Robert Jones Rivers's and Alfred Smith's estates, the estates of Augustus B. Wooldridge, John H. Moller, and John F. Berry had district court suits.

53. Historians have frequently found that throughout the antebellum South elite men were less likely to entrust their estates to their widows. See Rable, *Civil Wars,* p. 24; Censer, *North Carolina Planters,* pp. 105–11; Lebsock, *The Free Women of Petersburg,* pp. 35–50.

54. Marriage Records, Probate Records, CCCC.

55. Of fourteen divorces granted in the frontier era, ten wives can be ascertained to have married again. The other four cannot be accounted for. In the antebellum period four of thirteen were found to have remarried, while at least four were found single at a later date and did not remarry in the county.

56. Petition, *Mary Ann Sapp v. Basil G. Sapp,* Feb. 4, 1853, Docket File No. 766; Petition, *Charlotte Cherry v. Thomas E. Cherry,* Mar. 26, 1857, Docket File No. 1203; Petition, *Margaret Miller v. Theodore Miller,* Mar. 10, 1859, Docket File No. 1410; Petition, *Odeliah Besch v. Charles Besch,* Apr. 2, 1859, Docket File No. 1424; Petition, *William Bauer v. Julia Bauer,* Sept. 30, 1859, Docket File No. 1472; Deposition, *Wm. Byars v. Jacob Illg,* Apr. 24, 1861, Docket File No. 1589—all in CCDC. See also Bond and Mortgage Records, Book E, p. 359, Sept. 14, 1859, CCCC; Bynum, *Unruly Women,* pp. 77–83; and Cashin, *A Family Venture,* p. 111.

57. Petition and Answer, *Charlotte Cherry v. Thomas E. Cherry,* Mar. 26, 1857, and Nov. 4, 1857, Docket File No. 1203, CCDC.

58. *Charlotte Cherry v. Thomas E. Cherry,* Nov. 10, 1857, District Court Minutes, Book C, p. 1299, CCDC.

59. Bardaglio, *Reconstructing the Household,* p. 28; Bynum, *Unruly Women,* pp. 61–71; Fox-Genovese, *Within the Plantation Household,* pp. 102, 203; McCurry, *Masters of Small Worlds,* p. 89; Isenberg, *Sex and Citizenship,* p. 108.

60. *Margaret Miller v. Theodore Miller,* May 10, 1859, District Court Minutes, Book C2, p. 56; Amended Petition, Nov. 8, 1859, Statement of Facts, Nov. 12, 1859, Charge, Nov. 8, 1859, *Odeliah Besch v. Charles Besch,* Docket File No. 1424; Nov. 8, 1859, District Court Minutes, Book C2, p. 120—all in CCDC. Also see Bardaglio, *Reconstructing the Household.*

61. Censer, "Smiling through Her Tears," p. 46; Robert L. Griswold, "Law, Sex, Cruelty, and Divorce in Victorian America, 1840–1900," *American Quarterly* 38 (winter, 1986): 730–31; Stevenson, *Life in Black and White,* pp. 153–56.

62. Two divorce cases filed by women during the antebellum era are not taken into account here. One case was dropped, dismissed, or forgotten when war began and the district court ceased holding court and hearing cases. In the other case the defendant died before trial. See Petition, *Sylvania Olds v. Jno T. Olds,* Oct. 4, 1860, Docket File No. 1563; and Petition, *Catherine Peltzer v. Adam Peltzer,* Sept. 24, 1860, Docket File No. 1554—both in CCDC.

63. Petition, *Elizabeth Hahn v. Jacob Hahn,* Aug. 30, 1859, Docket File No. 1459, CCDC.

64. Griswold, "Law, Sex, Cruelty, and Divorce," p. 725; Censer, "Smiling through Her Tears," pp. 30–31.

65. Charge, *Elizabeth Hahn v. Jacob Hahn,* May 4, 1860, Docket File No. 1459; *Elizabeth Hahn v. Jacob Hahn,* May 8, 1860, District Court Minutes, Book C2, p. 185—both in CCDC.

66. Petition, Aug. 29, 1860, Charge of the Court and verdict, May 3, 1861, *Nancy Jane Cundiff v. Calvin S. Cundiff,* Docket File No. 1546, CCDC. Chief Justice John Hemphill is quoted in Censer, "Smiling through Her Tears," p. 35. For other instances of courts making class distinctions in cruelty cases, see Bynum, *Unruly Women,* p. 83; and Griswold, "Law, Sex, Cruelty, and Divorce," pp. 721–24.

67. Petition, *Elizabeth Bateman v. Thomas Bateman,* Aug. 24, 1853, Docket File No. 802, CCDC.

68. Petition, *Mary Ann Sapp v. Basil Sapp,* Feb. 4, 1853, Docket File No. 766; Petition, *Marie Albrecht v. Hubert Albrecht,* Sept. 8, 1855, Docket File No. 1065; Petition, *Sarah Dunford v. William Dunford,* June 13, 1857, Docket File No. 1240—all in CCDC. See also Petition, *Nancy Hope v. John Hope,* Sept. 2, 1854, Docket File No. 905, CCDC.

69. Petition, *Jacob Illg v. Sophia Illg,* Sept. 15, 1859, Docket File No. 1466; Petition, *Antone Rickis v. Martha A. M. Rickis,* Jan. 13, 1858, Docket File No. 1304; Petition, *Horace B. Pendleton v. Susan Cass now Susan Pendleton,* Mar. 30, 1857, Docket File No. 1206; Petition and Answer, *A. Fletcher Bridges v. Rachel A. F. Bridges,* Aug. 8, 1857, and Sept. 1, 1857, Docket File No. 1252—all in CCDC.

70. Charge, *Jacob Illg v. Sophia Illg,* May 7, 1860, Docket File No. 1512, CCDC. Despite his stunning charge to the jury, Sophia was found to have committed adultery with "one August Enke." Chances are good that the charge was true: Sophia married August Enke within the year. See Marriage Records, Book D, CCCC.

71. Petition, *Andrew Cryer v. Lydia Cryer,* Sept. 30, 1857, Docket File No. 1269, CCDC. See also Stevenson, *Life in Black and White,* pp. 5–6, 141–46.

72. Petition, *Sion Bostick v. Susan Bostick,* Sept. 6, 1855, Docket File No. 1064 (emphasis added); Petition, *Mary Ann Sapp v. Basil G. Sapp,* Feb. 4, 1853, Docket File No. 766; Petition, *Nancy Hope v. John Hope,* Sept. 2, 1854, Docket File No. 905—all in CCDC. See Bardaglio, *Reconstructing the Household,* p. 34.

CHAPTER 4. THE LAW OF THE MASTER

1. Deposition, *William P. Turner v. George S. Turner,* Feb. 9, 1871, Docket File No. 2318, CCDC.

2. Oldham and White, *Digest of General Statute Laws,* pp. 26, 120, 225, 504; Bardaglio, *Reconstructing the Household,* pp. 59, 64; Campbell, *An Empire for Slavery,* pp. 112, 113; Fox-Genovese, *Within the Plantation Household,* p. 307.

3. Fox-Genovese, *Within the Plantation Household,* p. 326; Bynum, *Unruly Women,* p. 10.

4. Colorado County Historical Commission, comp., *Colorado County Chronicles,* vol. 1, p. 428.

5. Narrative of James Green, Feb. 8, 1938, in George P. Rawick, ed., *The American Slave: A Composite Autobiography,* repr. in Bill Stein, ed., "The Slave Narratives of Colorado County," *Nesbitt Memorial Library Journal* 3 (Jan., 1993): 22. See also John W. Blassingame, *The Slave Community: Plantation Life in the Antebellum South;* Ann Patton Malone, *Women on the Texas Frontier: A Cross-Cultural Perspective,* pp. 33, 47; Darlene Clark Hine and Kathleen Thompson, *A Shining Thread of Hope: The History of Black Women in America,* p. 79; Brenda E. Stevenson, *Life in Black and White,* pp. 209, 226.

6. Deposition, *Nelson P. Smith v. Alfred Smith and A. B. Wooldridge,* Nov. 7, 1857, Docket File No. 1126, CCDC; Jacqueline Jones, *Labor of Love, Labor of Sorrow: Black Women, Work, and the Family from Slavery to the Present,* p. 12; Malone, *Women on the Texas Frontier,* p. 36.

7. Deposition, *William P. Turner v. George S. Turner,* Feb. 9, 1871, Docket File No. 2318; Interrogatory and other papers, *Thomas J. Adams and Martha Adams his wife v. John Hope,* Sept. 4, 1843, Docket File No. 248; Petition and Bill of Exceptions, *John Hope v. William*

Alley Admr. and Jane E. Naill Admx. of estate of William Naill, decd., Jan. 3, 1850, and Nov. 5, 1851, Docket File No. 636; Amended Answer, *Jesse W. Tanner v. A. Boyd Bonds,* Nov. 1, 1859, Docket File No. 1371—all in CCDC. See Malone, *Women on the Texas Frontier,* pp. 32, 36–37; Noralee Frankel, *Freedom's Women: Black Women and Families in Civil War Era Mississippi,* pp. 1–6; Jacqueline Jones, *Labor of Love,* pp. 13–28; Hine and Thompson, *A Shining Thread of Hope,* pp. 69–75; Stevenson, *Life in Black and White,* pp. 187–93; Cashin, *A Family Venture,* pp. 68–72; Fox-Genovese, *Within the Plantation Household,* pp. 35, 172–86.

8. Schedule 1 (Free Population), Schedule 2 (Slave Population), and Schedule 4 (Agriculture), Seventh and Eighth Censuses of the United States (1850 and 1860), Texas, Colorado County. In Texas as a whole, Randolph Campbell found that 94 percent of slaves (both male and female) belonged to masters in agricultural occupations in both 1850 and 1860; see Campbell, *An Empire for Slavery,* pp. 118–19.

9. Petition, *Ellen Lacy v. Beverly M. Lacy,* Sept. 7, 1865, Docket File No. 1813, CCDC; Narrative of Dick Dervin, June 11, 1943, from *The Eagle Lake Headlight,* repr. in Bill Stein, ed., "The Slave Narratives of Colorado County," *Nesbitt Memorial Library Journal* 3 (Jan., 1993): 3–4. See Jacqueline Jones, *Labor of Love,* pp. 29–30; Stevenson, *Life in Black and White,* pp. 192–97; Deborah Gray White, *Ar'n't I a Woman? Female Slaves in the Plantation South,* p. 129; Malone, *Women on the Texas Frontier,* pp. 31, 37; Frankel, *Freedom's Women,* p. 6; Hine and Thompson, *A Shining Thread of Hope,* p. 77; Ruthe Winegarten, *Black Texas Women: 150 Years of Trial and Triumph;* McMillen, *Southern Women,* pp. 12–47; Campbell, *An Empire for Slavery,* pp. 123–26; Fox-Genovese, *Within the Plantation Household,* pp. 157–67; John B. Boles, *Black Southerners, 1619–1869.*

10. Answer, Nov. 2, 1866; Deposition of Sarah Wright and Deposition of Adeline Bridge, Feb. 26, 1870; Deposition of Mary Wright, Mar. 5, 1870; *Thomas Donnell v. James Wright,* Docket File No. 2048; Petition, *O. Andrews et al. v. Cleveland Windrow,* May 5, 1860, Docket File No. 1535; Deposition of Amanda Milton, *William P. Turner v. George S. Turner,* Feb. 9, 1871, Docket File No. 2318—all in CCDC; See also Estate of John Logue, Feb. 26, 1861, Probate Minutes, Book E, p. 189, CCCC; Schedule 1 (Free Population), Eighth Census of the United States (1860), Texas, Colorado County.

11. Schedule 1 (Free Population) and Schedule 2 (Slave Population), Seventh and Eighth Censuses of the United States (1850 and 1860), Texas, Colorado County. In these households there were thirteen females and five males (one adult, one infant, and males four, ten, and sixteen years old). See Bond and Mortgage Records, Book E, p. 469, Aug. 17, 1860, CCCC.

12. Schedule 1 (Free Population) and Schedule 2 (Slave Population), Seventh and Eighth Censuses of the United States (1850 and 1860), Texas, Colorado County. See Frankel, *Freedom's Women,* p. 6; Cashin, *A Family Venture,* p. 68; Fox-Genovese, *Within the Plantation Household,* p. 167.

13. Schedule 1 (Free Population) and Schedule 2 (Slave Population), Seventh and Eighth Censuses of the United States (1850 and 1860), Texas, Colorado County.

14. Lauren Ann Kattner, "The Diversity of Old South White Women: The Peculiar Worlds of German American Women," in Patricia Morton, ed., *Discovering the Women in Slavery: Emancipating Perspectives on the American Past,* pp. 299–311.

15. Jacqueline Jones, *Labor of Love,* pp. 17, 28, 38; Hine and Thompson, *A Shining Thread of Hope,* p. 75; Stevenson, *Life in Black and White,* pp. 187–93; Fox-Genovese, *Within the Plantation Household,* pp. 177, 293.

16. Schedule 1 (Free Population), Seventh Census of the United States (1850), Texas, Colorado County; "First Census: A List of American Settlers on the Colorado District," in Colorado County Historical Commission, comp., *Colorado County Chronicles,* vol. 2, pp. 722–25. It is assumed that these five were actually slaves because they were listed as domestics (they would not be listed as slaves since it was illegal), no last names were listed for them, and they had "girl" and "boy" written beside their names.

17. "Reminiscences of James Williams Holt," p. 153; Charles William Tait to Brother Robt. Tait, Letters of May and June, 1854, Columbus, Tait Papers. See also Stein, "Consider the Lily . . . , Part 4," pp. 138–39. According to Angus McNeill's chronicler, he took the slaves he inherited from Mississippi to Louisiana, then to Texas; see Ernest Mae Seaholm, "The Angus McNeill Family," *Nesbitt Memorial Library Journal* 8 (May, 1998): 51–77.

18. Schedule 2 (Slave Population), Seventh Census of the United States (1850), Texas, Colorado County; Ellen Eslinger, "The Shape of Slavery on the Kentucky Frontier, 1775–1800," *Register of the Kentucky Historical Society* 92 (winter, 1994): 1–23.

19. The interstate slave trade and possible "slave-breeding" is controversial among historians. Most scholars still argue that male slaves were preferred in the interstate slave trade because of the heavier physical labor they could perform, thus leading to a slight male majority. For instance, see Stevenson, *Life in Black and White,* pp. 175–84; and Cashin, *A Family Venture,* pp. 50, 67. Ellen Eslinger's study of the Kentucky frontier found that there was a preference for younger slaves, but no preference for males over females; see Eslinger, "The Shape of Slavery," pp. 1–23. Frankel found similar patterns in Mississippi; see Frankel, *Freedom's Women,* pp. 2–3. Richard Lowe and Randolph Campbell looked at slave population as a whole in Texas, and because the proportion of males and females and representation of ages was approximately the same as in older southern states, they assumed that the majority of slaves came with their owners to Texas and did not participate in a slave-breeding trade; see Richard G. Lowe and Randolph B. Campbell, "The Slave-Breeding Hypothesis: A Demographic Comment on the 'Buying' and 'Selling' States," *Journal of Southern History* 42 (Aug., 1976): 401–12; and Campbell, *An Empire for Slavery,* p. 51. However, in Colorado County there is abundant evidence that many slaves were brought to the county *after* the owners initially settled there, whether they were left on plantations back east and brought later or they were bought.

20. Schedule 1 (Free Population) and Schedule 2 (Slave Population), Seventh Census of the United States (1850), Texas, Colorado County. Ann Patton Malone argues that one reason female slaves were preferred was for "company" to white women on the frontier; see Malone, *Women on the Texas Frontier,* pp. 26–30. Stephanie McCurry points out that among yeoman farmers who were looking for their initial investment in slaves, women were preferred because they were cheaper and their reproductive capacity would prove to be an "investment" in the long term; see McCurry, *Masters of Small Worlds,* p. 50. Many of the residents of Colorado County invested in slaves after their arrival in Texas. Therefore, lower prices and the "dual nature" of slave women's work would have appealed to them.

21. "Reminiscences of James Williams Holt," p. 56; Criminal Docket Files, CCDC.

22. Narrative of James Green, p. 13.

23. C. William Tait to father, Aug. 12, 1850, and Oct. 12, 1850, C. Wm. Tait Letters, 1844–54, in Charles William Tait Papers, Eugene Barker Center for American History, Austin, Texas. According to White in *Ar'n't I a Woman?,* "Whether or not slave women desired relationships with white men was immaterial, the conventional wisdom was that black women were naturally promiscuous, and thus desired such connections"(p. 38).

24. Benjamin Lundy, *The Life, Travels and Opinions of Benjamin Lundy* (1847), repr. (New York: Negro Universities Press, 1969); repr. (New York: Augustus M. Kelley Publishers, 1971), p. 41; quoted in Stein, "Consider the Lily . . . , Part 4," p. 140n. 41. See also Estate of William Alley, June 12, 1871, through Oct. 10, 1873, Probate Final Record, Book H, pp. 701–15, 720–21, 730–48, CCCC; Schedule 1 (Free Inhabitants), Ninth Census of the United States (1870), Texas, Colorado County.

25. Estate of William Alley, June 12, 1871, through Oct. 10, 1873, Probate Final Record, Book H, pp. 701–15, 720–21, 730–48, CCCC.

26. Slave Schedule, Eighth Census of the United States (1860), Texas, Colorado County; Malone, *Women on the Texas Frontier,* pp. 28, 42.

27. Narrative of James Green, p. 12; White, *Ar'n't I a Woman?,* pp. 28–46; Bardaglio, *Reconstructing the Household,* pp. 49–59; Hine and Thompson, *A Shining Thread of Hope,* pp. 94–99; Stevenson, *Life in Black and White,* pp. 239–46; Boles, *Black Southerners,* p. 132; McMillen, *Southern Women,* pp. 22–25.

28. Narrative of James Green, p. 12; Malone, *Women on the Texas Frontier,* pp. 28–43; Campbell, *An Empire for Slavery,* p. 201; White, *Ar'n't I a Woman?,* pp. 28–46; Bardaglio, *Reconstructing the Household,* pp. 49–59; Hine and Thompson, *A Shining Thread of Hope,* pp. 94–99; Stevenson, *Life in Black and White,* pp. 239–46; Boles, *Black Southerners,* p. 132; McMillen, *Southern Women,* pp. 22–25; Rable, *Civil Wars,* p. 36.

29. Malone, *Women on the Texas Frontier,* p. 47; Hine and Thompson, *A Shining Thread of Hope,* p. 79; Stevenson, *Life in Black and White,* pp. 209, 226; Boles, *Black Southerners,* p. 90.

30. Charles William Tait to father, Aug. 24, 1854, Tait Papers; Narrative of James Green, p. 12. Owners figured at least 5 to 6 percent of their profit would come from the natural increase of slaves. Many slaveholders, like Pinchback, would try to sell slaves who did not have children. See White, *Ar'n't I a Woman?,* pp. 68–69, 98–105, 156–57; Winegarten, *Black Texas Women,* pp. 27–28; Malone, *Women on the Texas Frontier,* pp. 38–41; Catherine Clinton, *Tara Revisited: Women, War, and the Plantation Legend,* pp. 31–34; Frankel, *Freedom's Women,* p. 13; Hine and Thompson, *A Shining Thread of Hope,* pp. 79–81.

31. Narrative of James Green, p. 12. In 1850, 41 percent of slaveholders owned five or fewer slaves. See Schedule 2 (Slave Population), Seventh Census of the United States (1850), Texas, Colorado County; White, *Ar'n't I a Woman?,* pp. 149–55; Winegarten, *Black Texas Women,* pp. 30–32; Eslinger, "The Shape of Slavery," p. 19; Jacqueline Jones, *Labor of Love,* pp. 31–36; Stevenson, *Life in Black and White,* p. 160.

32. Dangerous times in a slave community sometimes followed the death of the master or a marriage. At these times slaves were split up on the basis of fairness to heirs and not always on the basis of slave families. See Malone, *Women on the Texas Frontier,* pp. 41–48; Stevenson, *Life in Black and White,* pp. 209–24; Censer, *North Carolina Planters,* p. 140; Rable, *Civil Wars,* p. 39. In addition to being separated by sale, there was the likelihood of being separated by being "hired out" while the estate was settled. See Campbell, *An Empire for Slavery,* pp. 83, 161; Campbell, "The Slave Hire System in Texas," pp. 107–14.

33. Schedule 1 (Free Population) and Schedule 2 (Slave Population), Seventh and Eighth Censuses of the United States (1850 and 1860), Texas, Colorado County; Probate Records, CCCC; District Court Records, CCDC; Cemetery Records, Nesbitt Memorial Library.

34. Stein, "Consider the Lily . . . , Part 5," p. 7; Amended Petition, *John Crisp v. Mary Crisp,* Dec. 24, 1859, Docket File No. 1418, CCDC; Schedule 1 (Free Population) and Schedule 2 (Slave Population), Seventh and Eighth Censuses of the United States (1850 and 1860), Texas, Colorado County.

35. "Reminiscences of James Williams Holt," pp. 151–57, quotes on p. 153; "Reminiscences of Mrs. F. G. Mahon," *Nesbitt Memorial Library Journal* 9 (Jan., 1999): 41–46, quotes on p. 42.

36. Interrogatory, *Mary A. Hall and Edward H. Hall, administrators of Alexander Anderson v. Eli Mercer,* Sept. 9, 1844, Docket File No. 311, CCDC; Eslinger, "The Shape of Slavery," pp. 2–5; Campbell, *An Empire for Slavery,* pp. 51–56; Cashin, *A Family Venture,* pp. 32–70. Although Texas never passed a law making it illegal to teach a slave to read and write, the majority of southern states from which slaves moved had done so; see Winegarten, *Black Texas Women,* p. 22. Some slaves had messages passed along by their masters; see Cashin, *A Family Venture,* p. 70. Campbell and Pickens published a letter from a wife to her husband when they were separated during the Civil War, but it is unclear who actually wrote it and whether or not her husband had to have someone read it to him; see Randolph Campbell and Donald K. Pickens, " 'My Dearest Husband': A Texas Slave's Love Letter, 1862," *Journal of Negro History* 65 (fall, 1980): 361–64.

37. Schedule 1 (Free Population) and Schedule 2 (Slave Population), Seventh and Eighth Censuses of the United States (1850 and 1860), Texas, Colorado County; Amended Petition, *John Crisp v. Mary Crisp,* Dec. 24, 1859, Docket File No. 1418, CCDC; Winegarten, *Black Texas Women,* pp. 16–17; Eslinger, "The Shape of Slavery," pp. 4–13; Stevenson, *Life in Black and White,* pp. 179–222; Malone, *Women on the Texas Frontier,* p. 47.

38. Estate of William R. Turner, July 27, 1857, Probate Final Record, Book E, pp. 401–402, CCCC; Ann Patton Malone, "Searching for the Family and Household Structure of Rural Louisiana, 1810–1864," *Louisiana History* 28 (fall, 1987): 357–79; McMillen, *Southern Women,* pp. 12–47; Campbell, *An Empire for Slavery,* p. 161; Malone, *Women on the Texas Frontier,* p. 41.

39. Probate Records, Bond and Mortgage Records, Deed Records, CCCC; District Court Records, CCDC. The mother/child relationship was the most recognized throughout the South; see White, *Ar'n't I a Woman?,* pp. 132–34, 159; and Stevenson, *Life in Black and White,* pp. 213–22.

40. See Probate Records, Bond and Deed Records, CCCC; District Court Files, CCDC.

41. Not all sales of slaves were recorded in the courthouse. Probated estates recorded more transfers than any other type of legal proceeding. Other sales were most often recorded when a mortgage accompanied the sale, although simple sales were occasionally recorded. See Probate Records, Bond and Mortgage Records, Deed Records, CCCC. Campbell shows that slaves were hired out, sold, and mortgaged for extra cash. He documented one case of a six-week-old female being "mortgaged"; see Campbell, *An Empire for Slavery,* p. 164. There was no legal provision in Texas prohibiting separation of slave mothers and children; see Malone, *Women on the Texas Frontier,* p. 50.

42. Estate of Susan Ann Gardner, Estate of George W. Gardner, Guardianship of Robert Jones Moseley, Guardianship of William R. and James Hamilton Stevenson, Feb. 2, 1848, through June 24, 1861, Probate Minutes, Books C, D, and E, and Probate Final Record, Books C, D, and E, CCCC.

43. Office Sub Assistant Commander, Columbus, to Capt. W. H. Hrinnstead, Bureau Sub Assistant Hallettsville, Jan. 21, 1867; to Dr. C. P. Brown, Mar. 2, 1867; to Brt Maj Genl. A. Doubleday, Sub Assistant Commander, Galveston, June 4, 1867; to Genl Burr at Galveston, June 27, 1867; and to many others, in Letters Sent, Record Group 105, Bureau Refugees Freedmen & Abandoned Lands, National Archives, Washington, D.C. (all subsequent citations hereinafter referred to as BRFAL; refer to Record Group 105). Regarding

separation of families and the desire to reunite them after emancipation, see Winegarten, *Black Texas Women,* pp. 42−45; Barry A. Crouch, "The Freedmen's Bureau in Colorado County, Texas, 1865−1868—Part 3," *Nesbitt Memorial Library Journal* 8 (Jan., 1998): 3−5; James Smallwood, "Black Freedwomen after Emancipation: The Texas Experience," *Prologue* 27 (1995): 303−17; Peter Bardaglio, "The Children of Jubilee: African American Childhood in Wartime," in Catherine Clinton and Nina Silber, eds., *Divided Houses: Gender and the Civil War,* p. 226; Edwards, *Gendered Strife and Confusion,* p. 46; Hine and Thompson, *A Shining Thread of Hope,* pp. 148−51; Tera W. Hunter, *To 'Joy My Freedom: Southern Black Women's Lives and Labors after the Civil War,* p. 40; Jacqueline Jones, *Labor of Love,* pp. 55, 78; Leslie A. Schwalm, *A Hard Fight for We: Women's Transition from Slavery to Freedom in South Carolina,* pp. 151−55, 209, 267; Cheryll Ann Cody, "Sale and Separation: Four Crises for Enslaved Women on the Ball Plantations, 1764−1854," in Larry E. Hudson, Jr., ed., *Working toward Freedom: Slave Society and Domestic Economy in the American South,* pp. 119−42.

CHAPTER 5. CIVIL WAR

1. *Colorado Citizen,* May 30, 1860, p. 1. In the same issue a short snippet asked, "Why is the Union of these States like a marriage vow?" and answered, "Because it was entered in to never to be broken." Also see *Colorado Citizen,* Feb. 16, 1861, p. 1. Bill Stein points out that the editors did not necessarily react to Lincoln's election with calls for immediate secession. In the election of delegates to the Secession Convention, the *Citizen* endorsed A. H. Davidson and John Shropshire; the former supported secession while the latter opposed it. After Davidson and another secession supporter, T. Scott Anderson, were elected, the *Citizen's* editors "joined the chorus"; see Stein, "Consider the Lily . . . , Part 5," pp. 47−50. Ten other Texas counties with a majority German population did vote against secession. See John B. Boles, *The South through Time: A History of an American Region,* p. 295.

2. R. V. Cook in *Colorado Citizen,* Oct. 12, 1861, p. 2; *Colorado Citizen,* Mar. 2, 1861, p. 2. The editor's response to the representative's story was "Pretty good." See also July 6, 1861, p. 1; Aug. 3, 1861, p. 2; "A Great Feat," Aug. 10, 1861, p. 1; and Sept. 14, 1861, p. 1. For a discussion of the meanings of women's support and the reasons for glorifying women's sacrifices, see Clinton, *Tara Revisited,* pp. 139−59; and Drew Gilpin Faust, "Altars of Sacrifice: Confederate Women and the Narratives of War," in Clinton and Silber, eds., *Divided Houses,* p. 174.

3. "Ladies Meeting," *Colorado Citizen,* July 6, 1861, p. 2; Editor's Column, *Colorado Citizen,* Aug. 3, 1861, p. 2; "Banner Presentation," *Colorado Citizen,* Aug. 24, 1861, p. 1; and Letter from R. V. Cook, *Coloardo Citizen,* Oct. 12, 1861, p. 2. For examples in other parts of the South, see Drew Gilpin Faust, *Mothers of Invention: Women of the Slaveholding South in the American Civil War,* pp. 11−27; Whites, *Civil War as a Crisis in Gender,* pp. 30−31, 40, 47−49; Clinton, *Tara Revisited,* pp. 79−82; Rable, *Civil Wars,* p. 32.

4. "Hoops for the 'Braveboys,'" *Colorado Citizen,* Sept. 7, 1861, p. 2; John Samuel Shropshire to Caroline Tait Shropshire, Sept. 28, 1861, in "Civil War Letters of John Samuel Shropshire," *Nesbitt Memorial Library Journal* 7 (Jan., 1997): 62. See also Clinton, *Tara Revisited,* p. 57.

5. "Helen," *Colorado Citizen,* Sept. 21, 1861, p. 2; Whites, *Civil War as a Crisis in Gender,* pp. 10−24; Rable, *Civil Wars,* pp. 46−51, 139−42. Women were expected to repress their concern for relatives and kin for the good of the South and not only allow them, but

encourage them to go to war. See Faust, *Mothers of Invention,* pp. 17–18; Faust, "Altars of Sacrifice," pp. 172, 178; Clinton, *Tara Revisited,* p. 59.

6. John Samuel Shropshire to Caroline Tait Shropshire, Jan. 26, 1862, in "Civil War Letters," p. 69. See also Joan Cashin, "'Since the War Broke Out': The Marriage of Kate and William McLure," in Clinton and Silber, eds., *Divided Houses,* pp. 208–12. The Civil War, at least in the beginning, made even clearer to women their helplessness and dependence when they felt they had no role to play in the conflict; see Faust, *Mothers of Invention,* p. 22; and Whites, *Civil War as a Crisis in Gender,* pp. 31–37. Women knew more about running plantations than they admitted because the Civil War was not the first time individual women had been left in charge of the plantations; see Rable, *Civil Wars,* pp. 32, 113.

7. Rable, *Civil Wars,* pp. 113–15; Whites, *Civil War as a Crisis in Gender,* p. 38; Cashin, "Since the War Broke Out," pp. 201–12. As men were removed to battlefields, husbands and wives were made strangers to each other and to each other's lives; see Faust, *Mothers of Invention,* p. 10.

8. Faust, *Mothers of Invention,* p. 10; Cashin, "Since the War Broke Out," pp. 200–12; Randolph B. Campbell, *Grass-Roots Reconstruction in Texas, 1865–1880,* pp. 8, 30–31; Campbell, *An Empire for Slavery,* p. 231; Clinton, *Tara Revisited,* pp. 109–14, 149–52; Whites, *Civil War as a Crisis in Gender,* pp. 5, 62; Rable, *Civil Wars,* pp. 91–111; Faust, "Altars of Sacrifice," pp. 182–83.

9. Petition, *B. T. Ingram v. E. K. Turner,* Aug. 31, 1865, Docket File No. 1810, CCDC (quote); Boles, *The South through Time,* pp. 342–43; Clinton, *Tara Revisited,* p. 114; Cashin, "Since the War Broke Out," pp. 204, 208–12. Evidence exists for other soldiers from many different sources. For instance, in his wife's divorce petition Beverly M. Lacy is described as having been a soldier at home on furlough, but he was not one of the soldiers in the four Colorado County volunteer companies; see Petition, *Ellen Lacy v. Beverly M. Lacy,* Sept. 7, 1865, Docket File No. 1813, CCDC. Forty-one more soldiers from Colorado County but not listed in these companies can be found in the Widow's Confederate Pension Records. These were men who served in the army and had widows who survived until at least 1899 but never remarried, remained in Colorado County, and were in destitute enough circumstances to warrant a Confederate widow's pension. Undoubtedly, there were many more who served but did not meet all of those criteria. See Confederate Pensions, Colorado County, Texas, Texas State Archives, Austin, Texas. Of the men buried in existing Colorado County cemeteries, 156 were Confederate veterans, and at least 4 fought in the Union army.

10. *Colorado Citizen,* Oct. 12, 1861, p. 2; Colorado County Historical Commission, comp., *Colorado County Chronicles,* vol. 1, pp. 79, 904; District Court Minutes, 1861–65; Rupert Norval Richardson, Ernest Wallace, and Adrian N. Anderson, *Texas: The Lone Star State,* 4th ed., p. 234.

11. Clinton, *Tara Revisited,* p. 109; Whites, *Civil War as a Crisis in Gender,* p. 5.

12. Women elsewhere in the South also moved into the roles of taking care of businesses and working for wages during the war. A quote from Faust's *Mothers of Invention* reads, "Ladies keep the stores here now . . . their husband [*sic*] having joined the army" (pp. 80–90).

13. Deposition, *J. G. Walker v. James A. Darby et al.,* Apr. 17, 1866, Docket File No. 2032, CCDC.

14. *J. G. Walker v. James A. Darby et al.,* Apr. 17, 1866, through Mar. 2, 1869, Docket File No. 2032, CCDC. Although originally named as defendants, the plaintiff dismissed the case "as to V. D. Le Tulle and endorsers" before proceeding to a jury. See Mar. 2, 1869, District Court Minutes, Book D, p. 212, CCDC.

15. Bond and Mortgage Records, Book E, p. 622, Apr. 3, 1862, CCCC. For seven cases

see Amended Petition, *L. M. Newsom v. William J. Darden and wife,* Nov. 5, 1856, Docket File No. 1173; Petition, *Thomas J. Neavitt v. W. J. Darden and wife,* Apr. 18, 1857, Docket File No. 1224; Petition, *John Williams v. Darden and wife,* Feb. 18, 1858, Docket File No. 1307; Petition, *Woodson Coffee v. W. J. Darden,* Apr. 19, 1858, Docket File No. 1356; Petition, *Charles Schmidt v. W. J. Darden and F. A. Darden,* Mar. 14, 1861, Docket File No. 1645; Answer, *Blum and Mayblum v. W. J. Darden et al.,* May 6, 1859, Docket File No. 1425; Petition, *Blum and Mayblum v. W. J. Darden et al.,* Jan. 28, 1860, Docket File No. 1493—all in CCDC.

16. Bond and Mortgage Records, Book E, p. 658, Mar. 1, 1863, CCCC.

17. Deed Records Transcribed, Book L, p. 518, Mar. 20, 1865, CCCC.

18. Petition, *Robert E. Stafford v. Martha Pankey et al.,* Oct. 19, 1866, Docket File No. 2099, CCDC.

19. Indictment, *State of Texas v. William Thompson et al.,* May 5, 1866, Docket File No. 594; Petition and Deposition, *C. W. Nelson v. William Alley,* Apr. 2, 1866, and Feb. 25, 1867, Docket File No. 2040; Oldham and White, *Digest of General Statute Laws,* p. 313.

20. Estate of Eliza Grace, Apr. 28, 1862, Probate Final Record, Book F, p. 550, CCCC. See also Estate of Elvy Ann Carson, Aug. 27, 1866, Probate Final Record, Book G, pp. 41–45, CCCC.

21. Estate of Eliza Grace, Apr. 28, 1862, Probate Final Record, Book F, p. 550, CCCC.

22. Estate of O. P. Kimbrough, Apr. 29, 1861, Probate Minutes, Book E, p. 199; Estate of William J. Wright, Oct. 16, 1861, Final Probate Record, Book F, pp. 555–56; Estate of Abraham Alley, June 16, 1862, Final Probate Record, Book G, pp. 189–90; Estate of D. A. Hubbard, Nov. 24, 1862, Probate Minutes, Book E, p. 253; Estate of James Cone, Jan. 26, 1864, Probate Minutes, Book E, p. 300; Estate of J. C. Bullington, June 27, 1864, and Oct. 31, 1864, Probate Minutes, Book E, pp. 320, 328—all in CCCC.

23. Petition, *H. F. Dunson et al. v. Josiah F. Payne,* Sept. 16, 1872, Docket File No. 2882, CCDC.

24. Estate of C. Windrow, Aug. 25, 1862, through Oct. 30, 1865, Probate Minutes, Book E, pp. 11, 244, 263, 264, 276, 334, 342, 348, CCCC; Petition, *H. F. Dunson et al. v. Josiah F. Payne,* Sept. 16, 1872, Docket File No. 2882, CCDC; Estate of James W. Carson, Jan. 27, 1862, through Oct. 20, 1865, Probate Minutes, Book E, pp. 220, 239, 316, 317, 343–46, CCCC.

25. Estate of Jesse W. Tanner, Apr. 28, 1862, Probate Minutes, Book E, p. 231; Estate of Allen Kuykendall, Apr. 27, 1863, Probate Minutes, Book E, p. 277—both in CCCC.

26. Rable, *Civil Wars,* pp. 83–85; Clinton, *Tara Revisited,* pp. 114–15. Older families were often wealthier as well, so some, but not necessarily all, husbands in this wealth bracket were too old to fight in the army or be conscripted. See Petition, *Maria Dungan admx. of Frank Dungan, decd. v. Conrad Shupp,* June 4, 1867, Docket File No. 2151, CCDC.

27. The average age of those who chose to administer (thirty-five) was higher than the average age of those who chose not to administer (twenty-eight), with the biggest difference seen between those who chose to coadminister and others (average age forty-eight for coadministrators, thirty-two for administrators, and twenty-eight for no administrators).

28. "Hoops for the 'Braveboys,'" *Colorado Citizen,* Sept. 7, 1861, p. 2; Marriage Record Index, Book D, 1861–65, CCCC. Although 1861 witnessed a record number of marriages, the number was not significantly higher than the number of marriages during the antebellum years. Between 1853 and 1860 the number of marriages per year averaged forty-two: 1853—forty-four; 1854—thirty-nine; 1855—forty-two; 1856—thirty-two; 1857—forty-five; 1858—fifty; 1859—thirty-eight; 1860—forty-three. See Marriage Record Index, Books B, C, D, 1853–60, CCCC; Rable, *Civil Wars,* pp. 51–53.

29. Petition, *S. T. and J. Harbert v. Mary Toland,* May 4, 1865, Docket File No. 1803; Petition, *M. Reichmann and Co. v. H. L. Lackey and Louisa Odom,* Sept. 22, 1865, Docket File No. 1821; Petition, *Julia A. Curry v. A. Cryer et al.,* Sept. 22, 1865, Docket File No. 1819; Petition, *Elizabeth McAshan v. J. S. Hancock,* Mar. 19, 1866, Docket File No. 1978; *S. E. Kuykendall v. T. G. Schultz,* July 22, 1870, Justice of the Peace Docket Book, p. 104; Petition, *Noah Bonds and wife v. J. W. E. Wallace,* Oct. 12, 1865, Docket File No. 1846; Petition, *Lucy Byars v. B. M. Lacey et al.,* Oct. 17, 1865, Docket File No. 1862; Petition, *Mary A. Taylor v. Jno C. Slaton et al.,* Oct. 8, 1866, Docket File No. 2081, all in CCDC; Estate of Sarah A. Mason, decd, Mar. 31, 1862, Probate Minutes, Book E, p. 230, CCCC.

30. Petition, *Leonora Miller v. John D. Taylor,* Aug. 22, 1865, Docket File No. 1808, CCDC.

31. Petition, *B. T. Ingram v. E. K. Turner,* Aug. 31, 1865, Docket File No. 1810, CCDC.

32. Petition, *B. T. Ingram v. E. K. Turner,* Aug. 31, 1865, Docket File No. 1810, CCDC; Faust, *Mothers of Invention,* pp. 51–71; Faust, "Altars of Sacrifice," pp. 182–84; Drew Gilpin Faust, "Trying To Do a Man's Business: Gender, Violence, and Slave Management in Civil War Texas," *Gender and History* 4 (summer, 1992): 197–214; Jacqueline Jones, *Labor of Love,* p. 48.

33. Faust, *Mothers of Invention,* p. 32; Whites, *Civil War as a Crisis in Gender,* pp. 65–75, 89; Clinton, *Tara Revisited,* pp. 79, 144–45; Rable, *Civil Wars,* pp. 63–111; Faust, "Altars of Sacrifice," pp. 193–99; Bynum, *Unruly Women,* pp. 121, 130–50.

34. Colorado County Court Minutes, Book 2, pp. 424–25; Police Court Minutes Book, 1862–76, pp. 3–22.

35. Rable, *Civil Wars,* pp. 51, 193–95.

36. Petition, *Martha A. Conner v. Stephen Conner,* Sept. 30, 1864, Docket File No. 1788, CCDC; copy of marriage certificate, *Martha A. Conner v. Stephen Conner,* Apr. 30, 1866 (entered into evidence), Docket File No. 1788, CCDC. Faust found examples of conflict between the mothers and wives of absent soldiers as families combined without the presence of the one person who held them in common; see Faust, *Mothers of Invention,* p. 37.

37. Petition, *George Metz v. Sarah Metz,* Aug. 29, 1865, Docket File No. 1807, CCDC. They had married in 1849. In 1865 George was sixty years old and Sarah was thirty-two. See Marriage Records, Book B, CCCC; Schedule 1 (Free Inhabitants), Eighth Census of the United States (1860), Texas, Colorado County.

38. Deposition of Peninah Daniel wife of Wm. Daniel, Oct. 24, 1865, Docket File No. 1807, CCDC.

39. Petition, *George Metz v. Sarah Metz,* Aug. 19, 1865, Docket File No. 1807, CCDC; Bond and Mortgage Records, Book E, p. 96, Dec. 8, 1856, CCCC. Rumors abounded in the South about illicit affairs. See Faust, *Mothers of Invention,* p. 126.

40. Petition, *E. H. Blum v. Emma Blum,* Mar. 12, 1862, Docket File No. 1764, CCDC. Victoria Bynum, "Reshaping the Bonds of Womanhood: Divorce in Reconstruction North Carolina," in Clinton and Silber, eds., *Divided Houses,* p. 79; Bynum, *Unruly Women,* pp. 119–20.

41. Petition, *H. A. Tatum v. Jane Tatum,* Oct. 7, 1864, Docket File No. 1790, CCDC.

42. Answer, *H. A. Tatum v. Jane Tatum,* May 3, 1865, Docket File No. 1790, CCDC.

43. Ellen Lacy sued for divorce three times before finally pursuing the case to a jury. The first two cases were dismissed when Ellen chose to believe Beverly's protestations of reform.

44. Petition, *Sylvania Olds v. Jno T. Olds,* Oct. 4, 1860, Docket File No. 1563; Petition, *Martha Richardson v. Benjamin F. Richardson,* Apr. 5, 1861, Docket File No. 1710; Petition,

Martha Conner v. Stephen Conner, Sept. 30, 1864, Docket File No. 1788; Petition, *H. A. Tatum v. Jane Tatum*, Oct. 7, 1864, Docket File No. 1790—all in CCDC.

45. A "breakdown in expectations about men's and women's roles" within marriage occurred during the war. When men were no longer there to perform their function of protection, relationships were often strained as women and men sought new foundations for their marriages. See Faust, *Mothers of Invention*, p. 136; Rable, *Civil Wars*, pp. 59–61; Cashin, "Since the War Broke Out," p. 206.

46. Whites, *Civil War as a Crisis in Gender*, p. 5; Rable, *Civil Wars*, pp. 157–58; Faust, "Altars of Sacrifice," p. 198.

CHAPTER 6. LONG-AWAITED PEACE

1. Translation of letter from Helen Maas Ruhmann to Emma Jungbecker Ruhmann, Frelsburg, June 5, 1865, printed in Dorothy Beasley Ruhmann, *Ruhmann and Beasley Family Roots* (Portland, Tex.: Published by the author, 1994), p. 2.55. Men and women probably had different reactions to the war's end. While many men felt defeated, disheartened, and disappointed, many women celebrated the end of the destruction of lives and an end to the fear that their loved ones would die in battle. See Whites, *Civil War as a Crisis in Gender*, p. 139.

2. Campbell, *Grass-Roots Reconstruction in Texas;* Campbell, "Reconstruction in Colorado County," pp. 3–30; Colorado County Historical Commission, comp., *Colorado County Chronicles,* vol. 1, pp. 126–60; Richardson, Wallace, and Anderson, *Texas,* pp. 244–65.

3. *Colorado Citizen,* May 6, 1869, p. 2, and Oct. 12, 1871, p. 3.

4. *Colorado Citizen,* Mar. 16, 1871, p. 1, and May 11, 1871, p. 2; Edwards, *Gendered Strife and Confusion,* pp. 120–30; Rable, *Civil Wars,* pp. 230–33.

5. Eric Foner, *A Short History of Reconstruction, 1863–1877,* p. 56; Campbell, *Grass-Roots Reconstruction in Texas,* pp. 30–31; Richardson, Wallace, and Anderson, *Texas,* pp. 263–65; Colorado County Historical Commission, comp., *Colorado County Chronicles,* vol. 1, pp. 134–36; Rable, *Civil Wars,* pp. 221, 287–88.

6. Petition, *Ellen Lacy v. Beverly Lacy,* Sept. 7, 1865, Docket File No. 1813, CCDC.

7. Barry A. Crouch, "The Freedmen's Bureau in Colorado County, Texas, 1865–1868," *Nesbitt Memorial Library Journal* 5 (May, 1995): 71; Campbell, *An Empire for Slavery,* p. 249; Campbell, "Reconstruction in Colorado County," pp. 3–30; Narrative of James Green, p. 13.

8. *Colorado Citizen,* Mar. 16, 1871, p. 1; Petition, *Ellen Lacy v. Beverly Lacy,* Sept. 7, 1865, Docket File No. 1813, CCDC; Edwards, *Gendered Strife and Confusion,* pp. 117–18; Rable, *Civil Wars,* pp. 255–56; Whites, *Civil War as a Crisis in Gender,* p. 145; Scott, *The Southern Lady,* p. 107; Faust, *Mothers of Invention,* pp. 249–50.

9. Edwards, *Gendered Strife and Confusion,* pp. 102–104, 147, 167; Hine and Thompson, *A Shining Thread of Hope,* pp. 152–53; Jacqueline Jones, *Labor of Love,* p. 58; Whites, *Civil War as a Crisis in Gender,* p. 150. For a discussion of the reasons for the labor shortage, see also Roger L. Ransom and Richard Sutch, *One Kind of Freedom: The Economic Consequences of Emancipation.* The labor shortage increased calls for immigration into the county; see *Colorado Citizen,* Feb. 27, 1873, p. 1.

10. Office Sub Assistant Commander, Columbus, to Mrs. Elizabeth Turner, Columbus, May 17, 1866, Letters Sent, BRFAL; Hunter, *To 'Joy My Freedom,* pp. 28, 52; Jacqueline

Jones, *Labor of Love,* pp. 54−57; Rable, *Civil Wars,* p. 257; Schwalm, *A Hard Fight for We,* pp. 207−10.

11. Editor's Column, *Colorado Citizen,* Oct. 12, 1871, p. 3. See also "Special Notices," *Colorado Citizen,* Nov. 2, 1871, p. 2, where Mrs. Withers, "Professor of Music," thanked the people of the community for their kindness on the death of her husband. Ellen Lacy was teaching school to "support" herself in 1869, at least; see Petition, *Ellenora Lacy v. Beverly Lacy,* Sept. 13, 1869, District Court Docket File No. 2374, CCDC. See also Scott, *The Southern Lady,* pp. 107−10; Edwards, *Gendered Strife and Confusion,* pp. 140−41; Faust, "Altars of Sacrifice," p. 187; Rable, *Civil Wars,* pp. 244, 277−78; Whites, *Civil War as a Crisis in Gender,* p. 156.

12. Office Sub Assistant Commander, Columbus, to Superintendent of Education, Galveston, Jan. 18, 1867, Letters Sent; Office Sub Assistant Commander, Columbus, to Superintendent of Education, Galveston, June 14, 1867, Letters Sent; Office Sub Assistant Commander, Columbus, to Superintendent of Education, Galveston, Apr. 24, 1868, Letters Sent; Office Superintendent of Education, Galveston, to E. M. Harris Esquire Sub Assistant Commander, Columbus, July 11 and 18, 1867, Letters Received—all BRFAL. See Winegarten, *Black Texas Women,* p. 86; Ella Forbes, *African American Women during the Civil War,* p. 113.

13. *Colorado Citizen,* Feb. 22, 1872, p. 3, and Feb. 27, 1873, p. 3; Petition, *Mrs. B. Foote v. J. W. Johnson and J. P. Harris,* Jan. 22, 1872, Docket File No. 2779, CCDC; Police Court Minutes, 1862−76, p. 103, Oct. 14, 1867, CCCC; Mrs. E. Haskell to Major E. M. Harris, Sub Assistant Commander, Columbus, Aug. 29, 1867, Letters Received, BRFAL; *Colorado Citizen,* Feb. 22, 1872, p. 3.

14. Estate of John Bryan, Aug. 13, 1867, and Nov. 15, 1867, Probate Final Record, Book G, pp. 516−17, 520−21; Estate of Adolph Rhode, Dec. 5, 1867, Probate Final Record, Book G, pp. 707−709; Dec. 27, 1869, Probate Minutes, Book F, p. 80, CCCC. See Schedule 1, Ninth Census of the United States (1870), Texas, Colorado County. A. Doregan won her case in Justice of the Peace and the District Court against William Fondren "brought on open a/c for goods"; see Petition, *A. Doregan v. Wm. Fondren,* June 28, 1872, Docket File No. 2860, CCDC; Petition, Citations, and Answers, *C. & R Traylor v. W. C. Crebbs and others,* Jan. 19, Feb. 10, Feb. 27, and Feb. 29, 1871, Docket File No. 2615, CCDC; Criminal Execution Docket, 1867−71, Justice of the Peace notes, pp. 62, 63, 66, 81, 97, 104, 116, 117, 118, 229, 267, CCDC.

15. Petition, *T. P. Hubbard v. Mary Taylor and Saml. B. Dehart,* Apr. 10, 1866, Docket File No. 1998; Petition, *Julia A. Currie v. Gui Carlton (freedman),* Nov. 23, 1866, Docket File No. 2102; Agreement to Arbitrate, *Julia A. Currie v. John Hester,* Nov. 18, 1867, Docket File No. 2204; Petition, *Julia A. Currie v. David H. Crisp,* May 11, 1871, Docket File No. 2659, all in CCDC. Also, Schedule 1, Ninth Census of the United States (1870), Texas, Colorado County. Also, J. Ernest Goodman, Sub Assistant Commander, Columbus, to Mrs. Elizabeth Turner, May 17 1866, Letters Sent; Office Sub Assistant Commander, to N. C. Eason, Prairie Point, June 3, 1867, all in BRFAL. See also Sub Assistant Commander, Columbus, to Mrs. C. A. Eason, Aug. 20, 1867, Letters Sent; Sub Assistant Commander, Columbus, to Mrs. S. Haskell, Columbus, July 7, 1867, Letters Sent, all in BRFAL.

16. In 1860, 15 percent of families had sons eighteen or older, and this figure was 18 percent in 1870. Families with sons thirteen or older at home increased from 30 percent to 51 percent in 1870. See Schedule 1, Eighth and Ninth Censuses of the United States (1860 and 1870), Texas, Colorado County.

17. Out of 938 adult white women, 30 listed occupations other than keeping house, attending school, or at home; see Schedule 1, Ninth Census of the United States (1870), Texas, Colorado County.

18. Schedule 1, Ninth Census of the United States (1870), Texas, Colorado County; Scott, *The Southern Lady*, p. 107. Roan, or Ann, Guy listed "keeping house" and Mrs. Sarah Arnold listed "at home" as their occupations, although both made money by taking in boarders. Jane D. Greer listed her occupation as "keeping house" although conducting some type of trading.

19. Jacqueline Jones, *Labor of Love*, p. 46.

20. Schedule 1, Ninth Census of the United States (1870), Texas, Colorado County. See Jacqueline Jones, *Labor of Love*, p. 46; Winegarten, *Black Texas Women*, p. 43.

21. Edwards, *Gendered Strife and Confusion*, pp. 27–30, 110–36; Whites, *Civil War as a Crisis in Gender*, pp. 101, 134–46; Rable, *Civil Wars*, pp. 223–33, 266–72; Nina Silber, "Intemperate Men, Spiteful Women, and Jefferson Davis," in Clinton and Silber, eds., *Divided Houses*, p. 295. Drew Faust argues that southern women wished to shift some of their burdens back to the men in their lives after the war. Additionally, the attempt to form new relations with former slaves where the hierarchy of race was preserved undermined women's willingness to challenge the familial patriarchy. According to Faust in *Mothers of Invention*, "In the face of the frightening reality of black emancipation, however, white women came to regard the rehabilitation of patriarchy as a bargain they were compelled to accept" (p. 247).

22. This argument was first ably argued by Anne Firor Scott in *The Southern Lady*. Other historians still echo this view. The editors of *Divided Houses* claim that "white women gained a new sense of confidence in their ability to manage and make decisions, a confidence which many historians believe extended into the postwar period"; see Clinton and Silber, eds., *Divided Houses*, pp. 168–69. See also Clinton, *Tara Revisited*, p. 166.

23. Marriage Record Index, Book D, 1861–65, CCCC. Although 1861 witnessed a record number of marriages, the number was not significantly higher than the number of marriages during the antebellum years. Between 1853 and 1860 the number of marriages per year averaged forty-two (see chap. 5, note 28, for the breakdown by years). See Marriage Record Index, Books B–G, 1853–76, CCCC. In 1860 females made up 39 percent of the adult white population, while in 1870 they comprised 46 percent. In 1860 adult single white women constituted 19.1 percent of the adult white population, and in 1870 they represented 21 percent; see Schedule 1, Eighth and Ninth Censuses of the United States (1860 and 1870), Texas, Colorado County. The pressure to marry throughout the South remained great even in areas where there was a shortage of marriageable men. See Bardaglio, *Reconstructing the Household*, p. 130; Edwards, *Gendered Strife and Confusion*, pp. 130–31; Bynum, "Reshaping the Bonds of Womanhood," p. 328; Rable, *Civil Wars*, pp. 249–61, 281–83; Whites, *Civil War as a Crisis in Gender*, pp. 147–49. Other historians have questioned Scott's assertion that there was a generation of women without men; see Jacquelyn Dowd Hall and Anne Firor Scott, "Women in the South," in John B. Boles and Evelyn Thomas Nolen, eds., *Interpreting Southern History: Historiographical Essays in Honor of Sanford W. Higginbotham*, p. 476. Hall and Scott refer, in particular, to Jonathan M. Wiener, "Female Planters and Planters' Wives in Civil War and Reconstruction: Alabama, 1850–1870," *Alabama Review* 30 (Apr., 1977): 135–49.

24. Suzanne Lebsock's study found that despite the "radical" promise of reconstruction, despite women's relative "independence" during the war, and despite the rare opportunity

of drafting new constitutions, "few additional powers were granted to women during the entire period of Republican rule." Some historians found legal progress for women in the married women's property provisions included in the Reconstruction constitutions. Lebsock argues that in these states, "the Reconstruction period . . . but one phase of an ongoing process of reform that had begun in Mississippi in 1839"; see Suzanne Lebsock, "Radical Reconstruction and the Property Rights of Southern Women," *Journal of Southern History* 43 (May, 1977): 196–97. See also Lazarou, "Concealed under Petticoats," p. 42. Texas had enacted married women's property provisions in 1840, and therefore the Reconstruction laws on the matter were no advancement for Texas women. A Nov., 1871, law gave married women appointed administrators of estates the right to post a bond using their separate property as security even if their husbands refused to join as securities; see Gammel, comp., *The Laws of Texas,* vol. 7, p. 24.

25. Bond and Mortgage Records, Book F, p. 201, Feb. 7, 1868, CCCC; Petition for Injunction, *J. H. Murray and wife v. Jones McWilliams et al.,* Oct. 26, 1868, Docket File No. 2305, CCDC.

26. Petition and Answer, *James Courtney v. H. Kussatz,* Feb. 28, 1870, and Mar. 11, 1870, Docket File No. 2422, CCDC.

27. Deed Records Transcribed, Book N, p. 4, June 20, 1868; p. 187, Nov. 13, 1868, CCCC.

28. Petition, *Thomas H. Garner v. Philip E. Waddell et al.,* Feb. 27, 1868, Docket File No. 2243; Petition, *D. D. Claiborne v. P. E. Waddell and L. A. Claiborne,* Jan. 4, 1868, Docket File No. 2216; Petition and Decree, *Noah Bonds and wife v. Sion Bostick,* Mar. 16, 1866, Docket File No. 1975—all in CCDC.

29. Petition, *Emeline Cherry v. C. Burger and F. Otell,* Dec. 9, 1872, Docket File No. 2902, CCDC.

30. Oldham and White, *Digest of the Laws of Texas,* p. 696.

31. Petition, Sept. 9, 1870, Answer, Oct. 7, 1870, *Ernestine Illg v. Wm Burford, F. M. C.,* Docket File No. 2521; Feb. 27, 1871, District Court Minutes, Book D, p. 530—both in CCDC.

32. Petition and Answer, *Ernestine Illg v. Wm Burford et al.,* May 16, 1871, and June 9, 1871, Docket File No. 2667, CCDC.

33. *Ernestine Illg v. Wm Burford et al.,* Feb. 3, 1873, District Court Minutes, Book E, p. 440; Amended Answer, *Ernestine Illg v. Wm Burford et al.,* Oct. 9, 1873, Docket File No. 2667—both in CCDC.

34. Writ of garnishment, *Ernestine Illg v. Wm Burford et al.,* May 31, 1876, Docket File No. 2667, CCDC.

35. Bond and Mortgage Records, Book F; Deed Records Transcribed, Books L, M, N, and O—all in CCCC. Fewer freedmen and freedwomen were able to acquire land in Texas than in other southern states. Elsewhere they took advantage of government policies that allowed them to buy or rent federal lands. The federal government did not own any land in Texas. Although there was plenty of vacant land in western Texas, the state legislature passed laws prohibiting African Americans from homesteading there. See Merline Pitre, "A Note on the Historiography of Blacks in the Reconstruction of Texas," *Journal of Negro History* 66 (summer, 1981): 340–48.

36. Office of Sub Assistant Commander, Columbus, to S. M. Swenson, Apr. 11, 1868, Letters Sent; Swante M. Swenson, New York, to Edwin W. Stevenston, Sub Assistant Commander, Apr. 24, 1868, Letters Received—all in BRFAL. There is no evidence that Swenson ever lived in Colorado County.

37. Office of Sub Assistant Commander, Columbus, to George Thatcher, Aug. 20, 1867, Letters Sent, BRFAL. See also *Office of Sub Assistant Commander, Reuben Blackburn and wife et al. v. A. J. Smith,* and *George Williams and wife et al. v. George Thatcher,* p. 15, Docket Criminal and Civil, 14th Sub District of Texas, Aug. 20, 1867; Office of Sub Assistant Commander, Columbus, to D. Draub, Mar. 5, 1868; to George Turner, Apr. 24, 1868, Letters Sent; Office of Sub Assistant Commander, *Calvin Currey, c[olored], v. George Turner,* Docket Criminal and Civil, 14th Sub District of Texas; Liz Stevens to Office of Sub Assistant Commander, Dec. 28, 1867, Letters Received; Sub Assistant Commissioner, Docket Criminal and Civil, 14th Sub District of Texas—all in BRFAL. For reasons that few freedmen and freedwomen used courts, see Catherine Clinton, "Reconstructing Freedwomen," in Clinton and Silber, eds., *Divided Houses,* p. 318; Donald G. Nieman, *To Set the Law in Motion: The Freedmen's Bureau and the Legal Rights of Blacks, 1865–1868,* pp. 182–83; Schwalm, *A Hard Fight for We,* p. 261.

38. Barry A. Crouch, "The 'Chords of Love': Legalizing Black Marital and Family Rights in Postwar Texas," *Journal of Negro History* 79 (fall, 1994): 334–51; Winegarten, *Black Texas Women,* pp. 50–55; Bardaglio, *Reconstructing the Household,* p. 131; Bardaglio, "The Children of Jubilee," p. 226; Clinton, "Reconstructing Freedwomen," p. 307; Edwards, *Gendered Strife and Confusion,* pp. 45–47; Frankel, *Freedom's Women,* pp. 29–30; Hunter, *To 'Joy My Freedom,* p. 38; Schwalm, *A Hard Fight for We,* pp. 243–46; Smallwood, "Black Freedwomen after Emancipation," p. 315; Marriage Records, Books C2 and D, CCCC; *Colorado Citizen,* Dec. 14, 1871, p. 3.

39. Schedule 1, Ninth Census of the United States (1870), Texas, Colorado County. Other historians found similar patterns throughout Texas; see Smallwood, "Black Freedwomen after Emancipation," pp. 854–55; Campbell, "Reconstruction in Colorado County," p. 28; Crouch, "Chords of Love," p. 346; Winegarten, *Black Texas Women,* pp. 53–55.

40. Schedule 1 (Free Inhabitants), Eighth and Ninth Censuses of the United States (1860 and 1870), Texas, Colorado County. The numbers of single women involved in lawsuits do not include women acting as administrators of estates or minors. Overall there were roughly 942 total cases filed in district courts in the eight and a half years of the antebellum period and 1,208 cases in the eight and a half years of Reconstruction, a 28 percent increase; see District Court Docket Files, CCDC.

41. Estate of Robert H. Tobin, May 12, 1866, and Aug. 28, 1866, Probate Final Record, Book G, pp. 281, 287, CCCC; Petition, *A. V. Worthy v. Martha C. Tobin et al.,* Aug. 21, 1873, Docket File No. 2981, CCDC. Julia Ann Stalle also filed an application for property to be set aside to her the next Jan.; see Estate of F. Stalle, Feb. 10, 1866, and Jan. 28, 1867, Probate Final Record, Book G, pp. 496, 499; and Estate of W. B. Roever, Apr. 9, 1869, Probate Minutes, Book E, p. 236—all in CCCC.

42. Estate of William J. Harbert, June 15, 1867, Probate Final Record, Book G, p. 705; Estate of August Summerlatte, Feb. 12, 1872, Probate Final Record, Book H, pp. 278–81—both in CCCC.

43. Estate of O. B. Crenshaw, Sept. 6, 1865, through June 13, 1873, Probate Final Record, Book G, p. 67, and Book H, pp. 356–78; Probate Minutes, Book E, pp. 342, 353–55, 368, 369, 410; Estate of W. L. Patterson, Dec. 25, 1865, Feb. 26, 1866, and Aug. 27, 1866, Probate Minutes, Book E, pp. 360, 371, 392—all in CCCC. For the date of Don F. Payne's death see Cemetery Records compiled from gravestones in Colorado County, Nesbitt Memorial Library.

44. Estate of James Wright, Mar. 18, 1867, and Dec. 28, 1867, Probate Final Record,

Book G, pp. 582–85, Dec. 15, 1867, Probate Minutes, Book E, p. 501; Estate of Henry Ocker, Aug. 7, 1866, and Sept. 13, 1866, Probate Final Record, Book G, pp. 274–78; Aug. 28, 1866, Probate Minutes, Book E, p. 394—all in CCCC.

45. Petition, *Elizabeth Jackson v. Stephen Jackson,* Aug. 31, 1868, Docket File No. 2295; Petition, *Ilione C. Maynard v. Mendoza B. Maynard,* Sept. 24, 1868, Docket File No. 2301; Petition, *Mary Meddick v. Edward D. Meddick,* Feb. 28, 1870, Docket File No. 2418; Petition, *Anna E. Bridge v. Augustus Bridge,* May 30, 1870, Docket File No. 2465—all in CCDC. See also Faust, *Mothers of Invention,* p. 249; Bynum, "Reshaping the Bonds of Womanhood," pp. 320–33; Bardaglio, *Reconstructing the Household,* pp. 130–35.

46. Petition, *Elizabeth Jackson v. Stephen Jackson,* Aug. 31, 1868, Docket File No. 2295; Petition, *Virginia Holliday v. Daniel C. Holliday,* Feb. 9, 1870, Docket File No. 2404; Petition, *Anna E. Bridge v. Augustus Bridge,* May 30, 1870, Docket File No. 2465; Petition, *Wilhelmina Lach v. Rudolph Lach,* Aug. 13, 1872, Docket File No. 2872—all in CCDC.

47. Petition, *Henry Boone v. Emily Boone,* Sept. 24, 1872, Docket File No. 2889; Petition, *Henry Nelson v. Annie Nelson,* Dec. 11, 1873, Docket File No. 3011; Petition for Temporary Orders, *George Metz v. Sarah Metz,* Nov. 10, 1865, Docket File No. 1807—all in CCDC.

48. One wife in the frontier era received a divorce for bigamy. According to Mary Somerville Jones in *An Historical Geography,* "It was not only in the south that the majority of adultery cases were granted to husbands"(p. 52). See also Bynum, "Reshaping the Bonds of Womanhood," p. 327.

49. "A wife who charged cruelty rather than adultery may have been protecting herself from scandal rather than reporting the actual causes that drove her to seek a divorce"; see Glenda Riley, *Divorce: An American Tradition,* p. 124.

50. Petition, *Ellen Lacy v. Beverly M. Lacy,* Sept. 7, 1865, Docket File No. 1813; Nov. 3, 1865, District Court Minutes, Book C2, p. 452; Petition, *Ellenora Lacey v. Beverly M. Lacey,* Sept. 13, 1869, Docket File No. 2374; Oct. 11, 1870, District Court Minutes, Book D, p. 346; Petition, *Ellen Lacy v. Beverly M. Lacy,* Dec. 20, 1872, Docket File No. 2906; Feb. 24, 1873, District Court Minutes, Book E, p. 509—all in CCDC.

51. More African American women than men filed for divorce throughout Texas; see Winegarten, *Black Texas Women,* p. 54. Victoria Bynum found that in North Carolina among blacks and whites, men were more likely to file for divorce than women. However, she cites the changes in the laws which favored men's suits as the reason for this. Texas divorce statutes did not change in the postwar era. See Bynum, "Reshaping the Bonds of Womanhood," pp. 320–33.

52. Gammel, comp., *The Laws of Texas,* vol. 7, p. 424.

53. Petition, *Alcey Thomas v. John Thomas,* May 9, 1871, Docket File No. 2657; Petition, *Alcey Holmes v. Isaac Holmes,* Feb. 9, 1872, Docket File No. 2799; Answer, *Martha Harris v. Hiram Harris,* Feb. 9, 1872, Docket File No. 2762—all in CCDC.

54. Marriage Records, CCCC; Sub Assistant Commander, Docket Criminal and Civil, 14th Sub District of Texas, pp. 33, 36, BRFAL.

55. Petitions, *Alcey Thomas v. John Thomas,* May 9, 1871, Docket File No. 2657; *Cornelia Johnson v. Jack Johnson,* May 18, 1871, Docket File No. 2668; *Charity Whitley v. Dennis Whitley,* Sept. 28, 1872, Docket File No. 2746; *Martha Harris v. Hiram Harris,* Dec. 6, 1871, Docket File No. 2762; *Alcey Holmes v. Isaac Holmes,* Feb. 9, 1872, Docket File No. 2799; *Fanny Smith v. James Smith and J. N. Binkley,* Aug. 13, 1872, Docket File No. 2871; *Mary Susan Tatum v. Frank Tatum,* Jan. 21, 1873, Docket File No. 2917; *Rachel Virginia v. Charles Virginia et al.,* Apr. 24, 1873, Docket File No. 2939—all in CCDC. Clearly, just as many

freedmen and freedwomen did not bother with legal marriages, many others did not bother with legal divorces. See Frankel, *Freedom's Women,* pp. 29–31; Edwards, *Gendered Strife and Confusion,* pp. 45–58; Crouch, "Chords of Love," pp. 340–43; Smallwood, "Black Freedwomen after Emancipation," p. 313.

56. Verdict, *Rachel Virginia v. Charles Virginia et al.,* Oct. 8, 1873, Docket File No. 2939, CCDC.

57. Marriage Records, CCCC; Schedule 1, Ninth Census of the United States (1870), Texas, Colorado County.

EPILOGUE

1. Schedule 1 (Free Inhabitants), Seventh Census of the United States (1850), Alabama, Pickens County; Answer, *Mary M. B. Smith v. Henderson and Tooke,* Nov. 11, 1857, Docket File No. 1221, CCDC.

2. "Letter of James W. Holt," in "Documents, Letters, Reminiscences, Etc.," p. 57; Marjorie Bock Miller, interview with Angela Boswell, Apr. 2, 1996; Answer, *Mary M. B. Smith v. Henderson and Tooke,* Nov. 11, 1858, Docket File No. 1221, CCDC.

3. Estate of Augustus B. Wooldridge, Nov. 24, 1856, Final Probate Record, Book E, pp. 447–48; Marriage Records, Book D, p. 7—all in CCCC.

4. Motion to Quash bond, *Mary M. B. Smith v. Henderson and Tooke,* Nov. 4, 1857, Docket File No. 1221, CCDC. See also Estate of Alfred Smith, July 14, 1856, to Jan. 3, 1857, Probate Final Record, Book E, pp. 346–60; May 14–25, 1857, Probate Final Record, Book F, pp. 119–21; Probate Minutes, May 25, 1857, Book D, p. 495—all in CCCC.

5. *Digest of the Laws of Alabama,* 1857–58, p. 421; Deed Records Transcribed, Book K, pp. 324–25, 480, 483, Aug. 18, 1859, Aug. 27, 1859, Oct. 20, 1859, Nov. 10, 1859, and many more, Bond and Mortgage Records, Book E, p. 358, Aug. 27, 1859, and many more—all in CCCC.

6. Marjorie Bock Miller, interview with Angela Boswell, Apr. 2, 1996; Transcribed Deed Records, Book K, p. 387, Nov. 1, 1859, CCCC.

7. Petition, Sept. 30, 1864, Amended Answer, May 4, 1865, and Amended Answer, Nov. 10, 1865, *Martha A. Conner v. Stephen Conner,* Docket File No. 1788, CCDC.

8. *Weimar Mercury,* Oct. 11, 1890.

BIBLIOGRAPHY

ARCHIVES AND DOCUMENTS

Charles William Tait Papers. Center for American History, University of Texas, Austin.
"Civil War Letters of John Samuel Shropshire." *Nesbitt Memorial Library Journal* 7 (January, 1997): 61–70.
Colorado County, Republic of Texas, Tax Lists, 1840. Nesbitt Memorial Library, Columbus, Texas.
Colorado County, Texas, Cemetery Records compiled from gravestones. Nesbitt Memorial Library, Columbus, Texas.
Colorado County, Texas, Confederate Pensions. Texas State Archives, Austin.
Colorado County, Texas, Tax Rolls, 1849–1854. On microfilm at Nesbitt Memorial Library, Columbus, Texas.
"The Constitution of the Republic of Texas, March 17, 1836." In *Documents of Texas History*, edited by Ernest Wallace, pp. 100–106. Austin, Tex.: Steck Company, Publishers, 1963.
Digest of the Laws of Alabama. 1857–58.
"Documents, Letters, Reminiscences, Etc." *Nesbitt Memorial Library Journal* 6 (January, 1996): 53–57.
Gammel, H. P. N., comp., *The Laws of Texas, 1822–1897.* Vol. 7. Austin, Tex.: The Gammel Book Company, 1898.
Hartley, Oliver C. *A Digest of the Laws of Texas. . . .* Philadelphia: Thomas, Cowperthwait and Co., 1850.
Hunter, Robert L., comp. "Hunter & Combs-Dunlavy Bible Records." *Stirpes* 4 (September, 1964): 93–96.
Laws of the Republic of Texas, in Two Volumes. 2 vols. Houston, Tex.: Office of the Telegraph, 1837.
Letters. Reprinted in *Pioneer Texans: Montgomery and Thatcher Families and Their Descendants,* compiled by Dorothy Elkins Cox, pp. 168–244. N.p., n.d.
Letters. Translated and reprinted in *Ruhmann and Beasley Family Roots,* by Dorothy Beasley Ruhmann, pp. 2.55–59. Portland, Tex.: Author, 1994.
Leyendecker Family Papers. Center for American History, University of Texas, Austin.
Narrative of Dick Dervin, June 11, 1943, from *The Eagle Lake Headlight.* Reprinted in "The Slave Narratives of Colorado County," edited by Bill Stein. *Nesbitt Memorial Library Journal* 3 (January, 1993): 3–32.
Narrative of James Green, February 8, 1938. In *The American Slave: A Composite Autobiography,* edited by George P. Rawick. Westport, Conn.: Greenwood Press, 1977. Reprinted in "The Slave Narratives of Colorado County," edited by Bill Stein. *Nesbitt Memorial Library Journal* 3 (January, 1993): 3–32.

Narrative of John Thompson, October 16, 1937. In *The American Slave: A Composite Autobiography,* edited by George P. Rawick. Westport, Conn.: Greenwood Press, 1977. Reprinted in "The Slave Narratives of Colorado County," edited by Bill Stein. *Nesbitt Memorial Library Journal* 3 (January, 1993): 3–32.

Office of the Colorado County Clerk, Colorado County Courthouse, Columbus, Texas:
Bond and Deed Records, Book A, 1836–38.
Bond and Mortgage Records, Books B–I, 1838–73.
County Court Minutes, Book A-1840, 1839–41; Books 1–2, 1846–62; and Book A, 1867–70.
Deed Records Transcribed, Books B–X, 1837–73.
Final Probate Record, Books A–I, 1837–74.
Marriage Records, Books B–G, 1837–80.
Police Court Minutes, 1862–76.
Probate Minutes, Books A–F, 1837–76.
Probate Record Files, 1837–73.
Transcribed Marks and Brand Record, Book 1, 1837–85.

Office of the District Clerk, Colorado County Courthouse, Columbus, Texas:
Criminal Docket Files, 1837–73.
Criminal Execution Docket Record, Justice of Peace Records, 1866–71.
District Court Criminal Docket Record Book, 1866–73.
District Court Criminal Minutes, Book D, 1866–70.
District Court Minutes, Books AB–G, 1837–81.
Docket Files, 1837–73.

Oldham, Williamson S., and George W. White, comps. *A Digest of the General Statute Laws of the State of Texas.* . . . Austin, Tex.: John Marshall & Co., 1859.

Record Book of Luther Chapel, Columbus, Texas. Center for American History, University of Texas, Austin.

Records of the Bureau of Refugees Freedmen and Abandoned Lands. Record Group 105. National Archives, Washington, D.C.

"Reminiscences of James Williams Holt." *Nesbitt Memorial Library Journal* 6 (September, 1996): 151–60.

Roemer, Ferdinand. *Texas.* Translated by Oswald Mueller. San Antonio: Standard Printing Company, 1935.

Saint Peter and Paul Catholic Church, Frelsburg, Texas. Nesbitt Memorial Library, Columbus, Texas.

Schedule 1 (Free Inhabitants), Schedule 2 (Slave Population), and Schedule 4 (Agriculture). Seventh, Eighth, and Ninth Census of the United States (1850, 1860, and 1870), Colorado County, Texas.

NEWSPAPERS, BOOKS, ARTICLES, AND THESES

Andreadis, Harriete. "True Womanhood Revisited: Women's Private Writing in Nineteenth-Century Texas." *Journal of the Southwest* 31 (summer, 1989): 179–204.

Bardaglio, Peter. "The Children of Jubilee: African American Childhood in Wartime." In *Divided Houses: Gender and the Civil War,* edited by Catherine Clinton and Nina Silber, pp. 213–29. New York and Oxford: Oxford University Press, 1992.

BIBLIOGRAPHY

Bardaglio, Peter W. *Reconstructing the Household: Families, Sex, and the Law in the Nineteenth-Century South.* Chapel Hill and London: University of North Carolina Press, 1995.

Basch, Norma. "Equity vs. Equality: Emerging Concepts of Women's Political Status in the Age of Jackson." *Journal of the Early Republic* 3 (fall, 1983): 297–318.

———. *In the Eyes of the Law: Women, Marriage, and Property in Nineteenth-Century New York.* Ithaca and London: Cornell University Press, 1982.

———. "Relief in the Premises: Divorce as a Woman's Remedy in New York and Indiana, 1815–1870." *Law and History Review* 8 (spring, 1990): 1–24.

Bell, John. "Powers of Married Woman in Texas Aside from Statutes." *Texas Law Review* 6 (June, 1928): 516–18.

Biesele, Rudolph Leopold. *The History of the German Settlements in Texas, 1831–1861.* Austin, Tex.: Press of Von Boeckmann- Jones, Co., 1930.

Black's Law Dictionary. 6th ed. Saint Paul, Minn.: West Publishing Company, 1990.

Blassingame, John W. *The Slave Community: Plantation Life in the Antebellum South.* New York: Oxford University Press, 1972.

Boatwright, Eleanor M. "The Political and Civil Status of Women in Georgia, 1783–1860." *Georgia Historical Quarterly* 25 (December, 1941): 301–24.

Boles, John B. *Black Southerners, 1619–1869.* Lexington: University Press of Kentucky, 1984.

———. *The South through Time: A History of an American Region.* Englewood Cliffs, N.J.: Prentice Hall, 1995.

Bynum, Victoria. "Reshaping the Bonds of Womanhood: Divorce in Reconstruction North Carolina." In *Divided Houses: Gender and the Civil War,* edited by Catherine Clinton and Nina Silber, pp. 320–33. New York and Oxford: Oxford University Press, 1992.

———. *Unruly Women: The Politics of Social and Sexual Control in the Old South.* Chapel Hill: University of North Carolina Press, 1992.

Campbell, Randolph. *An Empire for Slavery: The Peculiar Institution in Texas, 1821–1865.* Baton Rouge: Louisiana State University Press, 1989.

———. *Grass-Roots Reconstruction in Texas, 1865–1880.* Baton Rouge and London: Louisiana State University Press, 1997.

———. "Reconstruction in Colorado County, Texas, 1865–1876." *Nesbitt Memorial Library Journal* 5 (January, 1995): 3–30.

———. "The Slave Hire System in Texas." *American Historical Review* 93 (February, 1988): 107–14.

Campbell, Randolph, and Donald K. Pickens. "'My Dearest Husband': A Texas Slave's Love Letter, 1862." *Journal of Negro History* 65 (fall, 1980): 361–64.

Cashin, Joan. *A Family Venture: Men and Women on the Southern Frontier.* New York and Oxford: Oxford University Press, 1991.

———. "'Since the War Broke Out': The Marriage of Kate and William McLure." In *Divided Houses: Gender and the Civil War,* edited by Catherine Clinton and Nina Silber, pp. 200–12. New York and Oxford: Oxford University Press, 1992.

Censer, Jane Turner. *North Carolina Planters and Their Children: 1800–1860.* Baton Rouge and London: Louisiana State University Press, 1984.

———. "'Smiling through Her Tears': Ante-Bellum Southern Women and Divorce." *American Journal of Legal History* 25 (January, 1981): 24–47.

Chused, Richard H. "Late Nineteenth Century Married Women's Property Law: Reception of the Early Married Women's Property Acts by Courts and Legislatures." *American Journal of Legal History* 29 (January, 1985): 3–35.

———. "Married Women's Property Law: 1800–1850." *Georgetown Law Journal* 71 (June, 1983): 1359–1425.

———. *Private Acts in Public Places: A Social History of Divorce in the Formative Era of American Family Law.* Philadelphia: University of Pennsylvania Press, 1995.

Clinton, Catherine. *The Plantation Mistress: Woman's World in the Old South.* New York: Pantheon Books, 1982.

———. "Reconstructing Freedwomen." In *Divided Houses: Gender and the Civil War,* edited by Catherine Clinton and Nina Silber. New York and Oxford: Oxford University Press, 1992.

———. *Tara Revisited: Women, War, and the Plantation Legend.* New York: Abbeville Press, 1995.

Cody, Cheryll Ann. "Sale and Separation: Four Crises for Enslaved Women on the Ball Plantations, 1764–1854." In *Working toward Freedom: Slave Society and Domestic Economy in the American South,* edited by Larry E. Hudson, Jr., pp. 119–42. Rochester, N.Y.: University of Rochester Press, 1994.

Colorado Citizen, 1857–61, 1865–66, 1869–73.

Colorado County Historical Commission, comp. *Colorado County Chronicles: From the Beginning to 1923.* 2 vols. Austin, Tex.: Nortex Press, 1986.

Columbus (Texas) *Times,* 1868.

Cott, Nancy F. *The Bonds of Womanhood: 'Woman's Sphere' in New England, 1780–1835.* New Haven and London: Yale University Press, 1977.

Crouch, Barry A. "The 'Chords of Love': Legalizing Black Marital and Family Rights in Postwar Texas." *Journal of Negro History* 79 (fall, 1994): 334–51.

———. "The Freedmen's Bureau in Colorado County, Texas, 1865–1868." *Nesbitt Memorial Library Journal* 5 (May, 1995): 71–106.

———. "The Freedmen's Bureau in Colorado County, Texas, 1865–1868—Part 3." *Nesbitt Memorial Library Journal* 8 (January, 1998): 3–31.

Edwards, Laura F. *Gendered Strife and Confusion: The Political Culture of Reconstruction.* Urbana and Chicago: University of Illinois Press, 1997.

Ely, James W., Jr., and David J. Bodenhamer. "Regionalism and American Legal History: The Southern Experience." *Vanderbilt Law Review* 39 (April, 1986): 539–67.

Eslinger, Ellen. "The Shape of Slavery on the Kentucky Frontier, 1775–1800." *Register of the Kentucky Historical Society* 92 (winter, 1994): 1–23.

Faust, Drew Gilpin. "Altars of Sacrifice: Confederate Women and the Narratives of War." In *Divided Houses: Gender and the Civil War,* edited by Catherine Clinton and Nina Silber, pp. 171–99. New York and Oxford: Oxford University Press, 1992.

———. *Mothers of Invention: Women of the Slaveholding South in the American Civil War.* Chapel Hill and London: University of North Carolina Press, 1996.

———. "Trying To Do a Man's Business: Gender, Violence, and Slave Management in Civil War Texas." *Gender and History* 4 (summer, 1992): 197–214.

Foner, Eric. *A Short History of Reconstruction, 1863–1877.* New York: Harper & Row, Publishers, 1990.

Forbes, Ella. *African American Women during the Civil War.* New York and London: Garland Publishing, Inc., 1998.

Fox-Genovese, Elizabeth. *Within the Plantation Household: Black and White Women of the Old South.* Chapel Hill and London: University of North Carolina Press, 1988.

Frankel, Noralee. *Freedom's Women: Black Women and Families in Civil War Era Mississippi.* Bloomington and Indianapolis: Indiana University Press, 1999.

Friedman, Jean E. *The Enclosed Garden: Women and Community in the Evangelical South, 1830–1900.* Chapel Hill and London: University of North Carolina Press, 1985.

Goodheart, Lawrence B., Neil Hanks, and Elizabeth Johnson. "'An Act for the Relief of Females . . .': Divorce and the Changing Legal Status of Women in Tennessee, 1796–1860, Part I." *Tennessee Historical Quarterly* 44, no. 3 (1985): 318–39.

Greer, D. Edward. "A Legal Anachronism: The Married Woman's Separate Acknowledgement to Deeds." *Texas Law Review* 1 (June, 1923): 407–22.

Griswold, Robert L. "The Evolution of the Doctrine of Mental Cruelty in Victorian American Divorce, 1790–1900." *Journal of Social History* 20 (fall, 1986): 127–48.

———. "Law, Sex, Cruelty, and Divorce in Victorian America, 1840–1900." *American Quarterly* 38 (winter, 1986): 721–45.

Gunderson, Joan R., and Gwen Victor Gampel. "Married Women's Legal Status in Eighteenth-Century New York and Virginia." *William and Mary Quarterly* 3d series, 39 (January, 1982): 114–34.

Hagler, D. Harland. "Down from the Pedestal: The Role of Women in the Antebellum South." In *Texana II: Cultural Heritage of the Plantation South,* The *Revised* Proceedings of a Humanities Forum Held at Jefferson, Texas, June 4–6, 1981, edited by Candace M. Volz and LeRoy Johnson, Jr., pp. 56–62. Austin: Texas Historical Commission, 1984.

Hall, Jacqueline Dowd. "Partial Truths: Writing Southern Women's History." In *Southern Women: Histories and Identities,* edited by Virginia Bernhard, Betty Brandon, Elizabeth Fox-Genovese, and Theda Perdue, pp. 11–29. Columbia: University of Missouri Press, 1992.

Hall, Jacquelyn Dowd, and Anne Firor Scott. "Women in the South." In *Interpreting Southern History: Historiographical Essays in Honor of Sanford W. Higginbotham,* edited by John B. Boles and Evelyn Thomas Nolen, pp. 454–509. Baton Rouge and London: Louisiana State University Press, 1987.

Hartog, Hendrik. "Marital Exits and Marital Expectations in Nineteenth Century America." *Georgetown Law Journal* 80 (October, 1991): 95–129.

Hine, Darlene Clark, and Kathleen Thompson. *A Shining Thread of Hope: The History of Black Women in America.* New York: Broadway Books, 1988.

Hogan, William Ransom. *The Texas Republic: A Social and Economic History.* Norman: University of Oklahoma Press, 1946.

Hudson, Mrs. Elizabeth, comp. *History of St. John's Episcopal Church Columbus, Texas, April 14, 1856–April 14, 1956.* N.p., 1956.

Hunter, Tera W. *To 'Joy My Freedom: Southern Black Women's Lives and Labors after the Civil War.* Cambridge and London: Harvard University Press, 1997.

Isenberg, Nancy. *Sex and Citizenship in Antebellum America.* Chapel Hill and London: University of North Carolina Press, 1998.

Jeffrey, Julie Roy. *Frontier Women: The Trans-Mississippi West, 1840–1880.* New York: Hill and Wang, 1979.

Jones, Jacqueline. *Labor of Love, Labor of Sorrow: Black Women, Work, and the Family from Slavery to the Present.* New York: Basic Books, Inc., 1985.

Jones, Mary Somerville. *An Historical Geography of the Changing Divorce Law in the United States.* New York and London: Garland Publishing, Inc., 1987.

Jordan, Terry G. *German Seed in Texas Soil: Immigrant Farmers in Nineteenth-Century Texas.* Austin and London: University of Texas Press, 1966.

Kattner, Lauren Ann. "The Diversity of Old South White Women: The Peculiar Worlds of German American Women." In *Discovering the Women in Slavery: Emancipating Per-*

spectives on the American Past, edited by Patricia Morton, pp. 299–311. Athens and London: University of Georgia Press, 1996.

Kerber, Linda K. "Separate Spheres, Female Worlds, Woman's Place: The Rhetoric of Women's History." *Journal of American History* 65 (June, 1988): 9–39.

Kerber, Linda K., and Jane Sherron DeHart, eds. *Women's America: Refocusing the Past.* 5th ed. New York and Oxford: Oxford University Press, 2000.

Kilgore, Dan. "Two Sixshooters and a Sunbonnet: The Story of Sally Skull." In *Legendary Ladies of Texas,* edited by Francis Edward Abernethy, pp. 59–72. Denton: University of North Texas Press, 1994.

Lale, Max S. "The Influence of the Press on Nineteenth-Century Texans: Robert W. Loughery and the Marshall *Texas Republican.*" In *Texana II: Cultural Heritage of the Plantation South,* The *Revised* Proceedings of a Humanities Forum Held at Jefferson, Texas, June 4–6, 1981, edited by Candace M. Volz and LeRoy Johnson, Jr., pp. 22–26. Austin: Texas Historical Commission, 1984.

Lazarou, Kathleen Elizabeth. "Concealed under Petticoats: Married Women's Property and the Law of Texas, 1840–1913." Ph.D. diss., Rice University, 1980.

Lebsock, Suzanne. *The Free Women of Petersburg: Status and Culture in a Southern Town, 1784–1860.* New York and London: W. W. Norton and Company, 1984.

———. "Radical Reconstruction and the Property Rights of Southern Women." *Journal of Southern History* 43 (May, 1977): 196–97.

Lich, Glen E. *The German Texans.* San Antonio: University of Texas Institute of Texan Cultures, 1981.

———. "Rural Hill Country: Man, Nature, and the Ecological Perspective." In *Eagle in the New World: German Immigration to Texas and America,* edited by Theodore Gish and Richard Spuler, pp. 36–44. College Station: Texas Committee for the Humanities by Texas A&M University Press, 1986.

Lowe, Richard G., and Randolph B. Campbell. *Planters and Plain Folk.* Dallas: Southern Methodist University, 1987.

———. "The Slave-Breeding Hypothesis: A Demographic Comment on the 'Buying' and 'Selling' States." *Journal of Southern History* 42 (August, 1976): 401–12.

Malone, Ann Patton. "Searching for the Family and Household Structure of Rural Louisiana, 1810–1864." *Louisiana History* 28 (fall, 1987): 357–79.

———. *Women on the Texas Frontier: A Cross-Cultural Perspective.* Southwestern Studies Monograph No. 70. El Paso: Texas Western Press, 1983.

McCoy, Ingeborg Ruberg. "Tales of the Grandmothers, II." In *Eagle in the New World: German Immigration to Texas and America,* edited by Theodore Gish and Richard Spuler, pp. 212–20. College Station: Texas Committee for the Humanities by Texas A&M University Press, 1986.

McCurry, Stephanie. *Masters of Small Worlds: Yeoman Households, Gender Relations, and the Political Culture of the Antebellum South Carolina Low Country.* New York and Oxford: Oxford University Press, 1995.

McIlveen, Sue Dunlavy, comp. *Footprints: The Dunlavys and Related Families.* N.p.: Private Distribution, 1988.

McKnight, Joseph W. "Texas Community Property Law: Conservative Attitudes, Reluctant Change." *Law and Contemporary Problems* 56 (spring, 1993): 71–104.

McKnight, Joseph W., and William A. Reppy, Jr. *Texas Matrimonial Property Law (Provisional Second Edition).* Dallas, Tex., 1994.

McMillen, Sally G. *Southern Women: Black and White in the Old South.* Arlington Heights, Ill.: Harland Davidson, Inc., 1992.

Moncrief, Sandra. "The Mississippi Married Women's Property Act of 1839." *Journal of Mississippi History* 47 (May, 1985): 11–25.

Myres, Sandra L. *Westering Women and the Frontier Experience, 1800–1915.* Albuquerque: University of New Mexico Press, 1982.

Nieman, Donald G. *To Set the Law in Motion: The Freedmen's Bureau and the Legal Rights of Blacks, 1865–1868.* Millwood, N.Y.: KTO Press, 1979.

O'Brien, Charles. "The Growth in Pennsylvania of the Property Rights of Married Women." *University of Pennsylvania Law Review* 49 (September, 1901): 524–30.

Paulsen, James W. "Remember the Alamo[ny]! The Unique Texas Ban on Permanent Alimony and the Development of Community Property Law." *Law and Contemporary Problems* 56 (spring, 1993): 7–70.

Paxson, Frederic L. "The Constitution of Texas, 1845." *Southwestern Historical Quarterly* 18 (April, 1915): 386–98.

Pitre, Merline. "A Note on the Historiography of Blacks in the Reconstruction of Texas." *Journal of Negro History* 66 (1981): 340–48.

Pugh, Nina Nichols, "The Spanish Community of Gains in 1803: *Sociedad de Gananciales.*" *Louisiana Law Review* 30 (December, 1969): 1–43.

Rabkin, Peggy A. *Fathers to Daughters: The Legal Foundations of Female Emancipation.* Westport, Conn., and London, 1980.

Rable, George C. *Civil Wars: Women and the Crisis of Southern Nationalism.* Urbana and Chicago: University of Illinois Press, 1989.

Ransom, Roger L., and Richard Sutch. *One Kind of Freedom: The Economic Consequences of Emancipation.* Cambridge, London, New York, and Melbourne: Cambridge University Press, 1977.

Reeves-Marquardt, Dona. "Tales of the Grandmothers: Women as Purveyors of German-Texan Culture." In *Eagle in the New World: German Immigration to Texas and America,* edited by Theodore Gish and Richard Spuler, pp. 201–12. College Station: Texas Committee for the Humanities by Texas A&M University Press, 1986.

Reynolds, Suzanne. "Increases in Separate Property and the Evolving Marital Partnership." *Wake Forest Law Review* 24 (summer, 1989): 240–333.

Richardson, Rupert Norval, Ernest Wallace, and Adrian N. Anderson. *Texas: The Lone Star State.* 4th ed. Englewood Cliffs, N.J.: Prentice-Hall, Inc., 1981.

Riley, Glenda. *Divorce: An American Tradition.* New York and Oxford: Oxford University Press, 1991.

Salmon, Marylynn. *Women and the Law of Property in Early America.* Chapel Hill and London: University of North Carolina Press, 1986,

Schwalm, Leslie A. *A Hard Fight for We: Women's Transition from Slavery to Freedom in South Carolina.* Urbana and Chicago: University of Illinois Press, 1997.

Scott, Anne Firor. *The Southern Lady: From Pedestal to Politics, 1830–1930.* Chicago and London: University of Chicago Press, 1970.

Seaholm, Ernest May. "The Angus McNeill Family." *Nesbitt Memorial Library Journal* 8 (May, 1998): 51–77.

Sedevie, Donna. "Women and the Law of Property in the Old Southwest: The Antecedents of the Mississippi Married Woman's Law, 1798–1839." Master's thesis, University of Southern Mississippi, August, 1996.

Silber, Nina. "Intemperate Men, Spiteful Women, and Jefferson Davis." In *Divided Houses: Gender and the Civil War,* edited by Catherine Clinton and Nina Silber, pp. 283–305. New York and Oxford: Oxford University Press, 1992.

Smallwood, James. "Black Freedwomen after Emancipation: The Texas Experience." *Prologue* 27 (fall, 1995): 303–17.

Smith, Bea Ann. "The Partnership Theory of Marriage: A Borrowed Solution Fails." *Texas Law Review* 68 (March, 1990): 689–735.

Smith, Daniel Blake. *Inside the Great House: Planter Family Life in Eighteenth-Century Chesapeake Society.* Ithaca and London: Cornell University Press, 1980.

Speer, Ocie. *A Treatise on the Law of Marital Rights in Texas.* Rochester, N.Y.: Lawyers Cooperative Publishing Co., 1916.

Speth, Linda E. "The Married Women's Property Acts, 1839–1865: Reform, Reaction, or Revolution?" In *Women and the Law: A Social Historical Perspective,* Vol. 2 of *Property, Family and the Legal Profession,* edited by D. Kelly Weisberg. Cambridge, Mass.: Schenkman Publishing Company, 1982.

Stein, Bill. "Consider the Lily: The Ungilded History of Colorado County, Texas, Part 1." *Nesbitt Memorial Library Journal* 6 (January, 1996): 3–34.

———. "Consider the Lily: The Ungilded History of Colorado County, Texas, Part 2." *Nesbitt Memorial Library Journal* 6 (January, 1996): 35–51.

———. "Consider the Lily: The Ungilded History of Colorado County, Texas, Part 3." *Nesbitt Memorial Library Journal* 6 (May, 1996): 63–94.

———. "Consider the Lily: The Ungilded History of Colorado County, Texas, Part 4." *Nesbitt Memorial Library Journal* 6 (September, 1996): 115–49.

———. "Consider the Lily: The Ungilded History of Colorado County, Texas, Part 5." *Nesbitt Memorial Library Journal* 7 (January, 1997): 3–59.

Stevenson, Brenda E. *Life in Black and White: Family and Community in the Slave South.* New York and Oxford: Oxford University Press, 1996.

Stowe, Steven M. *Intimacy and Power in the Old South: Ritual in the Lives of the Planters.* Baltimore and London: Johns Hopkins University Press, 1987.

Struve, Walter. *Germans and Texans: Commerce, Migration, and Culture in the Days of the Lone Star Republic.* Austin: University of Texas Press, 1996.

Stuntz, Jean. "Three Flags over Texas: Marital Property under Spanish, English, and Republic of Texas Law." Department of History, University of North Texas. Paper in possession of author, 1996.

Texas Monument (La Grange), 1851–53.

Townes, John C. "Sketch of the Development of the Judicial System of Texas. I." *Quarterly of the Texas State Historical Association* 2 (July, 1898): 29–53.

Turner, Elizabeth Hayes. *Women, Culture, and Community: Religion and Reform in Galveston, 1880–1920.* New York and Oxford: Oxford University Press, 1997.

Webb, Walter Prescott, et al., eds. *The Handbook of Texas.* 2 vols. Austin: The Texas State Historical Association, 1952.

Weimar Mercury, 1890.

Welter, Barbara. "The Cult of True Womanhood: 1820–1860." *American Quarterly* 18 (summer, 1966): 151–74.

White, Deborah Gray. *Ar'n't I a Woman? Female Slaves in the Plantation South.* New York: W. W. Norton and Company, 1985.

Whites, LeeAnn. *The Civil War as a Crisis in Gender: Augusta, Georgia, 1860–1890.* Athens and London: University of Georgia Press, 1995.

Wiener, Jonathan M. "Female Planters and Planters' Wives in Civil War and Reconstruction: Alabama, 1850–1870." *Alabama Review* 30 (April, 1977): 135–49.

Winegarten, Ruthe. *Black Texas Women: 150 Years of Trial and Triumph.* Austin: University of Texas Press, 1995.

Wortman, Marlene Stein, ed. *Women in American Law, Volume I: From Colonial Times to the New Deal.* New York and London: Holmes & Meier Publishers, Inc., 1985.

Wyatt-Brown, Bertram. *Southern Honor: Ethics and Behavior in the Old South.* New York and Oxford: Oxford University Press, 1982.

INDEX

ANGELA BOSWELL is associate professor of history at Henderson State University in Arkadelphia, Arkansas. She received her doctorate from Rice University and has written extensively on the history of southern women.

ISBN 1-58644-128-7

90000

9 781585 441280

ISSCW   305
         .4209
         764
         B747

BOSWELL, ANGELA
    HER ACT AND DEED

CENTRAL LIBRARY
12/07